SHATTERED DREAMS
A Mother's Pain

by

Christine Ledger

Word for Life Trust

Published by:
Word for Life Trust
3 Danestream Close, Milford-on-Sea,
Hampshire, SO41 0UR, U.K.
Tel/Fax +44 (0)1590 645216
e-mail: wflt@wflt.org

COPYRIGHT   2001 Christine Ledger

First published 2001

All rights reserved. No part of this publication may be reproduced, stored in a retrieval system, or transmitted in any form or by any means, electronic, mechanical, photocopying or otherwise, without the prior written consent of the publisher. Short extracts may be used for review purposes.

Unless otherwise stated, Scripture taken from the HOLY BIBLE, NEW INTERNATIONAL VERSION. Copyright © 1973, 1978, 1984 by International Bible Society. Used by permission of Hodder and Stoughton Limited.
ISBN: 1-903577-15-2

Printed and bound in Great Britain by Omnia Books Ltd, Glasgow

Contents

Page No

Acknowledgements

Foreword

Chapter 1 - Sorry Mum, It Hurts	11
Chapter 2 - The Early Years	16
Chapter 3 - Shattered Dreams	28
Chapter 4 - Dashed Hopes	45
Chapter 5 - Crying Out	64
Chapter 6 - Hanging On	83
Chapter 7 - A Measure of Healing	102
Chapter 8 - A Slippery Monster	121
Chapter 9 - Why God Do You Allow Suffering?	133
Chapter 10 - Relinquishing Ownership	148
Chapter 11 - The Dark Waiting Room	171
Chapter 12 - Fighting Despair	190
Chapter 13 - Blessings	207
Chapter 14 - Hidden Treasure	228

Shattered Dreams

Acknowledgements

The people mentioned in this book are real people - some are family members, some friends and others are patients whom I have counselled in the surgery. However in order to preserve the confidentiality and anonymity of some of those mentioned, their real names have been changed and their stories slightly altered to protect their identity. But I would like to thank them, for without their part in the story this book would never have found itself in print.

I am grateful for all the many people who have encouraged me along the way and made constructive comments, with special thanks to:

- the Rev Yvonne Richmond who was the first person to read the story, and spurred me on with the words "It has great potential" as she believed in this book;

- the Rev William Olhausen, who helped me clarify some of the theological issues;

- Mary Munday, a friend who has always been supportive and walked alongside me during this period of writing;

- Sue Batchelor, an art therapist who introduced Julia to the joys of painting after the onset of the illness, and designed the cover;

- Eileen Carey who has kindly written the foreword, and despite her demanding role as wife of the Archbishop of Canterbury, has always been prayerfully supportive.

- Last, but not least, a very special thank you to Christine Orme, without whom this book would never have been completed. We sat together for many an hour, laughing and crying as she helped me knock the first draft into shape! Her considerable skill in grammar and the use of language, together with suggestions on numerous aspects of the content, was invaluable.

My husband John, has been a great support and encourager to me in the writing of this book, and I would like to thank him and our two daughters, Julia and Fiona, together with their husbands, Geoff and Paul, for their permission to give glimpses into our family life. Each chapter begins with one of Julia's poems, many of which were written in the midst of very difficult times. I am grateful for her permission to include them, and also for the source of inspiration she has been to me in reading the manuscript and making suggestions, otherwise this book would not have been authentic. Her testimony of courage in being willing to make herself vulnerable and to allow this story to be shared openly for the sake of others, is characteristic of her generous nature for which I am thankful.

Finally I would like to thank "Word For Life Trust" and particularly Elizabeth Brazell for her enthusiasm and willingness to commit this story to print.

To God be the glory!
(Chris Ledger)

Foreword by Mrs. Eileen Carey

I am delighted to write the foreword to a book, which I believe, will be of enormous help and encouragement to others who have someone in their family, particularly a young person, suffering from a chronic illness.

I have known Christine, the author, and her family for 26 years and I can testify that this is a true account of Christine's struggles in coming to terms with the loss of her dreams for her daughter.

Julia, the daughter of Christine and John Ledger, has been suffering from Myalgic Encephalopathy, commonly called M.E., since her late teens. The result has been the loss of those wonderful years of growing up, her independence and the establishment of a fine career as a nurse.

The medical status of the illness has been questioned by many whom have viewed it primarily as a psychological illness. This, of course, is very hurtful to those suffering from this debilitating disease and those who care for them.

Christine, a trained counsellor, has already written a book entitled **'Caring for the Carers'**. This time roles are reversed - she finds herself as a carer, looking after her daughter Julia.

Christine's book is full of the entire range of human emotions and Julia, herself, contributes some moving expressions of her anguish at the beginning of each chapter.

The Christian faith that all the family share comes through clearly in this book, but that does not mean it is trite and simplistic. It is an honest account of how their faith has faltered at times.

Chris has shared her story and her pain with an openness and honesty that I know to be characteristic of her. I am sure that others caring for sick and disabled children will find the book a great help and gain a deeper understanding of the situation.

I warmly recommend '**Shattered Dreams - A Mother's Pain**'.

Mrs. Eileen Carey
Lambeth Palace

At some time the dark clouds will clear

and allow the sun to shine again.

Gradually the pain will become more manageable

and may even recede,

giving way to laughter and joy,

and a hope

that creeps out of the shadows,

brightening the future.

HIS WAYS ARE NOT MY WAYS!

I asked God to be challenged, in order that I should gain:
I wanted to be more like Him - and I was faced with pain.
I asked for the pain to be taken away; instead it seemed to grow
Sapping my youth, my health and strength - I felt my energy go.
Once more I asked to lose the pain; instead I lost my mind
Blanket-heaviness descended - no respite could I find.
I asked God then to give me His strength, weak, just where I lay:
He gave me joy to fill my heart and grace to face each day.
I cried out to God for healing, in a desperate plea;
He gave me perseverance to trust where I couldn't see.
I pleaded with God for comforters, but sadly no one came;
Yet God himself befriended me, soothing away my pain.
I groaned, 'God, stop my suffering!', in the plummeting depths of despair
He sowed in me hope as I rested and surrendered my life to His care.
I asked God to ease my frustration; his patience was the key
To cope with my incapacity and accept His will for me.
I had asked God for a challenge: I did not expect such pain -
God sent me physical suffering to bring me spiritual gain.

Julia

Chapter 1

Sorry Mum, it hurts
My heart is in anguish within me (Psalm 55:4)

"Oh Mum . . . . . it hurts . . . . I'm so sorry"

The words greeted me as I entered my daughter's room at King Edward VII Hospital in Midhurst where she was a student nurse. Hearing them my heart sank, but the sight of my twenty-year-old daughter drawn with pain, white faced, and with dark bags under her sunken eyes, made my stomach churn. Thoughts flashed at lightning speed through my mind.

"Julia, you look so ill . . . . Oh my goodness what's going on? . . . . you look so jaded and pale . . . . Has she got cancer? . . . . God, where are you? . . . . What's going to happen to her nursing training"?

Pushing these thoughts aside I sat on Julia's bed and holding her in my arms I heard myself say: "There's nothing to be sorry about; it's not your fault that you're ill, I'm here now to take you home."

Julia sank back on to the pillows, relieved that I was there to take over. She no longer had to hold herself together or think. A friend had all but packed her bag so I quickly finished gathering her toiletries together, pleased to do something that gave me some control in circumstances where I was beginning to feel life was out of control, because I couldn't understand what was happening to my daughter. Intermingled with my confusion and sadness, was a measure of anger. I felt angry, not with Julia, but somehow with life in general and to a certain extent with God. How cruel could life be? Julia was so happy at university. Probably for the first time in her life she had everything going for her and was enjoying life to the full; then, it seemed, the rug had been pulled from beneath her feet. How could God let that happen?

Somehow we got Julia into the car. On the way home I went through a confusing kaleidoscope of thoughts and emotions, thinking repeatedly, *"This can't be happening.... There must be an end to it soon...."* and crying out to God, *"What are you doing?"*

I recognised that to some extent I was in shock and needed space to work through the implications of what was happening. A battle raged in my mind. Being naturally optimistic, fleeting thoughts like, *"Oh, she'll get better soon"*, battled with the concept, *"Surely there must be something really wrong with Julia for her to have been unwell for nine months and now so ill she can hardly crawl from the nurses' home into the car"*. In my pain and confusion my natural reaction was to deny all this was happening, so in my heart I cried out to God, *"Please give me grace to face the truth."*

As we drove back on that summer's day in June 1991, Julia was too ill to chat, so we played a worship tape. Focusing on God through the music and words calmed my inner turmoil. Although I felt great pain inside, and the atmosphere in the car was sad, when I looked through the windscreen I was aware of a beautiful sunny day. The different shades of green soothed the eyes and the sky was a brilliant blue. I reminded myself of God's wonderful creative beauty, and the words, *Your faithfulness reaches to the skies.* (1) Somehow I managed to contain my overwhelming sense of sadness and the inevitable tears - at that time I sensed it was important to be strong for Julia. Only when I had settled her in her own bed that night, did I give way to my tears. It was good to feel my husband's loving and comforting arms around me. John felt as confused as I did. As we sat and talked together we began asking ourselves what was happening to our hopes and dreams for our daughter - were they being shattered?

The next day I asked Jill, one of the doctors from the surgery where I work as a counsellor, to visit Julia. She found Julia in so much pain from swollen and sore glands, as well as joint pains, that she didn't care what was going on. Jill arranged for some blood tests and I asked if John and I could come into the surgery a few days later to talk about the results. We were both now determined to keep pushing until we found out what was wrong with Julia. Sitting in the consulting room, Jill didn't beat about the bush. The test results were all negative. I found myself blurting out to Jill, "Do think Julia has M.E?" [1]

This thought must have been lurking at the back of my mind over the previous few months. Because I hadn't wanted to think that maybe this was Julia's problem I had stuffed the idea down deep into the recesses of my mind and denied it. Now I heard myself saying the words and having to face the fact that perhaps this was true, a reality I had been refusing to believe because it brought fear into my heart - fear about how long it would last; fear about other people's reactions; fear that Julia would be labelled a yuppy (way back in the 1980's, M.E. was known as Yuppies' disease); fear that people wouldn't believe that Julia was really ill. There were still people around who felt that M.E. wasn't real; it was for the weak and those who wanted to opt out of life. But I knew that there was no way Julia wanted to opt out of life. It didn't make sense: she was enjoying life too much.

This train of thought was interrupted as I heard Jill's response: "Well, in the absence of anything else showing up, I think Julia must have M.E. Her illness is presenting with the typical peaking and troughing of M.E. - when Julia exerts herself she gets worse and when she rests she gets better." My heart did a double flip. *"Oh no, I can't believe it. This can't be happening to our daughter."*

---

[1] Myalgic Encephalomyelitis refers to a disorder affecting the hypothalamus in the brain. It is also known as Chronic Fatigue Syndrome. These names describe a pattern of symptoms characterised in many different ways - the central feature being an unexplained persistent or relapsing fatigue, both physical and mental. The diagnosis rests on the basis of the clinical history as there are no validated laboratory or other tests to confirm it.

Immediately I was reminded of a young teenager we knew who had M.E. He had been a top table tennis player for England and had now been ill for four years. A few years earlier, Julia and her sister, Fiona, hearing that he was housebound with M.E. decided to visit him on their way back from school one day. On their return home, we sat as usual in the kitchen, drinking coffee and chatting about the day's events. They were both obviously very shocked at how M.E. had affected this young lad.

"Mum, he can't seem to do anything but sit around and watch a bit of TV. He hasn't even got the energy to type or read a book - it must be terrible". We had chatted on, trying to get our heads round what life must be like for him and I remember Julia saying: "If that was me I would go round the bend."

"Four years .... Go round the bend .... Four years .... go round the bend", the words rang in my mind, like an echo bouncing off cave walls. I threw up an SOS, *"Please Lord, may Julia not be that bad"*.

Eventually I managed to pull myself out of the numbness I felt and although I didn't feel I was making any sense out of anything, I breathed a sigh and said to Jill, "Well, at last we know what we are facing".

During the short car journey home, hot prickly tears poured down my face and John's comforting hand crept across to take mine. Feeling numb and speechless with shock we struggled to come to terms with what we had heard. As we walked into the house my legs felt like jelly and I felt sick inside but I knew we had to be strong for Julia. I whispered: *"Thank you that Julia hasn't anything like cancer, but please Lord, be all that we need at this time as we tell Julia she has M.E. and as we face all the implications of this illness".*

CHILD OF THE KING

Captured by God's love I stand and watch
The sunset in full glory radiating across the sky
The rainbow in soft watercolour painted through dark clouds
The tender love between mother and child
The glint of sunshine on the delicate petals of a rose
The trees gently stirring in the breeze
The pounding waves upon the sea -

And Father you put all this creative beauty within
I am a precious daughter of the King
Through the shedding of Christ's blood, his greatest act of love:
His dying in my place let flow life-giving grace in me,
Yet nothing I can ever do will pay the debt I owe.
I surrender my wrestling, my struggle, my strife,
Jesus, give rest - and find rest in my life
And when my feelings are running high
Changing, shifting as storm clouds in the sky
I will set my heart once more on you in faith
And see with your eyes, know my place
My inheritance as a daughter of the King.

Julia

Chapter 2

The Early Years

You knit me together in my mother's womb (Psalm 139:13)

At 4 am on a cold, frosty winter's morning in December 1970 I found myself being driven at a steady pace by my husband, John, to the Cheshire maternity hospital. I didn't feel quite as steady however - with contractions coming every 2 minutes I felt a measure of panic, yet also excitement that the long awaited birth of our baby was imminent. We had been trying for this baby for over a year before I became pregnant, so it was very much wanted. With no time for enemas or painkillers, I went into second stage of labour at 5 am. Being a nurse I knew that the baby would probably arrive by about 6 am, as normally mothers of first babies were not allowed to go longer than an hour in 2nd stage. However this was not to be . . . . Somehow this baby got stuck and it was not until 7.15 am with the help of forceps that Julia finally entered the world. The journey had been a struggle for her - was this an omen of what was to come?

Despite her birth-struggle, Julia was an easy, contented, happy baby who slept well (apart from the usual teething trouble!) She laughed and chuckled a lot and one day when we were in the car en route to my parents' home in the south we stopped to feed her. I don't know what triggered it . . . . but I began to laugh and she began to chuckle, and together we seemed to spark each other off to enjoy a fun mother/daughter giggle together - this ability to relate to each other in a non-verbal way would become very precious to us when Julia became so ill.

Eighteen months after Julia's birth we were blessed with our second daughter, Fiona. After Julia's contentedness we didn't know what had hit us when Fiona arrived! She cried and yelled throughout the day for about the first year of her life and even when I picked her up she was agitated and screamed. Fortunately she slept well at night. I felt very helpless with Fiona as I didn't seem able to comfort her in her distress, and Julia was obviously struggling to understand why Mummy couldn't make it better. As Fiona exercised her lungs with ear-piercing screams Julia would say, "Don't cry, Fiona, Mummy's holding you". In those early years of motherhood I began to learn that though mummies were there to make things better, sometimes they couldn't. I could only do my best and as my best was good enough for God I tried to let it be good enough for me. Thankfully, once Fiona became mobile she stopped screaming and then never looked back, developing into an outward going, confident, fun-loving and energetic child, whereas Julia was quieter, more serious, sensitive and creative.

John and I were so grateful to God for our two wonderful, healthy daughters who gave us much pleasure. When the girls were 4 and 3 years old, John's job in education took us from Wilmslow, Cheshire to the beautiful city of Durham. The girls settled happily in a Church of England primary school. Julia enjoyed the creative and academic sides of school life but was not at all sporty. She invariably came in last in the race around the school, and we would see our little plump bespectacled daughter bringing up the rear. I could see her distress and disappointment at coming last, and although we encouraged her and said we were still proud of her, I think inside she hurt a lot.

We encouraged the girls to participate in all the things little girls do: Brownies, playing musical instruments, swimming and ballet lessons. As a trained dancer I particularly enjoyed their ballet shows, but I had no illusions that they would ever be dancers! With the fun of enjoying the typical escapades of a cat who gave birth to kittens, and a hamster who chewed his way through Julia's dressing gown, we were like any other normal family. The girls had the usual sibling squabbles, but were also best of friends. We had many happy holidays together and at quite a young age they enthusiastically joined John and me in our love of walking. John was very fond and proud of his daughters and took a keen interest in all they did. "Let's have a rumple scrumple on the floor with you Daddy," was their frequent cry and as they grew older he would take them ice-skating.

When the girls were about 8 and 6 1/2 years they both became very ill at the same time with glandular fever, with fevers reaching 105 degrees F. I spent my time running between one and the other, tepid sponging them and helping them to drink, since neither of them could hold a cup to their mouths because their joints were swollen. As a nurse I didn't worry unduly about their childhood ailments as I knew they would recover in time, but after their recovery both seemed more susceptible to viral infections and at least once a year Julia would become ill with swollen glands, joint pains and high temperatures. This was to be an annual pattern until she finally became ill at university and this time her body never seemed to recover - she had M.E.

When Julia was 11 years old, we moved again, this time to Coventry. Although Julia settled in very happily to our church life and had friends there, school was a struggle. I don't think I ever realised the extent to which she was bullied; only as she got older did she say how unhappy she had been. As a counsellor working in a GP surgery, I have counselled many women who have tried to come to terms with the legacy of having been bullied at school. This sort of verbal bullying is abusive and can be just as destructive as physical or sexual abuse. I feel now that I let Julia down somehow in not addressing this issue, but I have had to reason with myself that at the time I didn't know to what extent it was going on, and I couldn't foresee the effect it would have on her. While this was going on at school, life at home had its stressful times as John was going through a very difficult time at work, and Julia was becoming a typical teenager; hence they started to clash with each other. Until this time Julia had always been daddy's girl but now their relationship was not what it used to be!

Within 3 years John had yet another move, this time further south to Reading. Fiona's reaction to this was one of anger and sullen silences towards John, as much as to say, "How dare you uproot me from a place where I am so happy?" Julia, however, seemed relieved to escape school, although didn't want to leave her church friends or move house. She was very understanding and sensitive about how hard it was for her dad and didn't make life difficult at all. In fact the impression we got from Julia was, "I'm OK." It was only years later that Julia was able to express to us that she actually had been far from OK as inside she felt emotionally upset but because the move was too painful to face and talk about she had 'closed off' her emotions. During our three years in Coventry there had been a number of other sad changes in our lives. Both my parents had died within five months of each other and the girls were deeply saddened at the loss of their Nana and Grandad. Although we hadn't seen them that frequently they used to come and stay from time to time and we had always had great fun together. Then a couple of weeks after we moved to Reading, my sister's husband died after a heart transplant. All the losses incurred in moving and relatives dying in a short span of time, left the girls feeling very insecure and upset.

Changing schools as teenagers of 13 and 11 years is difficult for many children, and in our case, to make matters worse there were no places at our local comprehensive school so the girls had to cycle to a school four miles away. With peer group pressure, the longing to be accepted that all teenagers experience can be very powerful. Within the first week Julia was aggressively cornered in the toilet and encouraged to smoke like the rest of the girls. She was able to withstand this pressure, but nevertheless their longing to be accepted drew our girls into difficulties. After a few terms at school they came home and asked if they could lose some weight as all the other girls were much thinner than they were, and they wanted to be like them. With hindsight, I can see that I made a big mistake - I said yes, providing they worked towards a sensible target weight. Unfortunately one thing led to another, and what with peer group pressure and sibling rivalry they both became anorexic. Fiona recovered quite quickly, but Julia continued to be anorexic for many years.

Slowly both girls settled into the school, and now Julia was much happier whereas Fiona became very quiet and withdrawn until she entered the 6th Form when she found her feet again and all her normal bounce and zest for life returned. Arriving as they did in Years 8 and 9, it was hard for them to break into existing friendship groups and living so far away from a community-based school no one lived near enough to pop in. Rapidly losing confidence, neither of them settled into any of the out of school activities which they had previously been involved in, so consequently they both went through a stage of being extremely lonely. Although academically they both excelled in their A - levels, the move to a new school and area again proved to be an emotional upset for them both. Another detrimental factor was that whereas in Coventry they had both been very happy in the Pathfinders Youth Group at church, in Reading neither of them found friends of their own age at church. Somehow they didn't seem to fit in. One friend said that on first meeting them on their arrival in Reading, they appeared to be unsophisticated but mature, very different from the local teenagers who were the opposite - sophisticated and immature.

Julia's childhood dream was to be a nurse, so it was with enormous pride and pleasure that John and I took her up to Great Ormond Street to start her training as a children's nurse. She had intended to do a 4-year combined children's and general nurse training, but for her intake they had changed the course to just children's training. Unfortunately the course really didn't suit her as it didn't stretch her academically and on her first ward experience she found herself working for a ward sister of the old dominating, cold and authoritative school. This sister was aggressively negative in her comments to Julia. In fact she was quite abusive, so not surprisingly Julia began to lose a lot of confidence in herself, and after becoming increasingly disillusioned with the course and with the stress of coping with that first ward experience she decided to leave Great Ormond Street after 9 months and start on a BSc degree course in nursing at Surrey University in 1990.

University life suited Julia tremendously well, and she settled down happily to the academic work, spending time socialising with friends, and experiencing many different activities: tap dancing, aerobics, swimming, and training for a parachute jump. She also became very involved in the Christian Union. The decision to move had been a wise one. After the difficult time at Great Ormond Street it was good to see her so happy but a dark cloud began to appear. About the third weekend of her first term Julia had a stomach upset, but appeared to not recover completely - she was very tired most of the time: having enjoyed swimming one week, she experienced muscle weakness throughout the following week, so dropped out of swimming.

During one of my visits towards the end of term I was sitting in her room having coffee and Julia was chatting enthusiastically about all that she was learning on her course. "Oh Mum, we read about chronic fatigue - it feels like I have it!" I chose to ignore this comment. Being a nurse the one thing I couldn't stand was hypochondria so I wouldn't even give myself permission to question the truth of what Julia said. I just dismissed it and thus forgot about the comment. At home with us over the Christmas holidays Julia *was* really tired all the time, and couldn't live at her normal pace. She slept most of the time and I innocently thought this was a normal student existence! But I wasn't worried, as I always looked on the bright side, believing the fatigue would pass and she would quickly recover.

During the spring term Julia began to pick up and I drove over to Guildford to take her out. Over coffee our chat was non stop. Julia was back to her normal energetic self. Babbling away nineteen to the dozen she relayed to me how happy she was and gave me the run down on all that she was doing. The previous weekend she had been away with the Christian Union and had had a wonderful, fun packed time. "Mum" she said, "I now know that I am OK as a person. I used to think there was something the matter with me as I couldn't relate to people at Great Ormond Street, but I now know there is nothing wrong with me. People like me, and I can relate to people". Under my breath I whispered a big, *"Thank you"* to God. As a mother I was so thrilled to see that Julia was beginning to have confidence in herself again and to enjoy life. But that night, on her way to a Christian Union meeting she slipped on a wet wooden walkway, hurting the bottom of her spine. After a long evening in casualty she was sent home with a prescription for painkillers and advised to rest. But not only did she bruise her spine - the shock to her body caused by the fall seemed to trigger extreme fatigue again. Feeling washed out most of the time with frequent stomach upsets and swollen glands in her neck, Julia was once more far from well. It was hard to take on board what was happening. One minute she was so well and enjoying life, then within a week she was ill again.

Somehow Julia managed to struggle on until the end of term. Easter was to be a special time, as she and a friend had booked to fly out to Geneva to visit Fiona who was with Youth with a Mission (YWAM) at their base in Lausanne, Switzerland. Obviously there was great anticipation and excitement for both the girls as they eagerly awaited their reunion and opportunity to chat together - and boy, could they both chat! Julia and Fiona were not only very close as sisters but they were also the best of friends. However Julia was barely well enough to go. When she arrived back at the end of term, tiredness had such a grip on her that she couldn't do anything. Sitting motionless and looking at everything to be unpacked, the tears flowed relentlessly for about an hour. This was not like Julia. To unpack and repack seemed too much of a mammoth effort for her, but somehow between us we managed to get her packed and en route to Switzerland. The visit went well, in spite of Julia having to spend some time resting on the bed and both the girls were thrilled with the opportunity to catch up with each other.

Julia returned to university for her nursing induction course at King Edward VII hospital, Midhurst which she enjoyed. However during the last few days on the ward, severe stomach pains began to plague her, so she went to the University Health Centre, but when all the blood tests came back negative the doctor just sent her away with a prescription for her spots!! Although we were all relieved when these tests proved negative, we were confused about why Julia was suddenly so ill again with glandular fever like symptoms and extreme fatigue. A few days later I had a very distressed phone call saying she couldn't cope, so I went straight away to collect her. By then I was beginning to feel very anxious about Julia but felt I could do something positive by bringing her home for some TLC (tender loving care). After about a week Julia felt somewhat better, so went back to Guildford, only to return home again after a few days. This became the pattern over the next few months, and although we had made contact with our local doctor, no one offered any advice on managing her fatigue.

On one occasion when I took Julia back to university I said, "You're not really better, are you?" Our eyes met. We looked knowingly at each other. We were lost, uncertain of what to do, yet knowing Julia didn't want to miss any more of her course. No words were necessary. Heavy-hearted I left her yet again wondering how long it would be before I received the next tearful phone call. I was totally confused as to what was going on. Normally Julia was as bright as a button but now she could neither concentrate on her work nor had the energy even to talk and spent most of her time in bed. Exams were looming and one tutor pushed her to take them all saying how brilliant she was and all she had to do was to pass them. Julia was not so sure as she couldn't even concentrate enough to revise more than a page or two at a time.

At about the same time as Julia's exams were due, Fiona and I went off to a Christian conference, entitled 'The Battle Belongs to the Lord." As the theme suggests this conference was very encouraging for us because we were battling to make sense of what was going on. We were in daily touch with Julia and were very distressed to hear that because of her low energy levels she had made the decision just to concentrate on taking one exam in the subject she thoroughly enjoyed. (In fact she passed this with 86%). Fiona and I prayed and fasted and sought God's heart for Julia. At the conference we sang "Jesus is Lord" many times, and although I had no idea what God was doing in Julia's life, I made a conscious decision to acknowledge that He was in control (even if I didn't feel he was!) - the battle belonged to Him. My deep personal faith was very important to me and I was blessed that John too had a deep faith. We had had the joy of seeing both our daughters come to know God as their Father at an early age and our Christian faith was something we could share as a family, as we talked and prayed together - little did I know then exactly how much our faith was to be tested.

Despite Julia having missed all but one exam, her tutors were very understanding and encouraged her to undertake her clinical placement, as arranged, at Midhurst at the end of June, and sit the exams she had missed in September. Still unwell, but better than before, she went off to join her friends on the wards. A couple of days later I received a phone call saying that she was very ill and asking me to collect her as soon as possible. In fact the medical staff had discussed admitting her to hospital but felt she would be better at home. Driving to collect Julia on that memorable journey, described in the previous chapter, my emotions were all over the place. I was too shocked, confused, anxious and numb to know what I felt or thought! I could see my immediate hopes of Julia being well enough to continue her course slipping away, and I couldn't help but wonder

The Early Years 25
to what extent her dreams too were being shattered.

THE RACE

Lord, once I ran races but now I sit listlessly here
My body, once agile, cries out, 'It's not fair!'
Now I'd panic at any outbreak of cheering from spectators
And have to retreat somewhere quiet to regain my poise.

I can't even remember what I've said to people
Names get muddled, I lose the thread of conversations
If I try to read my blurred eyes see just a line of words:
The relay line is severed to a mind that barely works -

A mind that seems covered by a thick, heavy cloud
Suffocating my thoughts, closing in like a shroud;
I'd falter now at the starting line, my body flashing 'can't do'
Messages to my brain, my joints one hot, dull nagging ache

The nausea is a distraction and I return back to my bed
Even there my mind haunts me, chilling nightmares - "I'm dead!"
I wake up suddenly dripping with sweat,
As if my body thermostat has just been reset.

I wish that the struggling could be over and done,
But with rest and God's healing a race I'll have won.

Julia

Chapter 3

Shattered Dreams

I think of you through the watches of the night (Psalm 63:6)

Memories of my happy, lively daughter were almost submerged in my fear for her future as we entered the house with the doctor's diagnosis still ringing in our ears. Struggling to keep our emotions in check we quietly went into the lounge where Julia was curled up on the sofa with her long arms wrapped round a hot water bottle. She looked very pale and ill, barely managing a smile. I knelt down placing my hand on her shoulder and John sat on the sofa and held her limp hand in his strong fatherly grasp. Looking on the bright side, (as ever!), I said, "Well, the good news is that all your tests have come back negative." Julia retorted "I'm not sure that that is good, I *am* ill - it would be easier if I knew there was something proven medically wrong with me." Disappointment was written on her face and I could see that she was struggling as she asked, "Did Jill say anything else?"

"Yes, it is most likely that you have M.E.". Julia turned her face away, a few tears glistening on her pale, drawn cheek. A stunned silence fell as we gave Julia time to take in what had just been said. Then the dam burst - sobbing accompanied by the words, "What will happen to my nursing ?" John gently replied, "It's not goodbye to your nursing career; you will get better". We heard the panic in her voice as she cried, "I'm not stopping university! I love it and I can't let my friends down - I'm going to be sharing a flat with them in October." Her determination to keep going came tumbling out as I sat feeling utterly helpless that I couldn't rescue my daughter from this situation, and I didn't know how quickly she would recover. When children fall and hurt themselves, mothers are there to stick plaster on and take control to make things better. But here I was with a twenty-year-old daughter who was in pain and my immediate thought was that there was nothing I could do to help her. However I quickly recognised that I *could* help her, by taking control of the situation so I said, "Julia, whatever it takes we will be with you in this and do everything we can to help you recover. None of us have chosen to be in this position. You don't want to be ill, and in no way do Dad and I want to see you ill and missing out on life . . . . but reality is, this is where we are. All we can do is trust God for his help and strength in this."

Our faith certainly helped us to take one day at a time, positive in the hope that Julia would quickly recover. Jill, our doctor visited Julia a day later and had a long chat to her about the illness, advising as much rest as Julia needed, with no sudden bursts of activity. During July Julia rested and did nothing; but knowing that she had to be better by August to start revising again was quite a pressure. By the end of July it became clear to Julia that she wasn't well enough to begin trying to revise, and so she made the decision not to go back to university for the time being. This gave her a measure of relief as she didn't have to battle on feeling so unwell, yet the thought of having to take a year out of university aroused deep feelings of disappointment

Although in my head I believed Julia's decision was right, my heart felt as if it had been pierced with a sword. That evening John, Fiona and I sat together on Julia's bed. We were so cut up, that all we could do was cry and hug each other. The comfort of feeling loving arms around us brought a measure of relief from the pain. We tried to be honest with each other about how much we were all hurting in our own ways and voiced our commitment to support Julia and one another during this difficult time. Then we ended up as we always did in difficult situations, praying and asking God for His strength and grace to cope.

My dreams for my daughter's future were beginning to be shattered. Although I was a nurse myself I had not pushed Julia into nursing, so my disappointment over the shattering of the dream was not so much specifically the dreams of seeing Julia nursing, but of seeing her happy and fulfilled in her chosen profession. Consequently I found my emotions were raw. Like many mothers hurting for their children, sleep at times evaded me at night, particularly in the early hours of the morning. The darkness and quietness surrounding me seemed to give full permission for my anxious thoughts to come out and play on my mind, and for my imagination to run riot. I knew it was important for me to manage these thoughts in order to have some sleep and somehow learn to starve my fears and feed my faith. Worship is a very important part of my relationship with Jesus so I decided to try and focus my attention on one worship song. These words very simply express the truth of the gospel and reminded me that in spite of experiencing difficulties here on earth, Jesus reigns in glory.

> *All hail the lamb enthroned on high,*
> *His praise shall be our battle cry.*
> *He reigns victorious, for ever glorious,*
> *His name is Jesus, He is the Lord.* (1)

I found that I would wake up with anxious thoughts immediately taking over so I would try to focus on the song and quietly sing the words in my heart . This gave me a measure of peace from my inner turmoil as thoughts bombarded my mind. Then they would set off again, and it took all my energy and determination to try and pull my mind back and focus on the song again. Over a period of time I found I could more quickly distract myself from my anxieties by singing these words and after about a year I found myself waking in the middle of the night with the words of the song already on my mind. Thus the darkness and quietness became a friendly and familiar corner of my world where I learnt to handle my imagination and turn to praise. If I found my mind wandering off along the path of anxiety, I immediately sang these words and invariably I was able to go back to sleep again.

Shattered Dreams

Once Julia had been diagnosed with M.E., a friend recommended a book on the subject which I ordered from W H Smith. One very hot, sunny August day I went into Reading to collect the book.(2) Emerging from the shop blinking against the strong sunlight, I quickly flicked through the pages. There, in print, were listed all her symptoms: flu-like illness, fatigue, muscle weakness and pain, headaches, poor sleep pattern, very cold extremities, increased sensitivity to noise and light, and problems with concentration and short-term memory. The only symptoms that Julia didn't appear to have were irritable bowel syndrome and muscle twitching! Reading this list made me face reality, and I think for the first time I recognised just how ill Julia was. I couldn't hold myself together and the tears flowed - just as well I could hide behind my sunglasses. Then I read something that really hit me between the eyes. In the early stages of M.E., 'taking enough time off work, as sick leave and holiday leave, to recover completely from that initial immunological stress will certainly prevent the illness from progressing any further and most likely return them to complete and full health.' Suddenly I was overcome with guilt. The *"if onlys"* came thick and fast: *"If only I had encouraged Julia to take time out from university when she was first ill . . . . . if only I had taken Julia seriously when she first said she thought she had chronic fatigue and if only we had pushed for a consultant referral, maybe she wouldn't be so ill now . . . . . if only I had insisted that she was to do nothing for several months . . . . ."*

I was overwhelmed by these completely irrational thoughts, feeling that I was to blame and that if I had done something different Julia would now be well. So often as mothers we blame ourselves for our child's mistakes and tragedies. *"If only I had given him more time,"* or *"If only I had given her more freedom."* As I walked down the high street, I barely knew what I was doing. I could hardly see, as my eyes were brimming over with tears and all I could hear resounding in my head were these self-accusations, *"I'm to blame. I could have stopped this."* But I wasn't the only one feeling guilty.

Subsequently Julia told me how she too struggled with guilt and self-blame and the *"if only"* for many years of her illness.

As I struggled to get rid of these irrational feelings of guilt I found myself withdrawing from Julia. Every time I looked at her I felt I was bleeding inside with self accusation, *"How could I be such a terrible mum?"* and, in Julia's words I became "quite mechanical" in my loving of her. My usual warmth and sensitivity became frozen. Over the next few days I became my own internal counsellor in order to work through my guilt. I recognised that when things don't turn out as I would like them to, it is very tempting to assume that if I had done something differently then the story would have a happier ending. It seems to be universal that mothers are quick to feel guilty, believing that they are the cause of what happens and saying, "it's all my fault." Guilt is a mother's occupational hazard! As mothers we can easily "beat ourselves up" about what we could have done differently, but nobody is a perfect parent and we can only do our best - God doesn't demand anything more. I have counselled many mothers who have felt this irrational guilt as somehow they thought they were to blame for their daughter's drug addiction or their son's homosexual relationship.

In his book, *When Bad Things Happen To Good People* Harold S Kushner describes how the roots of this feeling may lie in our childhood.

> "Psychologists speak of the infantile myth of omnipotence. A baby comes to think that the world exists to meet his needs, and that he makes everything happen in it. He wakes in the morning and summons the rest of the world to its tasks. He cries, and someone comes to attend to him. When he is hungry, people feed him, and when he is wet, people change him. Very often, we do not completely outgrow that infantile notion that our wishes cause things to happen. A part of our mind continues to believe that people get sick because we hate them . . . . Years later, should something bad

happen to us or around us, feelings from our childhood re-emerge, and we instinctively assume that we have messed things up again." (3)

Over the next few days my thoughts became more rational as I argued with myself that I couldn't be responsible for everything that happens in life and that blaming myself was punitive and destructive. I acknowledged that I wasn't perfect, and therefore probably had not been as wise as I might have been with Julia, but I had done my best. Looking at the evidence of what difference it would have made if I had told Julia she wasn't to go to Switzerland, or if I had tried to insist that she had to take time out from university, I began to realise that it would have made no difference as Julia would probably have listened but ignored my advice anyway! I had always encouraged her as an adult of 20 years to be responsible for her own decisions in life and I had never been a controlling, authoritative parent. On this occasion I wished that I had been more gently authoritative! However it was no use living in condemnation as it would get me nowhere. I reminded myself that Jesus didn't want me to live under a continuous, low-lying black cloud. On the cross He had entered the mess of my struggling humanity in order to set me free from condemnation, so I confessed my weakness to Jesus. I combated my guilt waves by saying, *"Thank you Jesus for dying for me on the cross and rescuing me from guilt."* and slowly over the next week or so I found a freedom from these self-accusations and feelings of guilt. This enabled me to relate to Julia again on an emotional level and I was able to reach out in love and compassion to comfort and to support her in her anguish.

There was however one occasion when I found it very difficult to support Julia in her decision. A few months earlier a friend in London had bought tickets for herself and Julia to see The Royal Tournament at Earls Court. The morning that she was due to go, Julia sat in bed torn between loyalty to her friend and an overriding fear of letting her down, and a recognition that as she felt so ill she needed to look after her own needs. I felt really angry that Julia decided to go, and fearful about how it might affect her. My feelings of helplessness as a mother surfaced again as I knew Julia had to make her own mind up, yet I also knew that the outing would be too much for her! However, having voiced my concern to Julia, Fiona and I insisted that she had to eat a decent meal at lunchtime before she went, in spite of her swollen stomach glands which caused dull aching when she tried to eat. Having waved Julia off on the train, I was aware that the anger I felt towards Julia's irresponsible decision would cause me a lot of stress if I didn't let it go, so I prayed *"Father, I place Julia into your hands , please protect and strengthen her whilst she is away"*. By the time I met her off the train the next day, I felt drawn and tired, and as I had anticipated, Julia returned absolutely exhausted. However the good thing was that psychologically Julia felt buoyed up as she had managed some social life! I came to recognise that in her grief Julia had panicked and had clung on to some normality (i.e. a social life) to stem the pain. But she had misjudged just how ill she really was and had therefore set unrealistic goals. It wasn't easy being a mum but at least this time I didn't feel guilty that Julia had made herself worse by going to London. That one *wasn't* my fault!

The other question I found myself asking was, *"Why has this happened"?* I wanted to be able to make sense of Julia's illness, in order to learn from it and move on. I could think of 101 reasons with no problem at all and they used to go round and round in my mind like a non-stop merry-go-round. We cannot escape the question of *"why"* something happens. "This little word *why* is no torrent of speech. It is only a little drop of three letters. Yet it can cause mortal injury to our souls." (4) In wanting to find an answer I became agitated and frustrated and certainly to some extent I was not at peace with myself. In fact sometimes I was so frustrated that I used to hop on my bike and cycle round the local cycle paths - anything to distract myself from this unanswerable question which began to haunt me.

I realised that one of the reasons I wanted an answer to the *"why?"* was that it would give me a logical explanation, a feeling that there is an order about life that makes sense. To live with life not making sense left me feeling more insecure. Also to find a logical explanation would help prevent this happening again to Julia, and indeed to anyone else. I don't think there is anything wrong with raising questions, pursuing possible answers and searching for reasons but if, after this process, no conclusions can be drawn, then it is time to let go. Well, it took me a long time to let go! Our computerised, televised age in which anything and everything must be disassembled, identified and classified doesn't help us to accept an unfathomable mystery.

After about a year of battling to answer this question, one day I found myself saying quite out of the blue, "You haven't been able to answer the question why after all these months so why don't you just accept the fact that you cannot make sense of why Julia is ill ." As soon as I had said these words to myself, I stopped battling and found a deep peace as I accepted that this illness was a mystery I couldn't solve. There were contributing factors which made her vulnerable, but no concrete evidence to answer the question *"why?"* As mothers when we find that our hopes and dreams for our child's life have been shattered, the other *Why?* we invariably ask is, *Why, God, do you let my child suffer?* Surprisingly this question was not at the forefront of my thoughts at that time - perhaps I was still in shock and numb with the pain. But it didn't stay locked away for ever. The whole question of why God allows suffering when He says He loves us, was something I explored later.

As I experienced the intensity of emotions accompanying the loss of my healthy daughter and the loss of expectations for her immediate future, I recognised the signs that I was in a grieving process. This wasn't the first time that I had been thrust into grief. When my parents died I had been unfamiliar with grief and it was like a stranger that came knocking on my door. I found it a very bewildering time. However, now that it felt more familiar, I knew what to expect. Having since spoken about the grief process and the stages of grief on counselling courses, and counselled many bereaved clients I am aware of some of the effects it can have on us. We are all very different and as mothers we will experience grief in very different ways as we travel through it at our own individual pace. There is no nice neat systematic sequence. In fact for some people it can feel more like riding a roller coaster as our emotions can send us zooming up to the top, to hang there for a few seconds, only to crash down with our stomachs feeling as if they have been left behind! By contrast, grief for other people can feel more like spinning round like a top, becoming quite dizzy with the speed at which several emotions can be felt all at once! The most helpful way for me to look at grieving is as a journey. *"The road is not straight, but winds and curves and doubles back on itself. On occasions, it is possible to emerge from a clearing or laboriously negotiate a pit - only to find oneself face to face with a landmark which at first seems new but which in fact has been encountered before, but from a different angle and via a different path. The journey can encompass rocky terrain which is arduous and costly to traverse, but also may include some clearings and even some stretches which feel like a desert. And the road certainly does not take the shortest route from A to B, but includes hairpin bends as well as relatively straightforward stretches. Much of this symbolism can be applied to the experience of people who are grieving; they may feel 'rocky' or unstable, arid or devoid of all feeling, and they may switch breathtakingly fast from denial to sadness and back to denial."* (5)

As I faced the pain of my own grief, I knew that it was not healthy to skirt around the perimeter of this loss. Instead it was important to walk through the centre of the pain, grief's very core, in order to work through the feelings and come out on the other side to continue life in a meaningful way. I have counselled many people who have become stuck in the grieving process because they couldn't face the pain - like the mother whose teenage son had been killed in a car accident three years earlier, but who had not allowed the tears of sadness to flow for fear that her feelings would overwhelm her; and the young teenager who was too frightened to face the pain of having a child with special needs, because she didn't want to feel out of control.

I gave myself permission to go with the flow of my grief. Consequently I found myself dealing not only with guilt and the tormenting questions that go on and on, but also with tears and sadness. I found that at some point every day the inner pain of my loss would be triggered or the pain I felt for Julia in her illness was so overwhelming that tears flowed. "Grief cannot be dry cleaned away, it must be washed in tears." (6) Sometimes I wanted to be private and cry alone, at other times I wept with John and occasionally with the girls. In fact it became quite a family joke that we could laugh about together: "Have you had your cry, today, Mum?" I had always cried easily for sentimental reasons, so the girls were quite used to seeing a weepy mum. But these tears were different. They were an expression of a deep inner pain of sadness that were part of my grieving process. It is often said that, "Tears are the safety valve of the heart." Fortunately I was blessed with Mary, a dear friend whose shoulder I could cry on at any time. She completely accepted me where I was and never judged me or said I shouldn't feel the way I did. A week or so after Julia had been told she had M.E., Mary popped her head round the door of my counselling room at the surgery. "How are things?" she asked. "Oh, have you heard that Julia has M.E., or Chronic Fatigue as it is sometimes called"? With those words the dam burst again, and my tears and pain burst over Mary like a torrent of swirling water bursting its banks. Between sobs I managed to blurt out all my fears: "Julia could have this for four years, like someone else I know, I can't bear the thought of that happening to her . . . . what will happen to her nursing career? . . . . How will she manage to cope? . . . . I can't believe this is happening, it hurts so much". Mary didn't try to stem the flow of tears with any trite, neat little answers, but just let me cry on her shoulder.

It is said that in response to any major loss there are about 50 gallons of tears to cry out, and I found this to be true. Tears are healing. Some people think that tears are a sign of weakness, and we Brits are known for our stiff upper lip, keeping all emotions in check. On opening a centre for the broken and hurting people in our society, the late Diana, Princess of Wales said, "There seems to be a curious conspiracy to suppress tears in our times."

But I believe that tears are a very important expression of inner pain and provided that they are not used as a manipulating tool they are a very natural expression of our humanity. When Lazarus, a close friend of Jesus, died, we read that *Jesus wept.* (7) Jesus wasn't afraid to express his feelings of sadness and it was important for me to be free to be myself and express whatever I felt in an appropriate way, provided the time and place were suitable. Obviously there were people with whom I would not freely share my pain as they either felt so embarrassed that they became uncomfortable, or they would start throwing Bible verses at me! Some people protect themselves from another person's pain by trying to give pat, trite advice about what the Bible says. One lady gave me a barrage of God's promises down the phone, and I ended up holding the earpiece away at arm's length! All I had wanted was someone to sit with me in my pain. But Mary was someone with whom I could be absolutely honest and be myself, and after a good cry I felt a great relief from the inner tension of fears and sadness.

Towards the beginning of August 1991 Julia and I set off for the university campus to talk to her tutors about taking a year out to give her time to recover. It was a beautiful sunny day, the sort of day I would normally really enjoy, but when I woke up that morning I had a sense of heaviness. We were going to have to face saying goodbye for the time being to the academic life that Julia loved. However so

Shattered Dreams 39

that Julia did not feel that she was loosing everything, we were happy that one part of her plans for the following academic year could still be fulfilled. She was still intending to keep her friendships alive by living in the flat with her friends in Guildford. As we drove into the university car park I was so distracted by my thoughts and emotions that I backed into a parked car and pranged it. I could have done without that! Trying to put the frustration of this event aside, we climbed slowly up the steps to the top of the science building, the cold starkness of the concrete walls reflecting the emptiness and numbness I felt inside.

My feelings of sadness and disappointment contrasted sharply with the warmth of Julia's tutor who met us with a welcoming smile. It was as if she was standing there as an expression of Jesus, welcoming us in our pain into His presence. The tutor couldn't have been more understanding as she herself had experienced a period of chronic fatigue after glandular fever in her life, so she understood Julia - a rarity! As Julia discussed her future with her tutor, it transpired that there was no problem about Julia rejoining the course a year later, as Julia was told that she was an excellent student. It was very affirming for Julia and myself to hear how much the department valued her and how sad they were to hear that she had to take a year out. Hearing such words of encouragement was comforting and soothing. As we drove out of the university I found myself holding back the tears as I inwardly whispered *"goodbye"* to the campus, while my hopes and dreams for Julia's student life, and for Julia herself, were put on hold. I turned to Julia and said, "That was difficult . . . . but God was with us." Leaning back in the car seat exhausted she was able to manage an audible, "Yes". Having said goodbye to her nursing studies, we then journeyed on to Midhurst to collect Julia's belongings from her room and to say goodbye to her nursing friends.

When we arrived at Midhurst most of her close friends were on the ward - I am not sure whether this made it easier or more difficult. I did most of the packing while Julia gave out the operational instructions since she knew what went where. We did this almost mechanically keeping our talking to a minimum and just addressing the task in hand. However my emotions were in turmoil as yet again I packed away the dream I had had of Julia being a natural compassionate nurse engaged in a career that she loved. I knew that if I broke down and cried it would not only be difficult for Julia but would also embarrass her in front of other nurses. So I held on tightly to my inner turmoil. But this had its consequences for when I was carrying some of the cases downstairs I wasn't thinking what I was doing, and thump, thump, down the stairs I fell, with the cases tumbling down behind me. With the inevitable crash at the bottom, I could not hold on to my inner turmoil any longer and warm tears slid from my eyes. At that point I just wanted the ground to swallow me up!

Fortunately I had no broken bones, I had just skinned my shin and shaken myself up. Desperately trying to hold back the tears I forced myself to laugh, saying with a grimace, "Typical me, I didn't look what I was doing . . . . does anyone want some hands on nursing experience to mop up the blood and put on a dressing?" One of Julia's friends took over and soon I was patched up. Some of the other nursing students had by now come off duty and Julia's closest friends, Anna, Caroline and Ango were standing in their crisp nurses' uniforms outside the nurses' home, ready to say goodbye. My longing for Julia to be among them seemed like a knife twisting in my heart. As we got into the car all her friends stood waving goodbye and full as ever of boisterous energy, shouted, "We'll keep in touch Julia . . . . hope you'll feel better soon . . . . we'll miss you . . . . see you in October in the flat."

As we began to drive home, the emotional pain of the day and the shock of falling down the stairs began to take its toll, to say nothing of the discomfort of my leg. I felt out of touch with reality, as if I was dreaming . "Mum, I'm not sure you're well enough to drive. I'll take over." "No, Julia . . . . . . I'm fine," I said as I tried to convince her that I was able to drive. "I can see that you're not OK, so pull over, and we'll swop places. I'm in a better place than you, so I'll drive." I didn't have any strength to argue, so without further hesitation we changed places. The resultant feeling of guilt began insidiously to creep into the pit of my stomach. *"This will make Julia even more exhausted and it's my fault. If I hadn't fallen down the stairs she would be able to rest and I could drive. The day has been emotionally exhausting enough for me - what must it have been like for Julia?"* All the way home I battled with these thoughts and feelings of guilt and it was such a relief to enter the safe haven of home.

John and Fiona were there to welcome us, and bombarded us with questions. "What did they say?" . . . . "What happened?" . . . . "What have you done to your leg?" Julia and I were quite irritable with them as we didn't want to have to do any more explaining, we just wanted to be left to "be". This was hard on John and Fiona as naturally they wanted to feel part of what had happened that day. I could see their look of astonishment and hurt at the way we were reacting, and muttered something like, "We don't want to tell you now, we'll talk about it later." So over the course of the evening, the day's events came out in dribs and drabs. When I went to bed that night, John and I prayed together as usual and as far as I was able, I handed all the day's events over to the Lord. *"Lord, you know how disappointed and shattered I feel about today's events. I place them all in your hands . You are Lord of the future please come and pour your healing grace upon Julia so that she is soon well enough to enjoy life again"*. As a result of this prayer I felt as if ointment had been gently massaged into my wounds and a great measure of peace obliterated all the inner turmoil - sleep came as a gift from God.

In the search to find appropriate help and advice for Julia we soon found ourselves visiting a consultant in London. There was the usual round of blood tests and the taking of Julia's past history -

something that Julia was to encounter repeatedly over the years. The consultant was helpful in various ways. Firstly, she brought more understanding of the factors contributing to why Julia was unwell - a build-up of physical and emotional stress brought on by many changes affects the body's natural immunity. Julia's history revealed she had experienced many stresses over the previous year - a very unhappy and difficult time at Great Ormond Street, stress to her body from inter-railing across Europe for a month; and then with only a few weeks to catch her breath Julia had been off to the new demands of university life. Secondly, Julia was advised to use only 70% of her energy and to learn always to keep some energy in the bank. This was easier said than done, as sometimes Julia didn't know how much energy she had to do things until she had used it all up! Lastly, the consultant advised a low dose antidepressant to help Julia with her sleeping patterns.

These antidepressants were to have a profound effect. Before Fiona commenced her course at Leeds University at the end of September we decided to have a family weekend away together in Cambridge. We were all prepared to accommodate Julia as far as possible in the activities and accepted that she would need frequent rests. During our meal there together on the Friday evening Julia said she felt as if the tablets had taken over and were driving her. In fact reading between the lines she appeared to be quite frightened by the effect, but knowing that starting on antidepressants can produce side-effects I encouraged her to keep taking them for the time being. On the Saturday we were able to park quite near the centre of Cambridge and began to wander round sightseeing. However, Julia was acting in a most bizarre way, as if she was high on drugs! One minute she was non-stop chatting, the next minute she sat on the path and flatly refused to move. I became increasingly worried about her and then to make matters worse she stormed off into the shops by herself. This wasn't the Julia I knew. Her erratic behaviour was also having an effect on Fiona who became quite upset about her sister. That evening we decided to halve the tablets and there was a definite improvement the following day. When we returned home we went to the doctor and discovered that apparently one of the possible side-effects of the tablets Julia had been taking was mania - that made sense; no wonder Julia had been hyper manic! With a change of prescription Julia, much to my relief, had no more problems. We have since learnt that people with M.E. are very sensitive to antidepressants and need to start on a low dose, and build it up slowly.

Julia continued to be very fatigued, with joint pain and swollen glands but was determined to go back to Guildford and share a flat with her friends. With Fiona starting at Leeds university, Julia was encouraged that her life was moving on, even though she wasn't going back to Guildford to study. John and I were fully supportive of Julia in this move as we were determined to help her in whatever way we could. As we journeyed back to Guildford with the car packed full of boxes and cases and Julia expectantly looking forward to a new phase of her life, John and I had great hopes in our hearts. In doing the most sensible thing by taking a year out, we anticipated that Julia would go from strength to strength and recover. Having seen some of our dreams for Julia shattered, we were now hopeful that the coming year would see Julia restored to health.

I'M NOT GOING BACK

My friends all go back to the usual mad life -
University style,
Joyful laughter, fun and wonder,
But for me the knife pierces further -
I'm **not** going back.
Boring lectures, books and papers,
Maybe the Library too?
You must be joking! They're far too busy
With sports, the union and CU -
But **I'm** not going back.
Dashing madly, from lecture to meeting
A life I knew so well.
Prayer meeting, tap dancing, friends to coffee
A hair-raising pace you can tell -
But I'm not going back.
This year its different, strangely quiet
My student life seems to be over
The clock ticks relentlessly, M.E., M.E.,
I need to recover
So I'm not going back . . .

Julia

Chapter 4

Dashed Hopes

. . . My prayers . . . . unanswered, I went about mourning (Psalm 35:13, 14)

"Bye. Have fun with your friends and take care of yourself." John and I drove away from the Guildford flat where Julia had moved back to live with her friends. It seemed a huge step forward, and part of me was bubbling with joy and hope. At the same time I had to admit to feeling a measure of sadness that she wasn't well enough to go back to the studies she had enjoyed so much, and there was a lingering concern - such as any mother would feel watching her child take a new step - hopefully on the way to recovery. Would she be able to manage? As John and I journeyed home we remarked on the beauty of God's creation in the breathtaking autumn colours, and asked Him to take care of Julia.

Over the next few months we were encouraged as we saw Julia slowly improving. She began to feel better and had more energy. Living with her flat mates was a great source of fun and encouragement and although she wasn't well enough to go out very much she enjoyed their company when they were in and sat listening for many an hour to the ups and downs of university life. However, being students they were out a lot, and consequently Julia was lonely at times so I used to drive over to see her every week or so. Sitting together in the small box room, because it happened to be the warmest room in the house, we caught up with each other's news and enjoyed each other's company, sometimes chatting about nothing in particular, the way women can! But we were not just two women, we were mother and a daughter. Since Julia's birth I had waited for the moment that every mother hopes for, when her daughter reaches adulthood and becomes a companion and friend, as well as a daughter. Julia and I were now able to enjoy that relationship.

As Julia grew in strength, ever enthusiastic for life she looked around for voluntary work. Sitting vegetating was not on her agenda - if anything her desire to be "doing" sometimes pushed her too far! I used to get annoyed when doctors and the media suggested that M.E. was for those who wanted to opt out of life. There was no way that Julia fitted into this category, and I knew without a doubt that if Julia was well she would be busy and active. When our children are misunderstood or treated unfairly our motherly instincts are to protect them. When we can't do so, we feel frustrated, and when I read or heard of uninformed judgment of M.E. sufferers I wanted to shout from the the rooftops, *"Hey, you've got it wrong! How dare you judge? Come and live with us; see the situation for yourself, and you'll revise your opinion!"* But something deeper than this was also going on. As a mother, I not only felt protective towards Julia, and wanted to set the record straight, but it was also as if my credibility as a mother was under attack, as if I was thinking to myself, *"If people don't believe what I say about my daughter, they can't trust me as a mother."* Once I recognised this irrational thought I was able to remind myself that I was a good enough mother and that it didn't matter what other people thought of me. My worth didn't depend upon other people's approval of me. I had been entrusted with two wonderful daughters, and God didn't demand perfection from me in my mothering - just a willingness to learn.

It is often said and it's probably true, that a mother knows her child better than anyone else does, so when other people come along and make comments which challenge a mother's perception, it is very easy for her to feel under attack, and being hurt, she reacts in anger. I have counselled mothers who recognised that their young children had special needs, or were in some way physically disabled, only to be told at first by the medical profession that there was nothing wrong. This experience leaves mothers thinking their judgment is not being taken seriously and leaves them feeling not only frustrated and angry, but with a loss of confidence as mothers with subsequent loss of self- esteem. Some mothers however, do the opposite, choosing to ignore the fact that there is something wrong with their child: the pain of facing reality is too difficult, so they deny the truth. A young mother, referred to me for counselling because her four year old had been recently diagnosed with special needs, couldn't accept it. She blanked out the fact that he would have to go to a special school and part of my work was helping her to face the pain of what she had lost (an expected healthy son) and to come to terms with what this meant for her.

The pain of my own loss became less intense as Julia grew stronger, and to see her becoming more involved in the community was very encouraging. One of the ways she worked as a volunteer was as a classroom helper. My sister-in-law, Cathy, was a teacher in a primary school in Hampshire and Julia would travel by train and bus to spend an afternoon in her classroom. At first she was so exhausted by the journey that just sitting in the room and being a presence was all she could cope with, but as she became stronger she was able to become more involved with the children. This interaction with other people outside the four walls of her room was a great confidence builder.

Working as a volunteer in her local church was another outlet Julia found. Fortunately the church was only about 100 yards down the road, and Julia greatly enjoyed helping in the office for a couple of hours every week and through this met the young pastoral assistant, James. Soon they were seeing more of each other. Julia wasn't really well enough to go out many times with James, but he used to pop round to the flat, and it was good for us to see Julia enjoying this relationship, with this very likable young man. Our hopes that Julia would be well enough to enjoy participating in life again were being realised.

To celebrate Julia's 21st birthday in December 1991 we organised a barn dance for family and friends in one of the University halls in Guildford. The day started really early for me: making the buffet meal; collecting helium filled balloons; arranging a basket of flowers; and collecting the cake. By the time Julia and James arrived from Guildford round about mid-day I was ready to sit down with them and put my feet up, watching Julia enjoy opening her presents. With the food preparation complete and Julia refreshed after an afternoon rest, we set off for Guildford with two car loads of drink and food. On arrival at the hall, John and James put up balloons and I set out the food with help from Julia's friends. In spite of it being cold and foggy outside, the hall was warm and welcoming and the band soon livened everyone up. Although Julia looked very pale and fragile, her flowing navy skirt worn with a cream blouse, and her long hair plaited and tied back gave her a feminine attractiveness. When the time came to cut the cake, which was beautifully iced with delicate flowers, Julia appeared to cope with being the centre of noisy singing! She sat down for most of the evening, but managed one rather stately dance and delighted in seeing her friends have fun. At the end of these birthday celebrations Julia looked absolutely shattered however, so sat quietly on some steps whilst a number of us cleared up. When we came to say goodbye, with Julia staying on in Guildford, she threw her arms round my neck and whispered, "Thanks Mum for all you have done; it was a great evening," and then went up to John and gave him a thankful hug as well. John and I caught each other's eyes as much as to say, "Phew! We're so relieved it went so well, and that Julia enjoyed herself."

It was good to have had my twin sister, Andria and her new husband at the dance, as well as my brother and his wife, Cathy. Unfortunately Cathy's daughter, Susan couldn't come as she was flat on her back in severe pain at home. Cathy and I talked together briefly about the pain Cathy felt as a mother - how difficult it had been for her to walk into a hall full of exuberant, energetic youngsters when her own daughter lay at home, hardly able to move. The pain of her own loss was made more acute by seeing other youngsters doing the things she longed for her daughter to be doing. I sensed that Cathy was putting on a very brave face, cheerful on the outside, but inwardly crying. Wearing a brave mask was something I knew all about, but on this occasion I didn't have to put it on! Seeing Julia well enough to celebrate with so many friends was a very special day, and gave me a great sense of joy and hope for the future.

This sense of relief that life was looking up for Julia, didn't last long. One morning the following week Julia phoned me in tears, "Mum, I feel ill again; all my glands are swollen and I ache all over." I tried to be reassuring over the phone, but my stomach was churning, *"O Lord, please don't let her become ill again"*. A few days later I collected Julia and with Fiona home from university we enjoyed a pleasurable Christmas with Julia picking up a little. Over the new year Julia went away with James to see friends. She was still far from well, and when she returned to James' house, all she could do was sit as she was too fatigued and exhausted to do anything. But as the early weeks of 1992 rolled on her health began to improve again and by February she was able to resume helping Cathy in the classroom, even walking the two miles from the station to the school. Cathy remarked on the phone that she could see a definite improvement: Julia looked so much better and could now cope well with the children as she seemed to have so much more energy. This improvement was sustained and Julia was able to go to the University's Valentine Ball; although she didn't dance, just to be there was a dream come true. Within a few weeks she then travelled up to Leicester to visit an old friend and a short swim in the local pool was another sign suggesting that she was on the road to recovery.

Then things started going downhill, again. Headaches and nausea returned and Julia began to experience such fatigue that she had to cut back on her activities. One bright cold, day I went down to visit her. We normally drove out to craft shops for tea, or went into town but on this particular day she didn't feel at all well, and the car journey out into the beautiful, cold frosty countryside didn't make things any better. It was as much as she could do to cope with the bends in the country lanes, let alone enjoy the scenic route. "Mum, I'm sorry, but I feel too nauseated and dizzy to stop for tea; we'll have to go home". Her drawn face, lined and grey said it all. Her lifeless eyes, with great panda circles under them were such a contrast to the sparkling eyes and lively, joyful faces that greeted us on our return to the flat. Anna, Ango and Jan were in the kitchen and as we entered all we could hear were squeals of delight and non stop chatter echoing round the place. Laughing and giggling they popped their heads round the kitchen door and greeted us, "Hi Julia - how was your trip out?" With all the energy she could muster, she mumbled "OK" and went and lay on her bed. I couldn't help but empathise with Julia's sense of isolation and loneliness at not being able to join in with the boisterous chatter of her flat mates, and recognised again how hard life was for her - longing to be well and able to join in the fun and laughter, yet lacking the physical strength to do so. The hurt I felt on Julia's behalf stirred up anger in me which I managed to contain until I had said goodbye to her and got in the car to drive home.

Once in the car, with no one but God within earshot, I let my anger out and told God exactly what I thought of him! *"You call yourself a loving God, how can you let Julia suffer like this? Can't you see the pain we're in? Where are you? I feel you've abandoned us. Do you really care?"* My emotions felt so raw and uncontainable that expressing them to God seemed to be the most constructive way to give vent to the pain. *"You don't play fair God, if you don't change the situation I am not going to speak to you . . . . . so there!"* Amidst my tears and shouting at God, I occasionally found myself also thanking Him for his goodness. *"But I give you all the honour and praise that's due your name."* What a mess I was in. It felt as if my emotions were on a roundabout, and I couldn't stop them - just as well no one could hear me in the car as this spewing out of all my anger, at times penetrated by words of praise, went on for the whole of the journey back to Reading!

Anger that comes out of pain and grief is a very normal response to loss. God gives us the ability to have emotions - they are normal, they are part of our lives. If we have a leg amputated, it hurts. Likewise if we lose a healthy child, it hurts. Expressing anger and flailing away at God for letting painful things happen, is a way of releasing and draining emotions. It doesn't mean we're unspiritual! Reading the Psalms of lament written by David was a great source of comfort to me because David illustrates the depths of a healthy human spirit as he deals honestly with devastating loss and all its attendant emotions. *My God, my God, why have you forsaken me? Why are you so far from saving me, so far from the words of my groaning?* (1)

Finding a constructive way of dealing with pain is a necessary way forward. Barbara Johnson, a mother who faced a different kind of sorrow from mine, when she came to recognise and accept that her son was gay wrote, "The most important thing is to DRAIN YOUR PAIN, release your anger much as a safety valve releases steam." (2) Allowing myself to acknowledge the pain and experience my emotions was my way of draining the pain and gaining release from inner turmoil. Researchers have learnt over the years, that those people who are able to let go of their emotions, either by crying or by means of some other appropriate avenue, enjoy better health overall.

Mixed up with my anger and the accusations that I threw at God throughout that emotional journey, was the comment, *"It's not fair that Julia can't enjoy life like her flat mates."* Now I had always accepted that life isn't always fair and had taught the girls to accept the unfairness of life as part of living in a fallen world. God may not seem fair, but it is important to hold on to the truth that He is just in all His ways. But in the hothouse of my raging emotions, my mind wasn't rational. It was saying *"It's not fair."* Every mother has been faced with the unfairness issue: little Luke comes running in at bedtime, and asks, "Why is Ruth allowed to stay up and watch telly and I have to go to bed? It's not fair!" The fairness question is universal, particularly when life throws at some people tragedy and heartache, whilst others appear to journey through life hardly touched by difficulties. Many mothers, who are single, either from choice, divorce or widowhood, wrestle with the question of fairness, but they are not the only ones. The most stabbing, hottest tears of a mother come when their expectant hopes and enthusiastic dreams for a child give way to suffering. This unfairness is there for mothers of the terminally ill and the disabled, for those whose children are enslaved by addiction or go off the rails. Sometimes life just isn't fair and bad things happen to good people.

In the conclusion of his book *When Bad things Happen to Good People* (3) Harold Kushner writes:
"Is there an answer to the question of why bad things happen to good people? That depends on what we mean by *answer*. If we mean 'Is there an explanation which will make sense of it all? - Why is there cancer in the world? Why did my father get cancer? Why did the plane crash? Why did my child die?' - there is probably no satisfying answer. We can offer learned explanations, but in the end, when we have covered all the squares on the game board and are feeling very proud of our cleverness, the pain and the anguish and the sense of unfairness will still be there."

But the word "answer" can mean "response" as well as "explanation", and in that sense, there may well be a satisfying answer to the tragedies in our lives".

"In the final analysis, the question of why bad things happen to good people translates itself into some very different questions, no longer asking why something happened, but asking how we will respond, what we intend to do now that it has happened".

Moving from the question, *why* to *what now* was a slow process going on within me. I began to discover that when I found myself asking *why*, I would more readily follow it up with questioning myself on *how* I could respond to the situation positively and would say "*OK God, what now?*" Victor Frankl, the famous Jewish psychiatrist who endured Auschwitz and other Nazi concentration camps observed that the people who remained strong and survived in these terrible conditions were those who had some future goal. Those prisoners who had a positive attitude in spite of the circumstances thrived, whereas those who blamed their environment and lost all hope often committed suicide. He fondly quotes Nietzsche's words, "He who has a *why* to live for can bear with almost any *how*." (4)

During that memorable car journey home, in the midst of my pain I was well aware that it was important to strike a balance between being honest with God and having a right attitude towards Him. By the time I arrived home, I had "drained my pain" and got it out of my system and although I felt like a wrung-out rag, I felt at peace within myself and with God, my Father. I had been able to pour all my rubbish into the heart of my heavenly Father and I had a sense that he had been holding me comfortingly in his arms. I was reminded of the times when as a child I used to go to my father and tell him amidst sobs that I was hurting, or how angry I was over something. He would gather me up in his arms, allowing me to spill it all out. He didn't have to say anything - just to feel safe in his arms, knowing he loved me was enough to soothe the pain. The desire to find a peace and a contentment in God, in the midst of suffering , became my prayer.

Any family adjusting to the changing circumstances of having an ill member in their midst will inevitably experience tension, and we were no exception! At times Fiona felt frustrated that Julia couldn't do very much and very occasionally they lost patience with each other. In one memorable incident Fiona cooked the evening meal for Julia, only to find Julia didn't like it - this ended up with Julia storming out of the house, in her frustration that she couldn't do things for herself. At times I found myself feeling angry with Julia for causing us so much pain and anxiety, which I rationally knew was through no fault of hers. One day I was surprised with myself for feeling really livid with Fiona, so much so that I was finding it difficult to talk to her civilly. As I reflected on what was happening I began to recognise that I felt angry with her for being so healthy and full of life, because it sharpened my pain for Julia. It was so confusing as I didn't really hate her for this. As I allowed this fleeting thought to rise up in my consciousness it was no longer a hidden intruder and in recognising what was going on I was able to let it go and move on to relate to Fiona again. John was not unaffected either - he became somewhat angry at times to see me upset and hurting. It sounds as if we were a very angry family! I don't think we were - I think we were just a normal family reacting to loss!

As we were all struggling with our own inner turmoil, Julia expressed her struggles in a poem she wrote round about that time, called

>   'God Understands'.
> "No other human being can fully comprehend
> My real inner suffering and physical bodily pain.
> I crouch inside a corner of a clear glass box
> No-one can get inside it -
> They can only stand and watch.
> Of course they can see when I'm crying,
> When I'm listless, or when I'm cross;
> But they cannot climb inside with me

Dashed Hopes

Into the clear glass box.
The searing pain piercing inside me,
Burns like a red hot rod
Stabbing, deeply wounding, for the
Healthy individual I'd been . . . once was.
Now I'm helpless, useless, at times a waste of space.
I want to cover the box with black paper
So you don't have to notice me in this state.
I know you've tried to break the glass,
Lift the lid . . . . . . get in . . . .
To reach my pain and feelings
Embedded deep within
I've got to leave my angry frustration and come to realise
That you'll never fully understand the welling pain inside.
But, I've found one empathetic person, who truly understands
Who can climb inside the clear glass box
And soothe the pain with His hands.
Yes, Jesus knows my suffering
He feels it in His heart
I don't need to . . . .
For He carried my hurts on the cross."

Julia gradually slid downwards and was home with Fiona for my 50th birthday celebrations over the Easter period of 1992. Returning from work on my birthday, I opened the front door and the girls surprised me with the noise of party poppers and loud cheers of "Happy birthday, Mum!" Once the hilarity had subsided, Julia went off to bed and didn't emerge again until we had our evening meal. As we sat round the table, John announced a surprise for me - he had booked tickets for the four of us at the Theatre Royal, Windsor for that evening. This was greeted with, "I'm sorry Mum, but I don't feel well enough to go," from Julia, quickly followed by Fiona saying, "I'll stay behind with Julia." "I'll see if I can find another couple to take the girls' seats," said John, departing for the study. I should have smelt a rat! But I didn't! I felt tearful at having to leave the girls behind as John and I set off for Windsor. Arriving at the theatre foyer suddenly John announced that he had got the wrong tickets - his face gave him away! Something was going on! Back in the car, I played along with the game as John blindfolded me so that I would have no idea where he was taking me! This had all been a ploy to get me out of the house so that food could be organised and guests arrive secretly for a surprise party! It was a wonderful evening and I was able to forget about the difficult time we were having. It was encouraging to see Julia well enough to join in by quietly sitting in the study so as not to be overwhelmed by too many people at once. However she paid the price, as over the following few days she was worse again.

A week or so later I kissed the girls goodbye as John was taking me away on a surprise weekend break for my birthday. I found myself flying off to Amsterdam to see the tulips in springtime. Part of me found it hard leaving Julia as she was far from well, but on the other hand I knew that Fiona was a really good sister to her, and able to look after her caringly. So I left with a spring in my step and a lightness in my spirit, determined to forget what was going on at home and to enjoy the time with John and the sights of Amsterdam. After a couple of very enjoyable days, on our way to hear the St Matthew Passion sung at the Concertgebouw, we decided to stop and phone home. Perhaps this was a mistake! Fiona answered and it was distressing to hear her nearly in tears and obviously very upset . "What's the matter, Fi?" I asked. The day's events tumbled out: in spite of Julia not feeling at all well, they had wanted to go out somewhere so Fiona had taken her in the car to some nearby shops but Julia had felt so fatigued that she could hardly walk. Returning home, they were preparing their evening meal with Julia cutting up the leeks, but she couldn't even manage this, and in her frustration threw them across the kitchen and stormed off in tears with, "I've got no energy to do anything." I tried to comfort Fiona by saying that Julia occasionally had a bad day like that, but would probably feel better the next day. Pulling herself together, Fiona then reassured me as she knew I would be upset as well, "Don't worry, Mum, I'll cope . . . . . you enjoy the rest of the holiday."

Putting the phone down, tears began to flow. I just wanted to go home and be there for the girls, but knew I couldn't. Somehow I managed to contain the rest of my tears so as not to spoil the evening for John who was looking forward to hearing the St Matthew Passion sung in German! Feelings of grief crashed over me, like a rough sea crashing over the rocks. Wave after wave overwhelmed me and try as I might, I couldn't stop them coming. I felt really mean and guilty because I was obviously upset and I knew that I was spoiling the evening for John, who was very gracious and tried to comfort me. When we lay in each other's arms in bed that evening, he took his Bible and read the 23rd Psalm. Sleep didn't come easily that night so I tried to focus and meditate on the words that John had just read to me.

The Lord is my shepherd. This phrase reminded me that at the heart of the Christian faith is a relationship between a human being and his Maker, between man and God. Images found repeatedly in Scripture are those of a father and child and a shepherd and his sheep. Meditating on the thought that God is my shepherd - gentle, kind, courageous, selfless, and compassionate, - I was comforted by the fact that He cares for me.

I shall not be in want. This statement is the sentiment of a sheep perfectly content with its lot in life and satisfied with his owner. These words conjured up an image of a sheep, so utterly contented in his shepherd's care that he didn't crave or desire anything more.

"Lord, help me to find a completeness in you," I whispered.

He makes me lie down in green pastures. Sheep will not lie down if they are frightened, tormented by flies or hungry. By diligently caring for the sheep the shepherd makes it possible for them to contentedly lie down. I could certainly relate to a sheep being frightened and unable to rest, as anxiety and foreboding aroused an inner unease which prevented me being able to relax and sleep. With the knowledge that my Shepherd has things under His control I prayed *"I can't cope with these anxieties - they're bugging me - I can't rest - please take over."*

He leads me beside quiet waters. Thirsty sheep become restless and search for water to satisfy their thirst. Likewise men and women can only be satisfied, when their thirst for spiritual life is fully quenched by the right sort of water. *Jesus said, "If anyone is thirsty, let him come to me and drink."* (5) In my mind's eye I saw a flock of sheep being led to beautiful, clear sparkling water and sensed the shepherd was calling me to come and discover afresh the living water - Jesus, the one who is with me in every situation.

He restores my soul. It is easy to assume that no one in the Good Shepherd's care could ever become so distressed as to need their soul restoring. But the reality is that this does happen. Like David, the author of this Psalm, I knew what is was like to be dejected and helpless, and echoed his words, *Why are you downcast, O my soul? Why so disturbed within me? Put your hope in God, for I will yet praise him, my Saviour and my God*. (5) I know of nothing which so quiets and restores my soul as the knowledge that God knows what he is doing with me .

As these thoughts were running through my mind, and images of a shepherd and his sheep flashed up on the screen of my imagination, I slowly began to unwind and find rest for my soul. I was conscious of God all around me and was assured of His care and concern for me and Julia, because He was with us in our circumstances. I was able to enjoy the remainder of our time in Amsterdam but was very relieved to arrive home. We returned to find that Julia had spent most of her time either in bed, or on the sofa in the lounge, and was not well enough to go back to Guildford after the Easter break. There was a tearful 'goodbye' to Fiona as she went back to Leeds, because we would all miss her. Full of beans and naturally noisy and fun loving, Fiona gave life some normality and she helped us to laugh and be cheery. We stimulated each other in an atmosphere that seemed heavy at times and I was well aware that Fiona was like a tonic for Julia. Although Julia was pleased that Fiona's life was going well, nevertheless, seeing her sister's career continuing to move forward contrasted starkly with the fact that hers was going nowhere. Stuck at home without Fiona around, and with no university friends to chat to, Julia felt abandoned, isolated and very lonely. However she had an outing to look forward to, as James had bought tickets to take her to a London theatre in May.

Julia felt a certain ambivalence about going to London: on the one hand she didn't really feel well, yet on the other she longed to do something with James and didn't want to disappoint him. We talked this through together and Julia decided to go. I thought it might do her good psychologically; as she was low and very lonely the theatre trip might break the stranglehold of isolation. In the event, however, it had a very detrimental effect. Arriving late at the theatre, James rushed Julia up the many flights of stairs. Rather than appearing weak and pathetic, Julia didn't say anything and ran up the stairs with him. We have subsequently found out from specialists that just climbing stairs can be very weakening for people with M.E., let alone running up about ten flights! Exhausted after this exertion Julia sat through most of the performance holding onto her seat trying not to faint or let the palpitations panic her.

This theatre trip to London hadn't helped Julia's recovery at all, and as she became worse, the to-ing and fro-ing between Guildford and home ended up with Julia living at home with my help for most of the time. During these weeks James' and Julia's relationship became strained and distant. He was usually busy and Julia had little energy in the evenings when he did phone to talk. She acknowledged that it must have been hard for James, to have a girlfriend with so little energy.

Thus, it was not a surprise, but nevertheless a shock, when James told Julia quite clearly that their relationship was finished. Julia was obviously upset and hurt but quickly accepted that being ill drained a huge amount of emotional energy from their relationship and caused confusion for them both - confusion because what Julia could do physically one day, she couldn't another, so the goal posts were always moving and consequently James never knew where he was. Julia wrote in her diary:
"Lord, thank you for preparing me for the words James spoke to me - to end the relationship. I wasn't surprised, but it was unexpected. I'm angry that M.E. has destroyed yet another part of my life. Upset that James couldn't love me when I'm very ill - it highlights to me I don't function as a healthy individual - I'm useless. In many ways I'm pleased that it has ended, because I can now save my emotional energy to put it to better use - to get well. I'm not well enough to work at a relationship and enjoy it. Lord, thank you for giving me James for company last term - I will treasure those times. Thank you for James' honesty today and for clearly showing me that my life is to take a different path."

By June of that summer, all our hopes for Julia's recovery were dashed. Acknowledging the fact that she was not well enough to look after herself, she made the painful decision to come home for good. Her hopes of rejoining her nursing degree course were now ruptured. Taking the painful step of writing to the university, she informed them that she wasn't well enough to rejoin the first year course again, and thanked them for all their support, help and concern. Another chapter of her life was closing.

As we packed up all her belongings in Guildford, it was as if once again we were packing up and saying goodbye to our hopes and dreams for part of Julia's life. She had said goodbye to James, who was no longer in her life; now she was having to say goodbye to her friends in the flat. In many ways this was more difficult as they had been part of her life for eighteen months. They reassured Julia that they would keep in touch, but as Julia said, "It's not the same as seeing them every day and being part of their lives." But they have been true to their word, and have kept in touch over the years which has been a great source of comfort and encouragement to Julia.

Although Julia's hopes for her university life in Guildford were dashed, I didn't lose hope that her health would improve and that God's grace would sustain us. I felt emotionally strong in the Lord with Julia coming to live permanently back at home with us. Little did I know at that time, that the pain I had experienced until then was only a taste of what lay ahead.

NO STATUS

I've been stripped of everything -
My health, my youth, normality;
Suddenly I'm left helpless and weak,
Hopelessness engulfing me
Frailty shadowing me
Despair encircling me.

There's nowhere I can hide . . .
Even in the darkest corner reveals another photo-slide
A picture of a healthy girl fully involved in life -
Fun-loving, busy, active, till the cruel and sharp-edged knife
Severed every strand:
Her body, her mind, university.

But, no-one remembered to ask me, "Do you mind?"

I had no option anyway; my life slipped through my hands
I watched it trickling away from me, like the timer with its sand
My heart felt pierced and wounded with a red-hot searing pain
Grieving for precious things I'd lost, which may never be mine again.

Julia

Chapter 5

Crying Out

Listen to my cry for I am in desperate need (Psalm 142:6)

"*OK, Lord, what now?*" was the question playing on my mind as one day slipped quietly into another with Julia at home. Plagued by headaches, nausea, swollen glands and the usual aches and pains and extreme fatigue, Julia spent most of the day either in bed or resting on a sun bed in the lounge. But the physical pain that she was suffering was nothing compared to the sense of loneliness and isolation from being away from her close university friends - she wouldn't have chosen to be at home, she would rather be with her peer group. Of course her friends were much more fun than Mum and Dad, who were boring in comparison! Naturally, she had more in common with her friends. What 21 year old daughter would choose to become dependent upon her mother again to be bathed and have her hair washed? Fiercely independent, Julia found this very frustrating, and what with all the other losses in her life, it wasn't surprising that anger began to surface.

It is often said that our nearest and dearest get the full brunt of one's pain, because they are the safest people to be real with. This proved true, as Julia got angry with me over issues that would never have bothered her when she was well. Sometimes nothing I did was right! This led to some mother/daughter conflicts, and at times my patience was pushed to the limit. I was furious with her one day as I had gone to the trouble to buy her some sweets, and she nearly hit the ceiling because they were not what she wanted. I nearly hit the ceiling too, but rather than yell at her and throw them back in her face (which I felt like doing!), I went for a walk to calm down. Another day I told Julia how cross I was with her as she was being difficult, and in her anger she took the car keys and drove off. This caused me great concern and guilt for she hadn't driven for months. *"What if she has an accident?"* However, much to my relief she safely returned having worked out her frustration - she just desperately needed space as she felt imprisoned in the house. The tedium of her life created tension.

Many a time I cried out to God for grace to hold my tongue so that I would not bite back with words that would destroy what little self-esteem Julia had left. I was often reminded, *"Reckless words pierce like a sword, but the tongue of the wise brings healing."* (1) Words are very powerful and have the ability to bless or curse. "Sticks and stones may break my bones, but words can never hurt me", was the playground retort when I was at school. But words have the capacity to prey upon our minds and sting feelings in a way that no physical blow ever can. I have counselled many people whose lives have been ruined by emotional abuse, where destructive words have been thrown at them so continually that they have ended up believing what was said. Annie, whose mother had repeatedly told her that she was "stupid", and "a problem child" ended up believing nothing good about herself as she couldn't do anything right. This resulted in Annie acting out the belief that she was indeed stupid, instilled into her by her mother, so that in fact she was perceived as being stupid. It took many months of counselling before she was able to break free from the curse of the words and begin to accept that those words had been a lie.

So, being well aware of the psychological damage that can occur as a result of destructive words said in the the heat of the moment, I was determined to watch my tongue. Consequently I used to walk away from Julia if she was getting angry with me. This gave me time to calm down, and space to think, and remind myself not to take it personally, recognising that her anger was a symptom of grieving. It was easy for me to walk away from the situation but Julia had no space to retreat to on her own, or anything to distract her, as she could never get away from illness, parents, and home, and thus felt confined and trapped. Julia was aware how mean she was to me at times, and would always take responsibility and apologise for her actions or words. Sometimes, after the heat of the moment, we were able to talk through the issues rationally and even laugh together, then offer each other forgiveness where appropriate. I thank God that I held my tongue and never let out some of the rubbish that was running around in my head when we had a conflict. In a constructive way, I was able to be honest and tell Julia how difficult I found life when she was angry, but I was careful not to blame her for being ill. In needing so much care at home, Julia was aware how the situation was affecting my life and I didn't want her to feel guilty about it. Believing that words can bring healing, I spoke comforting words of love to her and reassured her of my support. Sowing seed of love in my daughter was and always is a privilege, as this *Love Chapter for Mothers* shows so well.

The Love Chapter for Mothers

"If I talk to my children about what is right and what is wrong, but have not love, I am like a ringing doorbell or pots banging in the kitchen. And though I know what stages they will go through, and understand their growing pains, and can answer all their questions about life, and believe myself to be a devoted mother, but have not love, I am nothing.

If I give up the fulfilment of a career to make my children's lives better, and stay up all night sewing costumes or baking cookies at short notice, but grumble about lack of sleep, I have not love and accomplish nothing.

A loving mother is patient with her children's immaturity and kind even when they are not; a loving mother is not jealous of their youth, nor does she hold it over their heads whenever she has sacrificed for them. A loving mother does not push her children into doing things her way. She is not irritable, even when the chicken pox has kept her confined with three whining children for two weeks, and does not resent the child who brought the affliction home in the first place.

A loving mother is not relieved when her disagreeable child finally disobeys her directly and she can punish him, but rather rejoices with him when he is being more co-operative. A loving mother bears much of the responsibility for her children, she believes in them; she hopes in each one's individual ability to stand out as light in a dark world; and she endures every backache and heartache to accomplish that.

A loving mother never really dies. As for home-baked bread, it will be consumed and forgotten, as for spotless floors, they will soon gather dust and heel marks. And as for children, well, bright new toys, friends and food are all important to them. But when they grow up it will have been how their mother loved them that will determine how they love others. In that way she will live on.

So care, training and a loving mother reside in a home, these three, but the greatness of these is a loving mother.

Dianne Lorang (2)

Nevertheless I can't pretend that having Julia back home was easy, because we had no idea when it would end. Like most couples, when their last child goes off to university or leaves home, John and I had anticipated that we would have the freedom to do what we wanted, instead we were suddenly confronted with Julia becoming fully dependent upon us, like a baby. When a stone is thrown into a pond, the shock waves ripple out. It was as if a big stone labelled HURT had been thrown into the pond of my life, and the shock waves rippled out into many areas. One of the areas affected was my work.

I thoroughly enjoyed working part time as a practice nurse and a counsellor in a very large GP surgery nearby, where the doctors and staff are mostly Christians. Recognising that looking after Julia drained my energy and emotional resources, I felt it was necessary to reduce my hours, to give me more time to look after Julia. Work was a welcome distraction - a place where I could forget about being a mum and a carer, although I couldn't always escape from the pain of the situation. Entering the surgery one Monday morning, a group of young receptionists, some of whom were students of Julia's age, were chatting and laughing as they shared together what they had done over the weekend. This was in such sharp contrast to Julia's life, that I went into the nurse's room and burst into tears. That room saw many a tear shed in secret as I cried to God, asking him to give me the strength to hold myself together in order to get on with the job in hand. Thankfully, this He did. The surgery staff were very supportive to me, but I tried to keep my home life and work life separate and not to talk to people at work about my pain. However there were one or two people to whom I could go and ask to pray with me if I was really struggling. One of our secretaries, Dilys, had a son who had become mentally ill after having M.E. for many years. As another mother in pain she was very supportive to me and wrote a letter saying, "Words are so inadequate, but here goes:-

Dear Chris
My heart really went out to you this morning.
I do know how you feel.
I spent the first years like this.

It seems as if everyone is going happily about their business and no-one seems to care. You get so angry, frustrated, frantic and resentful that no-one is doing anything, while your child is languishing at home. You want them to feel the hurt that you do, the unfairness of it all.

I sought as much medical advice as I could, but not being medically trained myself, I left it to them and as they didn't offer any solutions, I stopped fighting.

The days run into weeks, then months and inertia sets in and you settle for what you have!

I admire your spirit. If you don't fight for her then no-one else will.

But, please take care of yourself, stay strong, take a break, try not to let it get you down (easier said than done!!!)

It is like a heavy ache that never goes. You need to put it on hold for your sanity though.

Please don't go pop.

If you need me for ANYTHING - to visit Julia with you (bring a video that we can watch together) talk, cry, pray, please say, dump what you need to on me.

I saw a brilliant film two weeks ago - 'The Dream Team' - sounds a pathetic title but it was really hilarious. It was about four psychiatric patients that go out on a day's outing to see a football match with their doctor. One thought he was Jesus, one thought he was a doctor, one couldn't talk. The doctor gets beaten up which leaves the four patients causing chaos in New York. However, they end up as heroes. This film was a bit close to home but it really cheered me up.

Anyway Chris, I love you.

Dilys"

Another very supportive group of people were friends at our church. A few years earlier we had felt called by God to join the ministers, Denis and Elizabeth Brazell working in a very needy Urban Priority Area of Reading. Whilst at their church both John and I trained as Lay Ministers, and in working with them as fellow staff members we established a deep friendship. They suggested that we meet regularly to pray together for Julia. The only time we could all fit this in to our busy lives, was a weekly 10 pm prayer time. More often than not we went on until about midnight, but this was a small price to pray for the loving support we received. Slowly the time together evolved into a prayer partnership, as the four of us began to share our own weaknesses and concerns on a personal level. John and I benefited from sharing our pain because the mutual support made us stronger and our lives richer. Many from the church joined us in prayer and fasting to seek God's heart for Julia's healing, and on one of these occasions someone had a picture of a bucket being filled up with water, drop by drop, and when it was full, it overflowed. It was suggested that God was telling us as a church to keep praying, however little, as it would be like another drop of water in the bucket. Eventually there would come a day when the bucket would overflow and our prayers would be answered. Sometimes we told Julia that as a church we were praying and fasting, but at other times we didn't tell her as I think she felt under some pressure to feel better afterwards! It was really interesting to observe that nearly every time we prayed in this way, whether Julia knew this was going on or not, she seemed to get worse! Who can fully understand God or the forces opposing Him and us?

Spiritually I was confused - I was crying out to God to show me some meaning and purpose in our situation, and to reveal more of Himself to me. My faith was being stretched like elastic, and avidly I read scripture so as to keep my faith alive. *Trust in the Lord with all your heart, and lean not on your own understanding; in all your ways acknowledge him, and he will make your paths straight.* (3)

Who has understood the mind of the Lord? (4) These words challenged my faith as I began to recognise that I wanted a God who moved according to my agenda, not His! Accepting that He might do things contrary to my wishes wasn't easy - I was still disappointed that Julia was ill. I realised that in journeying along the road of suffering I had a long way to go until I could come to the place of complete and utter surrender of all my hopes and dreams. The journey was bumpy and I never knew what was round the next corner, but I was learning to focus on God as He is, rather than the way I would like him to be. This was to be a continual struggle, but it became easier as time went on.

At another spiritual level I became aware that I was taking offence at God because I was angry with him - angry that He appeared to be turning a deaf ear to our prayers for Julia, who had now been ill on and off for a couple of years. It felt as if He had abandoned us. Although rationally I knew that God would never desert us, on the emotional level it certainly felt as if He had! I was challenged by the words that Jesus spoke to the messengers of John the Baptist, *Blessed is he who takes no offence in Me, and who is not hurt or resentful or annoyed or repelled or made to stumble (whatever may occur)* (5). These words occur in the story where John the Baptist sent his followers to ask Jesus, "*Are you the one who we have been looking for?* " (i.e. Are you the Messiah?) The men found Jesus healing many sick and blind people - it appeared that Jesus wanted these men to observe what he was doing so that the evidence of his work was sufficient to identify him as the Messiah. Then he replied with these words, "*Blessed is the man who takes no offence in Me* ." It was as if Jesus was conveying the message, You may not understand everything but you will be blessed if you hold on to me In other words, set aside your preconceived ideas and trust me.

No wonder I had lost my joy - I had taken offence. I was hurt, and to some extent resented God, because He didn't appear to be doing anything about our situation. I was angry as I watched Julia's ability to live life to the full being ripped from beneath her feet. It was important for me to face this truth - I resented God and to some extent in my heart I had turned my back on Him. I had ignored my buried anger to the point where it was affecting my relationship with God. Handling my anger inappropriately had led me to resentment and to taking offence. The Apostle Paul made a plain distinction between anger and resentment. In his statement, "*In your anger do not sin."* (6) Paul was saying get angry, be angry, ... but be careful. Paul knew that anger can lead to resentment and bitterness if not handled carefully and he was saying acknowledge and express your anger, but don't let it lead you into any form of resentment or bitterness, because that is a sin. In other words, its OK to feel angry, but what you do with that feeling is of vital importance. Because hitherto I had failed to deal appropriately with my anger, it had been simmering away like a stew in a slow cooker and, without my realising, it had turned into resentment. Recognising that I had fallen into sin, I then poured out my anger before God and asked him to forgive me for allowing my anger to turn to resentment and fester away inside. As I knelt at my bedside it felt as if God was cleaning my heart out - the anger was being washed away, and the corners of resentment were being scoured out, making everything inside me fresh and clean again. I echoed the words of David, *Generous in love - God, give grace! Huge in mercy - wipe out my bad record. Soak me in your laundry and I'll come out clean, scrub me and I'll have a snow white life.* (7) As I sensed the warmth of God's accepting love, I cried, "*Thank you, I love you and know that you love me. Help me to trust you, even when I don't understand."*

A few weeks later I became aware of another disturbing feeling lurking in the shadows of my heart - self pity. Although I felt somewhat ashamed in discovering the ugliness of my humanity, I was comforted by the thought that feelings of anger, resentment and self-pity are a normal response to loss. Mental health "experts" tell us that our confusing emotions are perfectly normal, but many Christians struggle with this, thinking that they have failed as a

Christian if they experience these "bad" emotions. But emotions cannot be bad. Each feeling is a truth in its own right. It is what we do with our painful emotions that is the key to health. My training as a counsellor helped me to recognise that if I didn't face these deeply disturbing feelings I could easily deny that they existed, or consciously or unconsciously throw them at Julia. Denial is a refusal to face our inner emotions and it was tempting to push these feelings down behind a mask that was smiling to the world. If I had done that, the feelings would have been buried, not dead, but alive, until such time as I dealt with them.

The danger in ignoring and repressing feelings is that they can re-emerge in other ways. We are whole people, made up of body, mind and spirit and when one area is hurting it can affect another as I saw with another client, Betty. In counselling Betty, it became apparent that she had ignored and repressed her powerful feelings over the death of her son. These feelings of anger and self pity had been somatised into bodily aches and pains. As soon as she recognised these deep feelings and chose to let them go, the aches and pains disappeared. Facing the truth is never easy for any of us, particularly when the truth is ugly and I didn't like facing the reality that I was having a "pity party".

I discovered this unwelcome pity party going on inside me through a throwaway remark from a nursing friend, Val. Sadly, she also had M.E., but was never as ill as Julia and occasionally she was well enough to go out. Chatting over coffee one day, we were exchanging our progress in coming to terms with and coping with M.E. Val had her own particular struggles, and I had mine. But at that period of my life I couldn't get in touch with why I wasn't totally at peace with myself. As we got up to go, she said, "You know Chris, God wants you to be totally content in this situation - that is his heart for you, to find your peace in Him." Something in these words made me continue to chew on them and I began to ask God to show me why I wasn't fully content in the situation with Julia so ill.

The words, *'I have learned the secret of being content in any and every situation.'* (8) became a challenge to me and I cried out to God to teach me this secret. *"Father, I cry for help to you. Enable me to find a completeness in you so that I am content and at peace in my circumstances."* In answering this cry from my heart, God showed me the very thing that was stopping me enjoying a deep contentment - a pity party.

Self-pity is unattractive and full of itself. My pity was a self-centred attempt to deal with my pain. "Poor old me, life's unfair" were the words being jubilantly shouted at the unwelcome party deep within myself. In the loneliness of suffering, self-pity can easily take root and I found myself simply wallowing in it. Recognising this and reminding myself that I am responsible for my feelings, I took myself in hand and gave myself a stern talking to. Confessing my sin to God wasn't an admission that I'm a terrible person. I knew I was a sinner and I was open to the dark corners of my life being exposed to God's healing grace. As a human being I couldn't avoid sin, but I could learn to recognise it. So in acknowledging and confessing my self-pity, an inner peace soon took its place. However, I didn't always find it easy to discern the point where my real grief, with all its accompanying emotions, began to turn into self-pity. But once I was able to identify that a pity party was in progress, I began to control any impulse to let it continue.

While I was struggling with all this, time and life marched relentlessly by for Julia with little change in her physical health. Her days seemed short and uneventful. Because she wasn't sleeping well at night, she stayed in bed until about 1-2 pm, then dragging on some clothes she would stagger downstairs where the rest of the day was spent in the lounge, either quietly resting or watching TV. On a really bad day I would read to her and just sit and keep her company. But I am naturally a fairly energetic person, who likes to be doing things, so I didn't always find it easy sitting with Julia for long, as I found her pace of life very slow and frustrating - but then so did she!

Julia longed to be well enough to be up and entering into life. It felt as if my daughter's life had ground to a halt, and I was helpless and impotent to do much about it. The energy that arose from these frustrations became so strong at times, I found the only way that I could deal with it was to get on my bike and take a short, quick quarter-hour ride round local roads! At least the traffic drowned my shouts of frustration! On returning home, considerably less agitated, I was then able to be supportive again.

One highlight for Julia during those long summer months, was a surprise visit from Fiona who travelled all the way down from Leeds to see her. Although this was ostensibly for Father's Day, Fiona and I had secretly arranged it as I was going to be away in Germany.

As I flew out of the country I felt a freedom from my responsibilities in caring, having handed them over to John and Fiona and I savoured the gift of being involved in something I found so fulfilling. As a member of "Christians in the Caring Professions" (CiCP) I went with Dr. Derek Munday, the senior partner of the GP practice where I worked and his wife, Mary, to lead workshops and speak at a Christian medical conference. The weekend had its contrasts - from being involved in reconciliation between denominations in one meeting to preaching at another meeting where I illustrated my talk from my own personal suffering; from walking in the beautiful countryside to sitting amongst two hundred German Christians hungry for God; from tears to much laughter. In the midst of all this I felt so alive and the strong message that came through really clearly to me was that God was shaking me, to get rid of all the junk in me that wasn't of Him so that . . . . *"the unshakeable essentials stand clear and uncluttered. Do you see what we've got? An unshakeable kingdom! And do you see how thankful we must be? Not only thankful, but brimming with worship, deeply reverent before God. For God is not an indifferent bystander, He's actively cleaning the house, torching all that needs to burn, and he won't quit until it's all cleansed. God himself is Fire! "* (9) I returned from that conference with a deeper sense of what God was doing in my life - shaking off all the bits that were not of Him, so as to fashion me more into His likeness and purify my heart.

Recognising and understanding the process I was going through enabled me to be far more understanding and supportive to Julia, but it didn't take away all the pain. One beautiful, hot cloudless summer's day, my instinct was to go out into the garden and enjoy the warmth and sunshine, with the temperature in the 80's. By contrast, Julia was cold and shivering inside. Lying on a sun bed in the lounge, feverish with swollen glands, all she could do was snuggle under her duvet with a hot water bottle, whilst I was in a sundress and sipping ice-cold drinks to keep cool. I think at times Julia was too ill to realise what she was missing but she did try and keep cheerful. On this particular day, I suggested that we watch a video, anything to keep the atmosphere light and full of laughter. We laughed together at an amusing comedy and forgot ourselves and our pain. Although naturally I would have rather been outside in the sunshine, being stuck indoors was worth everything just to see Julia able to laugh and enjoy life a little.

Because I was aware that life was rather tedious for her, day in and day out, I tried to be creative in breaking the monotony. Sometimes I put an armchair in the kitchen, so that Julia could watch me baking, or suggested we play a simple game for ten minutes or so; at other times I was plain silly just to make her laugh! Having visitors was difficult as Julia didn't have the energy to cope with them. When Julia had left Guildford earlier that summer, I had phoned three of her old school friends who lived locally and told them how ill she was, encouraging them to keep in contact with her as she needed them. I told them that Julia might be too ill at times to see them or speak to them on the phone, but just hearing that a friend had phoned to enquire how she was doing, was of great encouragement to her. It brought a smile to her face, and was a tangible way for her friends to say, "You're not forgotten". We all need the love and encouragement of friends in our lives as we are created to live in relationships, not alone. I have noted in my counselling work, that those who have good supportive family and friends, and thus don't feel forgotten and rejected by the world, do better than those who have no one.

Although I was doing my best in encouraging others to support Julia, she still felt very lonely. This was expressed in her diary:

> "At the moment I just want to give up fighting. What's the point? Why bother? I don't make any progress if I help myself or not. I am lonely and have no close friend nearby I can talk to or visit. Everyone is too busy to visit me for half an hour a week - good excuses - but if Christians CARE and really pray for folk they'd be on my doorstep. Yes, it's OK if you break your leg, or go to hospital, everyone's round in a flash. But with M.E., I'm forgotten especially when they see me on a good day - I look really well and able - how looks betray the inside body. Lord, please listen to my pathetic cry for healing, and loving care, and friendships from folk. Thank you . . . Amen".

It was becoming increasingly clear that Julia was making no real progress as she continued to feel very fatigued and ill. Occasionally she had a good day when she felt well enough to go out, but she was too weak to walk very far, so we obtained a wheelchair. Although I know that at first Fiona felt strange and a little awkward taking her sister out in the wheelchair, she never said anything. As an energetic young person Fiona found it very hard that Julia was so incapacitated, but she was mature enough to overcome her own feelings and be fully supportive. At first Julia, too, felt uncomfortable using the wheelchair: she felt a fraud, because it wasn't as if she couldn't walk at all. But by this time she knew that walking one day would have a detrimental effect on her a few days later. Returning one afternoon from a short walk, the girls were obviously a bit down. An unexpected meeting with Jane, a girl whom they had known at church, was the cause. Having not met since schooldays, they had stopped to catch up with each others' news. However Jane had ignored Julia. Speaking over Julia's head she asked Fiona how Julia was! Julia was obviously hurt at being treated as if she wasn't present; and Fiona felt very angry that a friend from the past could be so rude as to behave as if Julia wasn't there. Giving the girls an opportunity to talk about this led to a discussion about how some people can easily feel embarrassed when someone is ill, as they don't know what to say or how to cope. So rather than say or do the wrong thing, they end up not relating at all. We also talked about the feelings that people can have about wheelchairs - how wheelchair users can feel second class citizens, and indeed, can be treated as such; another difficulty can be the result of different eye levels, causing the person in the wheel chair to feel inferior because they are literally looked down on. For me, the wheelchair symbolised that this M.E. was becoming part of our life as it showed no signs of abating. Like the wheelchair, it looked as if it were here to stay for the time being.

With the summer of 1992 slipping by, Julia, John and I began to discuss the next step for Julia. Was she well enough to move out into a nearby flat we own? John is an only child so when his mother died in 1987, he was left some money. After prayerfully considering many options we finally felt that God was leading us to buy a flat for young women in our church who were not able to afford the tremendously high rents in our area. Within days of this decision, having looked at a few properties, we found an ideal top floor masionette, with two bedrooms, lounge, kitchen, garage and small garden. Because it was so light and airy, John and I remarked to each other that we liked it so much that we could live in it if we ever had to! We didn't mention this to anyone else, but once the paper work was completed we offered it to a young single girl in our house group. Her reaction was to burst into tears. She then went on to explain that she had to move out of her current accommodation and had asked God to provide affordable rented accommodation for her by the end of the month. God was Sovereign - the day we offered the flat to her was the end of the month. Since then, we had had four girls living in the flat at different times, and now in the Autumn of 1992 it was becoming vacant again. Little had we known when we originally bought it, that one of our daughters would want to move in.

"Dad, can I move into the flat?", was the question John found himself being asked one hot summer's day. So the three of us sat down and discussed the issues. Julia still needed a lot of support in the way of shopping, washing, getting meals, and on bad days bathing and washing her hair, as well as needing company. However, the flat was very conveniently placed nearby. Cycling via a pathway only took 3-4 minutes, and the longer way round by car was barely a mile, so it would be easy for me to pop in most days to see Julia and to take meals round. We decided that Julia would move in the Autumn and we would support her in having a measure of independence again. The flat seemed such a wonderful provision for her, and we were so thankful that God had led us to buy it years before for other needy girls. Now our daughter, in her need, would hopefully be blessed by living in it. Another encouraging answer to prayer was her flat mate, Marie, a student at Reading University. They had previously met before Julia was really ill, when they had shared a room at a university Christian Union weekend for leaders and had got on very well together as they were both lively and bubbly. Marie didn't know that Julia was ill at home, but had heard on the grapevine that a room was available to rent, so had phoned John for more details. During the second telephone conversation with him, the penny dropped and she asked if he was Julia's father. How we all rejoiced that Julia and Marie were going to share the flat together - things couldn't have worked out better.

Having waved Fiona off again, to start her second year at Leeds

University in the Autumn of 1992, Julia began to think about moving into the flat. Marie moved in first and Julia followed several weeks later when she felt well enough to cope with a move. Packing all her belongings (yet again!) was slow , of course, as Julia could do only a little at a time. Every afternoon for about a week, she would sit on her bed and I would get everything out of drawers and cupboards. Amidst a quiet enthusiasm that life was on the move again, Julia decided what needed to be packed. Because we took it slowly it didn't seem too burdensome and the day soon arrived when having previously taken most of her boxes round to the flat, I drove her round to her new home. My emotions were all over the place: I was pleased for Julia taking this next step; but although I was doing all I could for her I still felt a sense of helplessness and just seeing her struggle as she tried to cope with everyday life was very painful. I left Julia sitting in her new bedroom, which had been been painted afresh by Fiona and although she was looking pale and wan, she managed a cheery smile as if to say, "I'm here now". I was grateful for the beginning of this new phase of her life, and whispered, *"Thank you Lord for what these circumstances will become in your hands."*

HANGING ON

Lord I'm hanging onto the edge of a cliff top -
Another push and I'll fall;
I'm at the end of my tether, I'll lose my grip
With any more pain - not matter how small.

But Lord, I know you'll never test me beyond my
Endurance. You'll lift me up onto level ground
But I'm tired from dangling here so long
My my strength is fast running out.

Lord please give me patience in waiting,
Your comfort in the depths of my pain
A reassuring hand to hang on to
And grace to bear each hour, each day.

Lord I thank you for the dangling on the cliff top
For it's in our dangling we learn
To cling desperately on to you and rely
On your perfect timing, in your master plan.

Julia

Chapter 6

Hanging On

Why do you hide yourself in times of trouble? (Psalm 10:1)

Settling happily into her new home, Julia enjoyed the coziness and warmth of the flat and the friendship of Marie was a great blessing. Her bubbly personality was like a ray of sunshine for Julia. Although it must have been hard for Marie sharing a flat with someone so ill, she accepted Julia where she was. Conversely, it was painful for Julia to be a bystander, watching Marie lead a full and energetic life, while longing to be in that place herself. In order to prevent any misunderstanding about our expectations, I had a quiet word with Marie, assuring her that I didn't expect her as a flat mate to take any responsibility for looking after Julia. It would have been totally unfair to have placed her in the role of a carer. Her relationship with Julia was that of a friend; I continued as the carer.

Caring for Julia involved taking her meals round most weekdays - I became quite a dab hand at "Meals on Wheels"! Knowing how lonely Julia felt, I would sometimes take my evening meal round and eat with her so as to keep her company. But when she had a bad patch I used to have to go round to get her lunch as well, as she couldn't even open a tin of soup or prepare anything else. During these periods I also would give her baths, wash her hair, and help her to get dressed each day. Many a time I received a phone call asking, "Mum, are you free, can you come round and wash my hair in the bath?" These phone calls would come at any time of the day. Because some days Julia felt too ill to do anything, getting up seemed like a mammoth task. Consequently a bath and hair wash could take place late morning, afternoon or even early evening. Sometimes after a bath Julia was too fatigued to get dressed immediately, so she would lie on her bed in order to recover some energy before the next activity of getting dressed. When she was home with us, John and I sometimes found her lying flat out on our bathroom floor wrapped in a towel, recovering enough to be able to stagger back to her bedroom. One of the benefits of living in the flat for Julia, was that it only took a few steps to go from one room to another, whereas our home was bigger and the stairs had to be negotiated as well. During the afternoons I often popped round to see how she was. I found it particularly hard to cope when I found the curtains drawn to shut out the sunlight and Julia still in bed. It felt as if I had already done a day's work, and Julia hadn't even been well enough to get up. I was still finding it quite difficult to adjust and accept the situation and I began to start dreaming and having nightmares.

One night I woke up in a cold sweat, having dreamt about being robbed. A man had walked into my home in the darkness of night and robbed me of everything valuable. As I awoke, I instantly knew that it was Satan trying to rob me of my peace and joy, and everything dear to me, including my daughter. My immediate response was, *"How dare you come and try to rob me. God has blessed me with abundant life."* So I stood firm and asked the light of Christ to come and fill my heart with His peace. Another dream I had was of a fire. Finding myself being caught in scorching flames in a large building, I was trying to find an escape route for Julia. Somehow the rest of the family and other people from the building had found their way out and I could see them through large plate glass windows, all standing on the lawn outside, watching as Julia and I tried to escape. Dragging Julia behind me, we ran down smoke filled corridors. To my horror I found one door locked after another and I couldn't find a way out. I banged on the windows, crying for help but no one came to rescue us. Then in my dream I heard these words, *"When you walk through the fire, you will not be burned; the flames will not set you ablaze."* (1) Gasping for breath I woke up with tears streaming down my face as I felt frightened, utterly helpless and imprisoned in a burning furnace. In gaining consciousness I knew that it was God who had spoken these words of comfort to me and slowly the fear and sense of impotence gave way to a deep peace. God was in control. Although there didn't seem to be an escape route for Julia from this illness, nevertheless I knew that God was with us. I offered my tears and sense of helplessness to God, knowing how utterly dependent I was on Him - only He could reach out and rescue us. A few months later I had another vivid dream in which I saw a coffin being carried to the gates of heaven. I asked God for discernment for this dream. My immediate thought was perhaps the coffin represented the loss of Julia's healthy life, but in continuing to seek God's heart, I sensed that it was to do with my will. I was being challenged to let go of what **I** wanted in terms of Julia's illness and what I **didn't** want in terms of my enforced continuing role as a carer. The stark reality was that it was my desires that God wanted in that coffin. Just as Jesus in his suffering had cried out, *"My Father, if it is possible, may this cup be taken from me. Yet not as I will, but as you will."* (2) I too uttered these words to my heavenly Father. I was comforted in the thought that Jesus also had experienced deep anguish and suffering. He knew how I felt as my pain seemed to be growing deeper into an unresolvable heartache.

This heartache was again opened up on fireworks evening that autumn. Over the years, celebrating the fifth of November had given us, as a family, many happy memories as we had always made a special outing with the girls to a big fireworks display. Wrapping up warm in hats, gloves and scarves, pulling on welly boots and making flasks of hot drinks were all part of the family tradition. That year, although Julia couldn't go anywhere, John and I bought some fireworks, so that at the very least she could watch them from her window rather than let the celebrations pass by. It was a very cold, frosty night and not wanting to miss out, Julia decided to join us outside. John carried her downstairs warmly wrapped up and, having packed blankets around her as she cuddled a hot water bottle in the wheelchair, we pushed her into the garden. Aware that Julia felt far from well, we were a bit subdued, but made the usual noises

"Oh . . . . ah . . . . " as we watched the colourful fireworks and waved sparklers around. It was good to have a fun time together and to see Julia enjoying herself, albeit for only ten minutes. As we left the flat that evening, John and I shared together our delight in the fact that we were able to do something special for Julia, but both of us acknowledged how we hurt inside. Normally when I felt the pain of loss, I cried, so I was quite surprised that the usual tears didn't come flooding out. Something was changing. Somehow the pain had gone deeper than tears and I felt numbed by the anguish and ache in my heart.

It was as if God knew that the pain was going deeper because a few days later, He sent someone to comfort me. Doing the weekly shop I turned round and came face to face with Tricia. I was only acquainted with her as another Christian lady and we had barely had a conversation before. Taking one look at my face, worn with anguish and creased with months of pain, she gave me a bear-hug. Apparently she had heard about the difficult time we were having and felt that God had told her to support and pray for me. She had some understanding of our situation as whilst abroad as a missionary she had experienced a similar illness to M.E. and had been healed. As she told me this, tears slipped down my cheeks as I was so touched that someone whom I didn't really know well and whom I hadn't even asked, offered to support me regularly. Meeting together a couple of times a month was of great comfort and strength. Tricia was also to become a great source of blessing to Julia.

A few weeks after the firework evening, Julia had gastric flu and was so ill that I brought her home to nurse. The emotional strain of having to cope with these ups and downs was draining me and I began to feel very weary; but not as weary as Julia. Understandably she felt fed up and despondent with feeling unwell all the time, and having to come home and be dependent upon her mother again wasn't easy. Consequently irritability surfaced from Julia's feelings of helplessness and loss of control. However Julia's gracious nature was always quick to surface and she expressed her love and thanks to me with a bouquet of flowers. It was her way of saying, "Thanks, Mum." Once recovered from the gastric flu and feeling strong enough to cope, a few weeks later Julia returned to her flat once more.

Not only was I feeling weary with the fact that this monster of an illness was just going on and on, but I continued to battle with other dark shadows that were uncomfortable and ugly. Cycling to work I passed young teenagers full of life and laughter, making their way to school. Their exuberance and energy touched me deeply and gave rise to envy. I felt jealous that these youngsters had something that I wanted for Julia - life and energy. This unwelcome visitor, jealousy, joined the other emotions of anger, self pity, fear, loneliness and sadness - all were an inevitable part of being hurt by life's circumstances. It was as if there was hardly a breathing space between recognising and dealing constructively with one emotion, before another one emerged. Sometimes they crept silently out of their corner, and at other times they announced themselves with extreme ferocity. It didn't matter how they arrived, they had to be dealt with, and this time I was facing jealousy and envy - a green eyed animal. My cry of *"It's unfair!"* had turned into something deeper - jealousy - a strong desire to have what I did not have.

Seeing these young girls, I would speculate as to what they might do when they left school - thinking how fortunate they were to be healthy. Unconsciously I had been comparing Julia with them. In a world that constantly compares people, ranking them as more or less successful, or more or less clever, I automatically measured my children against all the others. Mary Silver, a psychologist said, "I can't imagine anyone who hasn't experienced envy at one time or another. To be human is to compare ourselves with others." (3) When I hear about the kindness and goodness of other youngsters, it is hard not to wonder whether Julia would be as kind as they if she were well. When I see trophies, medals and rewards being handed out to special people, I cannot avoid asking myself why that hasn't happened to Julia. After all, she is in the university of suffering and deserves a medal for perseverance. Comparing is a waste of time and energy and one day I was sharply interrupted with the question. . . . *"What is that to you? You must follow me."* (4) These words were spoken by Jesus to his disciple, Peter after having just told Peter what kind of death he would experience, by which he would glorify God. Seeing John, another disciple, Peter then inquired of Jesus, *"Lord, what about him?"* (5) In other words, having heard how his death would be, Peter wanted to know what sort of death John would have. Peter's curiosity was sharply rebuked by Jesus saying something like - if I want him to live, so be it, what concern is that to you? You must follow me. I sensed that Jesus was rebuking me for harbouring jealous thoughts that other young girls had something Julia hadn't got. Speculating on what might become of such and such a girl was not my concern, as it is not my place to question what God wants to do in someone else's life. God never compares. Even though I knew in my head that this is true, I found it hard to accept. My responsibility is to keep my eyes fixed on Jesus and follow Him closely. He loves the uniqueness of every man and woman without ever comparing. Thereafter, whenever I found myself having jealous thoughts, or comparing Julia with others, I would remind myself of Jesus' words, *"What is that to you? You must follow me."*

A few weeks later, I was challenged by these words at an even deeper level. The situation wasn't getting any easier and I was increasingly feeling frustrated that I couldn't get on with my life, as caring for Julia took up so much time. There were no signs of improvement and reluctantly I was having to accept that my life was having to change, whether I liked it or not. Driving into Reading to do some shopping, I was chatting away to Jesus as I often do, about how I felt. *"Lord, I'm not enjoying being a carer - its OK for a while, but I've had enough, I want to get on with my own life. Suppose Julia is like this for years?"* I was immediately pulled up with the words, *"What is that to you?"* *"It's everything to me"*, I shouted back to Jesus. *"You're not here on earth having to do the caring, it's easy for you to say that. I don't want to have to be a carer for years."* Then in sharp contrast to my shouts of indignation, the small, quiet voice whispered, *"Come, follow me"*. I knew I couldn't refuse the invitation to follow Christ, there was no choice, I didn't want to go my own way. By this stage of the conversation, I had stopped the car at traffic lights, and with tears flowing down my cheeks I replied, *"Yes, Lord I will follow you, and if that means being a carer for the rest of my life I will follow. My life doesn't belong to me, it belongs to you."* When I arrived home I immediately went into the kitchen and said, *"Lord, do you want me to go down on my knees before you just to show you that I meant business when I said that I would follow you."* A gentle, loving voice replied, *"No, I have seen the sincerity of your heart and that is sufficient."*

This experience had quite a profound effect on me. God had met me with His gift of grace. Grace is a divine act of intervention that breaks into our humanity, enabling us to experience God's presence and power, in ways we would never have experienced them for ourselves, in order to be the people God wants us to be. This concept is illustrated in one of Paul's letters. He pleads with the Lord to take his thorn in the flesh away - in fact in all honesty he admits that in his handicap Satan's angel had done his best to get him down and push him to his knees - and then God replies, *"My grace is sufficient for you, for my power is made perfect in weakness."* (6) Paul was given a gift of grace that strengthened him, making weakness a triumph and a joy. One effect of God's grace operating in my own life at this point was that He gave me the desire and the power to do what I couldn't do for myself. He had intervened and changed my desire into one of being less self-centred in following Him, even if that meant being a carer for the rest of my life. This was clearly a gift from God - He had stepped into my life without me asking Him to do so. As I continued to ask for grace sufficient for the day, and the power to do His will I felt the burden of caring lifted, and discovered a new energy and zeal to serve the Lord. Hereafter, caring for Julia was for me an act of worship.

Feeling so much lighter in my spirit was reflected in my whole being, as friends and family remarked how much better I looked and that I seemed to have regained some of my bounce. When Fiona came home for the Christmas break she said how much more I was like my old self. For me a mark of the change was that I could handle talking to a youth group about a God who is faithful in all circumstances. The talk came from my heart, not my head! I can remember seeing a poster years earlier that said something like "Faith isn't faith until its all you have to hang on to". When life seems easy we often depend upon our own skills and abilities and we only turn to God when we have exhausted our resources. Now in the difficulties I was learning to walk humbly and become more dependent on God. He was the one I was learning to hang on to, just as someone drowning hangs on to a raft in a stormy sea as the only means of survival, I was learning how to hang on to God. Having been quite a self sufficient sort of person, dependence for me was not defeat, but growth.

As I was becoming more dependent upon God, Julia was becoming more dependent upon me as her life continued to yo-yo up and down. This was becoming the norm, and it was difficult to expect anything different. Her 22nd birthday in December was quietly celebrated with a brief visit from her university friends one day, and a couple of other friends another. By now Julia rarely went out. With Christmas looming, she didn't want to miss out on the celebrations, so managed to sit through half an hour of a carol service, but that was enough. Within a few days she was feeling very ill again with a virus. "When will it ever finish?" I cried out one day with Tricia. This sense of desperation and helplessness soon began to fade as we read together Psalm 103, and began to praise Jesus for who He is: *Praise the Lord, O my soul; all my inmost being praise his holy name.*

Hanging On 91

With Fiona home for Christmas, Julia also joined us for that period. Having her at home for 24 hours a day soon revealed how ill she was, and how little she could do. Facing reality was painful and I cried most of the night of Christmas Eve. Normally our Christmases were full of fun and laughter, but this year a quiet heaviness pervaded the home. I was struggling to keep the balance between feeling empathy for Julia, without too much sympathy creeping in. If I allowed myself to be upset by Julia's distress, or in my sorrow pity her, I would become less effective in looking after her. On the other hand, if I didn't feel empathy for her suffering I could be seen as uncaring. So I tried not to commiserate too much with her, and instead, concentrated my mind and energies on supporting and helping her to get better. Lavishing sympathy and pity on my daughter might temporarily have helped her feel better, but in the long run I don't think it would have been of benefit.

Whenever we go through trials, our thoughts will determine the path we take. This was highlighted in a book Fiona gave me for Christmas, *Maybe it's Time to . . . Laugh Again* (7) The message resonated within my spirit and this book was such a tonic to read. Even the first chapter heading "Your Smile Increases your Face Value" caused me to smile inwardly.

> "I have discovered that a joyful countenance has nothing to do with one's age or one's occupation (or lack of it) or one's geography or education or marital status or good looks or circumstances. As I wrote earlier - and will continue to write throughout this book - joy is a choice. It is a matter of attitude that stems from one's confidence in God - that He is at work, that He is in full control, that He is in the midst of whatever has happened, is happening, and will happen. Either we fix our minds on that and determine to laugh again, or we wail and whine our way through life, complaining that we never got a fair shake. We are the ones who consciously

determine which way we shall go. To paraphrase the poet:
>'One ship sails east
>One ship sails west
>Regardless of how the winds blow.
>It is the set of the sail
>And not the gale
>That determines the way we go'". (8)

Laughing one's way through life depends on nothing external. Regardless of how severely the winds of adversity may blow, we set our sails toward joy."

This book didn't offer a mere diversion to coax me to ignore life's hard realities and hide behind a mask, but it drew on sound biblical principles drawn from the writings of Paul to the Philippians. I was challenged by Paul - although he was under arrest in Rome, his writings continually refer to joy. Reading this book helped me to focus again on the fact that I had a choice in how I could respond in our difficult circumstances. I could either be joyful and smile or be a whiner and go around grumpy with a long face. The choice was mine. This was easier said than done and although I didn't whine, and tried to give smiles away, I couldn't honestly say I was *always* joyful!

Moving into 1993 the path ahead was unknown as no one could predict Julia's recovery, yet I clung on objectively to God's faithfulness that He would heal her. Attending a European workshop with Christians in the Caring Professions (CiCP), I asked God to give me a sign. I knew intellectually that God was with me in the situation, but I longed for something more tangible so as to keep my hope and faith alive. Through a prophecy God reminded me that the rainbow was a symbol of His faithful promise. It was as if God was saying, *"As the rainbow is a sign that I will never again destroy all life with a flood, so it is a sign to remember that I have promised to heal Julia."* Being typically human, I struggled in totally believing those words,*"Was it really God speaking, or are these my thoughts"?* So just to make sure I had heard correctly I asked God to confirm these words to me again. *.."If this is really you God, please speak to me again about the rainbow."* The next morning, in the worship time, a man sang out a song about looking through a glass window and seeing a rainbow, a sign of God's promise. Overcome with emotion and total amazement of how gracious God was to reassure me in such a way, inwardly I fell on my knees with an outpouring of thanks. A month later in February I was at another CiCP conference, this time teaching on a counselling course. Just like a child who keeps running back to his father and says, *"Did you really say that?"* I again asked for confirmation. This time God spoke to me by drawing my attention to a poster in the book shop - it was of a rainbow. Then journeying home along the M1 I saw a beautiful rainbow in the sky. I felt very humbled and privileged that God had spoken hope into my life in such a way and I asked him to help me to hang on to this promise.

In the meantime, Julia had deteriorated and by March 1993 she was spending most of her time either in bed or on the sofa. It was as if she had glandular fever continually. Living in the flat was very monotonous for her, as one day drifted into another and although I continued to visit most days this didn't completely address her loneliness. Occasionally she would come home for a few days, if she really couldn't cope by herself, but preferred the flat as it was smaller and warmer. Because her brain felt so 'foggy' reading was out of the question, so Julia passed the time by doing needlework and watching TV. Being confined to the flat, the one thing she missed was being part of a worshipful community of people. This very real lack in her life was solved by a thought that came from Tricia. Not only was Tricia supporting me, but she also used to regularly visit Julia who always appreciated her company. They got on like a house on fire as Tricia was like a breath of fresh air, never staying longer than ten minutes, thus leaving Julia refreshed rather than drained, which often happened when visitors stayed too long.

When Julia voiced her longing to be part of a worshipping group of people, Tricia suggested a wonderful idea. She would arrange for the teenagers from her church, many of whom played musical instruments and enjoyed singing, to regularly come round to the flat. Arriving with keyboard, clarinet and flute, about half a dozen youngsters would squeeze into the lounge and spend about half an hour worshipping God. Depending on how she felt, Julia was free to join in; or just sit quietly in the lounge and listen; or remain in her bedroom on her bed. No expectations were put on her. These times of worship strengthened Julia and were the highlight of many a month. God in His grace, was hanging on to Julia in the midst of her illness, and Julia was hanging on to God. She was always very interested to hear what God was doing in the church and other people's lives and in spite of her circumstances she had a real genuine interest and concern for others.

I appreciated this support from other young people - it showed that they cared, and that Julia wasn't forgotten. This was a tangible expression of God's love and it went a long way to communicate to Julia that God was looking after her needs. I was always particularly touched when a young person came up to me with a word of encouragement. In one evening service that I was leading, feeling low I inwardly cried out, *""Lord, be the lifter of my head."* Somehow God in his grace and strength carried me through the service, and at the end Gail came up to me. Gail, was a young girl in early twenties in our church, who had also been at Leeds university with Fiona. So she knew us well and had visited Julia on a number of occasions. Whispering in my ear she said, "Chris, I'm so excited as I saw a picture of Julia dancing." This was such an encouragement to me and I walked out of church feeling much brighter. A few weeks later I had another encouragement when I was praying in the middle of the night. I saw Jesus rescuing Julia from a thick wood; carrying her up a hill; then setting her down in a beautiful garden. Then, just as a big London musical stage scene changes, the scene in the garden began to move and break up to give way to Julia standing in the middle of a city - involved in life again. Feeling totally astounded I said, *"Lord, give me the patience to wait until this promise becomes a reality."*

By the end of June that year Julia had reached a better plateau for about five weeks - it was the best she had been for over a year. How I enjoyed seeing her have more energy to do things, although when she became tired, irritability was still not far away. Seeing some improvement sustained I began to think that maybe at long last Julia was on the road to recovery. Sadly, this was to be short-lived as the old symptoms came back again and she relapsed. By now Marie had finished her degree and left the flat , so Julia was by herself. Seeing how unwell Julia was, Fiona, home for her summer holidays, stayed in the flat for a few nights to keep her company. This appeared to work well as they both enjoyed each other's friendship, and Fiona was able to contain her natural exuberance and refrain from bouncing around at 100 mph so as not to wear Julia out! Although Fiona's busy social life was in painful contrast to Julia's non-existent one, I didn't detect any barrier between the girls because of this. I had always encouraged Fiona to lead her own life to the full and not to feel guilty about her life in comparison to Julia's, and Julia always enjoyed hearing what Fiona was up to, although she acknowledged to me that deep down she was jealous of Fiona and it hurt a lot to see her sister enjoying what she longed for.

Later that summer, with Julia slightly better, they both drove down to Dartmouth with Gail and her sister, Antoinette, for a holiday. The terraced house that was given to them for a week had the most marvellous views overlooking the sea. The beauty of the spectacular scenery was a real blessing to Julia, and watching from the large bay windows she enjoyed many holiday events such as the Red Arrows RAF Display Team and an unexpected firework display. It was a wonderful gift that these holiday festivities came to her as she wasn't well enough to go out and be part of the crowd. While Fiona and Gail explored the local countryside, burning off their natural exuberance and energy in chatting and walking, Julia and Antoinette stayed behind, talking and using their creative talents in painting. During this short period I had a great sense of freedom as I didn't have to think about meals or pop round and make sure Julia was all right. This respite from caring was a welcome break.

Although I had adjusted to the role of a carer, nevertheless I found it at times totally draining. Earlier that summer I had found myself saying several times, *"I can't cope,"* as I felt so drained of emotional energy. Then one day I realised that it wasn't really that I felt I couldn't cope, but that hiding underneath that comment were the words, *"I don't want to cope."* I didn't want to walk the path I was treading. Unknowingly I had slipped into a negative thought pattern. When, as mothers, we give out continually and our emotional tank empties, it's very easy for self-defeating thoughts to creep in. They need watching as they can become very destructive. These thoughts are very powerful as research has shown that in our subconscious we speak to ourselves at about 1500 words a minute. Normal talking speed is around 200 words a minute. So telling myself that "I can't cope" at 1500 words a minutes, was self-defeating. Having identified what was going on, thereafter every time I caught myself saying these words I changed them to, *"With God's help, I can cope,"* which was a far more constructive way of dealing with my self-defeating thoughts. Consequently over the next few weeks the words, "I can't cope" lost their power and I began to face the responsibilities of caring with greater enthusiasm.

As the warm, bright summer merged into the coolness and darkness of autumn, Julia's few good spells merged into a continuous, dark and long tunnel of infirmity. Fevers, night sweats, swollen glands and blinding headaches were all part of the scenery. Giving out energy in adjusting to her new flat mate, Louise, and missing Fiona who had gone back to Leeds, Julia became quite low. As a result I was struggling to keep positive and bright and it was such a relief to share my inner turmoil with some close friends in a group called,

Kiriath. This group of seven, including some doctors from the surgery, had met regularly for years to talk about our inner struggles, how biblical principles impacted our lives; and to be accountable to each other. It was very releasing to talk honestly about the three strands I was battling with - anxiety, grief and trusting God. The non-judgmental acceptance of the group was very therapeutic. We had often talked about the consequences of Christian triumphalism - an attitude that was to be found in many charismatic churches preaching doctrines of prosperity and success, which suggest that there was no room for inner turmoil and struggles for a Christian. But this isn't reality. As a group we wanted to be real and honest with ourselves and each other. It is in facing our inner struggles that we grow, and this group was a healthy environment for me to do that in. Reflecting on all that I was going through one of the group asked me if I felt that God loved me. Without any hesitation, I replied, "Yes, I know God loves me." I had no doubts. In my childhood I had been loved by a wonderful father, and I knew that my heavenly Father would never stop loving me. He loved and accepted me for being me, which embraced all my doubts and struggles. I didn't have to prove anything to Him, he knew me inside out, warts and all!

In October of that year, I took Julia to a healing conference run by a small fellowship called, Sozo. We had first learnt of Sozo through friends as they had heard that God was doing amazing things through this small church based in Romsey. Sozo is a Greek word meaning healed, saved and whole and this small free independent fellowship seemed to have a special anointing for the healing of M.E. We had read their booklet in which many people testified to having been completely healed with this ministry. Having gently coaxed Julia to go, I set off with her for a four day healing conference with a hope and expectation that God in his grace would bring her to a greater place of health and wholeness.

Arriving at the conference centre at the Methodist Hotel in Weston-super-Mare I wheeled Julia into the reception area for registration.

The atmosphere welcoming us was one of love and acceptance and nothing was too much trouble as I took Julia up in the lift to our bedroom, whilst others brought up our bags via the stairs. We were shown into a basic but comfortable double room, that had a most glorious view over rooftops to the sea beyond. The beauty of the calm sea as still as a mill pond with the sun reflecting on its surface, spoke to me about the peace and glory of Jesus. My prayer was, *"Jesus, the giver of life and health, may we meet with you over the next few days."*

As Julia wasn't well enough to sit up for very long, I had taken along a lounger to put up in the conference room as it was obviously much more comfortable for her to lie down and rest. When I asked if I could put the lounger in the room I was at first met with a rebuff and a no, as there wasn't enough room. Feeling slightly taken back, I politely but firmly said that Julia wasn't well enough to sit for long spells and needed a lounger. I didn't find it very easy fighting for Julia but knew that if I, as her mother didn't speak up for her, no one else would. Being a person who naturally feels more comfortable in conforming than confronting, I found it difficult to take a firm stand. Reminding myself of how Jesus fought for the weak and vulnerable gave me the courage to speak up. In the event it turned out fine, and they arranged for the lounger to be taken into the conference room, placing it against the wall. I could quite understand what they were saying as the room was small and when they had about 40 people packed in, there was no room for manoeuvre. The hotel staff were very helpful over meals and were obviously used to adapting to ill people on the conferences. I used to collect our meals on a tray and take them upstairs to eat in the bedroom as Julia wasn't well enough to go down to the dining room.

Having been involved in prayer ministry myself, I was comfortable with all the different approaches at each session and felt drawn closer to God through the worship in the evening. Julia managed only the later morning session, rested during the free period in the afternoons and attended the evening worship and ministry time. What really struck me about the Sozo community was that they were not only a loving community, but they had such an expectant faith. They had seen God do great things and expected him to touch people's lives that week. As a community their expectant faith to see God move was far greater than I had ever experienced before. As the conference proceeded many people began to testify about how God's healing power was touching them. A lady who came walking in on crutches was now walking unaided.

Halfway through the morning of the last full day, Marion, the pastor announced that she was going to pray specifically for all those who had M.E. By now she knew who was who and scanning those present she realised that Julia wasn't there - she was still in bed. Encouraging me to bring Julia down as soon as possible, I shot upstairs to find Julia sitting on her bed, trying to dress. "Come on Julia, Marion is going to pray for all those with M.E. and sent me to encourage you to come down. Let's not be too long in getting down there." Julia was so slow in getting dressed that I became quite frustrated with her. "It'll be all right mum, don't fuss, I can't go any quicker." After what seemed like hours, but was probably only a few minutes, we eventually arrived in the conference room and Julia went forward to join the others for prayer. Nothing specifically happened for Julia, and as usual she went back to bed for the afternoon whilst I went out for a walk.

On returning I found her sitting in a chair in the bay window crying. "It's not fair mum, I have just seen one of the other girls with M.E. who previously could hardly walk, just walk up the steep hill. Why her and not me? I feel so ill - I'm not any better." Trying to get things into perspective for her, I replied "Yes, it is unfair Julia and it is disappointing that you are no better. . . . . but first and foremost we are here to meet with Jesus, . . . we are to look to Him, rather than look for healing." She just sobbed her heart out as I put my arms around her, and I quietly prayed that she would be given grace and strength to cope with her disappointment. When the tears eventually came to an end I suggested that we prayed that it was more important that Jesus became the centre of our lives, and that if she was healed it would be a bonus. This we did and peace began to soothe her anguish.

During the worship that evening a young couple came and prayed over Julia who was curled up on her lounger, feeling nauseated with a migraine. Becky, the young lady had been more or less been bed ridden for a couple of years with M.E. and had been completely healed at a similar Sozo conference about a year earlier. There was something very innocent and beautiful in seeing another young couple showing so much love in ministering to Julia. At the end of the evening an invitation was given to go forward for a blessing, which I did. In the meantime Becky had quietly encouraged Julia to worship; and then led her to the front for prayer. As I sat there watching and praying, tears streamed down my face as the Holy Spirit touched me. Then I saw Julia straighten up, lifting her hands in an attitude of worship (something she couldn't have done previously as she hadn't the strength in her arm muscles). When she turned round to come back she looked different, she moved differently and her face was so radiant and happy. Catching each others eyes from a distance we both knew that God had touched her. Words were of no relevance as we threw our arms round each other and amidst tears and laughter shared this very precious moment together. "Mum I feel so different. I reached out and touched Jesus and He's healed me. The heaviness has gone and I feel so full of joy."

HIS RIGHT HAND HOLDS ME

Lord don't let go of me; I cannot see
I'm surrounded by a thick white blanket
The foggy fingers even wrap themselves around my feet.
Lord, I don't know where I'm going
Where are you taking me?
The path is invisible, I can't even see the signpost to direct me
At times I become frightened and panic
But your hand clasps me tighter - it reassures.
At times I become frustrated and indignant
I want to go faster but then I trip and fall;
You stop to pick me up from the ground, a crying child
I feel your firm hands beneath my arms,
Your figure enshrouded - a silhouette in the mist.
At times anger rises in me - I want to know where the path leads.
I stop and shout out loudly,
But you stop and whisper - "Stopping only slows".
At times the fog thins to nothing and we can take a rest
It's then I see your face clearly
Compassionate eyes, a joyful smile, a radiant love.
Thank you Lord, your gentle hand never slips from mine
I trust you in the path we take
And one day I'll arrive.
Julia

Chapter 7

A Measure of Healing

God, I called for help and you healed me (Psalm 30:2)

Still reeling from the excitement and wonder of what had just happened, the main thought whirling around in my mind was that the long awaited promise that Julia would be healed, was now a reality. God had been faithful and true to his word to us, and for this I was overwhelmingly thankful. Once our initial emotional response of tears and excitement had died down we made our way back to the bedroom. But Julia could hardly contain herself - she said it was as if Jesus had lifted off all the heaviness and fatigue from her limbs and obliterated all her other symptoms - for the first time in years she felt well. In her obvious joy she leapt onto the bed and shouted at the top of her voice "Thank you Lord," then she jumped down and said, "I'm hungry, I'm going downstairs to get some chocolate from the tuck shop." About five minutes later she came bursting into the room clutching some chocolate bars, exclaiming, "It's so wonderful to be alive and well, I have just run back up the stairs," (several flights), and she did a twizzle in the middle of the room . I could see the delight written all across her face - just the sheer joy of being able to go and choose to buy herself some chocolate - a little thing she hadn't been able to do for several years.

Having feasted and celebrated on coffee and chocolate, we eventually turned our thoughts to going to bed. But before we did this, we thanked God for His faithfulness and His gift of healing. However in our elation, sleep evaded us. It was as if the flood gates to life were open and out tumbled all the things Julia could start doing again - visit her friends; go on holiday; drive a car; go out shopping; walk in the countryside; visit the seaside; see more of Fiona . . . . and the list went on and on. We had such fun imagining all the things she could now get up to. Having exhausted this list we then tried to quieten our minds and sleep. After a short spell the silence was broken with a whisper, "Mum, are you still awake?" I giggled and replied, "Yes, I'm enjoying thinking of all the normal things in life you can now get up to - I can take you to the theatre again, and we can go to Wimbledon." Still wide awake we then thought of all the people who had prayed for Julia and remembered them one by one - thanking the Lord for each of them, and asking for blessings to be poured down upon them. Perhaps turning our thoughts in thankfulness to God might help us eventually sleep! But it didn't. In spite of periodically trying to be quiet and sleep, one of us would think of something else and we would be off chatting away again. "Hey, have you thought about this . . . . and what about that . . . . ?" and so it went on until about 5 am. Finally, exhausted with excitement, we fell asleep.

When we eventually came to the next morning Julia seemed to be fine, but a little tired. However, I was more than a little tired! But we were still bubbling over with joy and thankful hearts. Skipping breakfast we went for a short walk in the early morning sunshine - the pleasure of being able to walk with my daughter was very precious; this was something we hadn't been able to do together for over a year. In the final meeting that morning one could sense the powerful presence of the Holy Spirit and Julia expressed her love to the Lord in dancing.

Quietly I thanked God for the picture that Gail had given me a few months earlier - Julia dancing in worship. God was faithful to his promises. With the conference ending at mid-day, on our way home we parked the car on the sea front and strolled along the promenade. Not content with a sauntering walk, we ventured onto the golden sands and had a fun time kicking the sand and making patterns. What freedom - I relished the enjoyment of being able to do simple normal things with my daughter. It was such a treat. On the way home in the car Julia said, "I would like to go up to Leeds tomorrow and surprise Fiona, do you think Dad will drive us up?" This request caught me on the hop as my mind was not adjusting to this new situation as quickly as Julia's. Appearing calmer than I probably felt inside, I replied, "I'm sure he will, and Fiona will be so thrilled to see you." With that, Julia settled down and slept for the rest of the journey home.

On arriving home I went in first ,with Julia following close on my heels, shouting out, "Hi Dad, we're home." But no answer. Entering the kitchen and looking through the window, I said, "Look he's up the garden. He doesn't know we're home yet." So Julia jumped up and down waving her arms about trying to catch his attention, shouting, "Dad, we're back." John eventually saw us, waved, and came in, greeting Julia with a big hug. She blurted out, "I've been healed," and giving him no time to catch his breath or ask any questions, let alone take in what had happened, Julia was off again, "Dad, will you take us up to Leeds tomorrow, I want to surprise Fiona." John seemed paralysed with shock and amazement - he was stunned in seeing the change in Julia. As he hugged her, he broke down in tears and said, "Oh, I'm so thrilled to see you looking so much better . . . I can't get over it." When Julia had first become ill, John was out of the house working so it didn't really impact his life very much. But since he had taken early retirement earlier that year and spent more time at home, the reality of how ill she was had shocked him quite deeply. Being around during the day he saw for himself how debilitated she was and often spent an afternoon with her at the flat keeping her company. Now he was so overjoyed to see her so much better that I guess like me, he would have done anything she wanted to celebrate her new life. "Of course we can go up to Leeds tomorrow if that's what you want to do."

The next day was a Saturday and we made some discreet phone calls to Fiona's friends so as to arrange a surprise visit when we would find her in. Plans were made to arrive in Leeds early evening and for Julia to stay with Fiona, whilst John and I bed and breakfasted somewhere. Pottering around at home that Saturday morning, catching up on washing etc. I was aware that Julia was up, dressed and playing the piano. But I didn't make any comment - I took Julia's improvement in my stride. However Julia herself was quite upset that neither John nor I had said anything to acknowledge the fact that she was up, dressed and playing the piano for the first time for years, and we had not encouraged her in it! It appeared that Julia felt so insecure that she wanted her improvements to be noted. I wondered how easy she was finding the transition - but all this soon got lost in our excitement in travelling up to Leeds.

Arriving in plenty of time, John and I went and booked in at a B&B and then drove round to the large terraced house that Fiona happily shared with four other students. They were very supportive of one another as they all had family problems with illness and other difficulties. So having heard all about Julia's struggles, Fiona's house mates were delighted to be involved, and later told me that they had enjoyed the secrecy of it all. Hardly able to contain myself in anticipating Fiona's reaction, John and I decided to keep in the shadows, so that Julia alone would be standing on the doorstep. Ringing the front doorbell, Julia stood there in joyful expectation, knowing that Fiona was going to be told to go and answer the front door. The suspense bought tears to my eyes, then the door opened. With total shock and amazement on Fiona's face, she exclaimed, "Julia, what are you doing here?. . . ". "I wanted you to know, I've been healed," and with that the predictable hugs and tears flowed.

Sitting in the living room amidst the shrieks of delight from Fiona and her house mates, Julia shared her story. It was such a cosy scene: Julia and Fiona sat together on the settee, bantering away as sisters do; the other girls sat on the floor, interjecting with comments at times; whilst John and I sat quietly listening, not able to hide our big grins! In a way John and I felt superfluous to the scene, as the action and the chatting was taking place amongst the youngsters - seeing Julia join in gave me a deep sense of joy and released in me an inner flow of thanks to God. I was still astounded by what was happening. Eventually John and I left the girls talking and went off to quietly slip into bed. We were both shattered with the events of the last few days.

Meeting up with our daughters the next morning was a great pleasure - seeing the delight on their faces and hearing their non stop prattle warmed our hearts. I was assured that their chatter hadn't gone on all night! Piling into the car we set off for the church Fiona attended and found ourselves parking about 100 yards away. It seemed amazing that Julia could walk this distance without any difficulties. For the first time for years it was as if we were a normal family: we were able to do something all together; we didn't have to limit our activities because of Julia; and we didn't have to use a wheelchair. We then went out for lunch which was greatly enjoyed by all. Walking from the restaurant back to the car, and out of Julia's earshot I asked Fiona how she felt about the miracle. Her reply wasn't what I expected. She found it a bit freaky and was still struggling to adjust and take it in. Seeing her sister standing on the doorstep the evening before was such a shock, that she could hardly call it enjoyable! But obviously she was delighted in seeing Julia well and able to do things again. Finally our time together drew to a close and having said our goodbyes we left Leeds to journey back home to Reading. Not surprisingly as soon as the car hit the motorway Julia slept - she must have been tired with all the emotional energy she had expended. When we came to stop at a Service Area for a drink, she was too tired to leave the car and just carried on dozing.

After a lie in the following morning Julia was up and making arrangements to do things. I found myself waving goodbye to her as she drove off down the road in the car, in spite of not having driven for over a year. As she turned round and waved back to me, her face was a picture. With a grin from ear to ear, it was as if she was saying "This is wonderful . . . freedom!" She was off to tell Alison, her GP, what had happened. (Jill, her previous doctor had left the surgery). Unlike other patients we knew whose doctors didn't accept

M.E., Alison was very understanding of Julia as she had experienced M.E. at first hand, having had a friend suffering with this, living with her for some time. Consequently Julia trusted her and they had a really good patient/doctor relationship. Being a Christian as well, Alison was also able to share in what God was doing in Julia's life. Arriving back from the surgery she came into the house shouting, "I'm back .... it was wonderful being able to drive myself again ... Alison was thrilled."

After spending a few days at home recovering from all the excitement, Julia returned to the flat. Now feeling much better and not wanting to shirk responsibilities she took on jobs around the home she hadn't done for years. Forgetting that her muscles had been inactive for a long time, Julia pulled a shoulder muscle in scrubbing the kitchen floor. This gave her some pain and having already pulled a ligament in her hand when driving the car for the first time, she was beginning to feel in the wars. However this didn't dampen her enthusiasm for life. Her greatest sense of freedom came in visiting the library and being able to manage a 10 minute walk to Asda and do her own light shopping. Julia enjoyed being independent again and although she had her off days, she was slowly improving and getting stronger. Spiritually she was very much alive to God and gave a wonderful testimony in church where there was not a dry eye to be seen. Gail's mother was so touched by Julia's story that she put her trust in God that evening. I was reminded of the picture God had given me a few months earlier of Julia being taken from a place of isolation and being planted back into the hustle and bustle of life again - this was His work in Julia's life to His glory.

Journeying through life, we often find that times of blessings are spoilt by minor irritations - and for Julia this was in the shape and form of fleas! Within two days of returning to the flat, Julia became bitten by fleas - there had been no problem with fleas in the flat before, but for some unknown reason they began to make their presence known. The inexplicable thing was that they attacked Julia rather than her new flatmate, Louise. At one time she had over one hundred flea bites over her legs alone, which prevented her from being able to rest and relax as she itched so much. We tried different powders, sprinkling it in corners of all the rooms and the cupboards, but even spraying Julia with special lotion didn't seem to stop the fleas enjoying her! Praying against these fleas didn't appear to have any effect either, and in the end coping with the swollen bumps got her down. However after a couple of weeks the flea invasion appeared to die down and life carried on as normal - it is very interesting to note that Julia has never been plagued by fleas in the flat since then.

When Fiona came home for a weekend in November, she was amazed at how much Julia could do. They enjoyed doing things together that they hadn't been able to do for years: a trip to the cinema; and an afternoon shopping in Reading. Fiona remarked how surprised she was in having just returned from traipsing round the shops together, that instead of collapsing, Julia still had the energy to enthusiastically show me what she had bought - a skirt and blouse. In fact she even put them on and we had something of a dress parade. At 5 ft 8 ins tall and slim, she looked very elegant - she hadn't lost her touch at selecting clothes that suited her well. Being able to walk into a shop and choose new clothes for herself was another significant achievement. Fiona was quite amazed by seeing Julia so much better, and she and I spent many a moment acknowledging together our thankful hearts as life was becoming more normal again. Fiona was enjoying doing things with her sister, and John and I were enjoying seeing Julia relishing life.

A few weeks later I stood on the station platform, waving her off on a train to Guildford to see her university friends. I was a little concerned that she was getting back into life too fast - but perhaps I was an over anxious mother! She even insisted on stopping off at the shops in Reading first. I tried to suggest that maybe one activity such as travelling to Guildford was sufficient to cope with and it might be wise to consider dropping the shopping idea - but no, Julia was going full steam ahead. However, visiting her university friends was much harder than Julia anticipated. Their lives were so busy that she felt like an outsider, out of place, which led to the inevitable feelings of isolation and sadness. She also felt pressurised by their fast pace of life and was hurt by their lack of understanding that she couldn't keep up with their speed as she was still recuperating and adjusting. In contrast to this experience, she visited James' parents, Roger and Elizabeth, where she was met with total understanding and acceptance of where she was. They were thrilled to see her and their love soothed some of her pain.

A week after Julia's return from Guildford, our quiet Sunday evening was interrupted by a phone call from Julia in the flat. In tears she told me the sad news that James' father, Roger, had died suddenly. Roger and Elizabeth had lovingly supported Julia during her time at university and she was very fond of them, and they likewise of her, so this loss was understandably distressing. When Julia had visited Roger a week earlier, he had been profoundly touched in seeing how God's healing grace had restored Julia to health. In the middle of their conversation he had stopped and paused - it was as if he became lost in the wonder of God's greatness. Perhaps he had caught a glimpse of heaven. Consequently the last week of his life was given over to joyfully thanking God for His faithfulness and goodness. Journeying to Guildford for his thanksgiving service, Julia not only felt sad, but also anxious about meeting James again. She hadn't seen him since they had split up. However in the event, there was no need to worry as there was no tension between them both as they greeted each other at the end of the service. Their relationship had ended without any animosity.

On our way home from the funeral we stopped off to do some shopping for Julia's birthday party, which was in a few days' time. Standing at the check out with a laden trolley Julia was unusually slow and quiet. I thought that this was probably a reaction to Roger's funeral. "Are you OK?" I asked her. "I don't feel well - all my glands are swollen again." I was dumb-struck - I didn't know what to say. Part of me wanted to shout, *"You can't be ill, you are healed!"* and another part of me cried, *"Oh my goodness, is her health being snatched away again?"* Discarding both of these thoughts I replied, "Oh dear, that's disappointing . . . . . . let's get you home quickly and after a good rest I"m sure you will feel better tomorrow." A rather unconvincing, "I hope so" was the response. I prayed all the way home in the car, thanking God for Julia's measure of healing and declaring that the enemy had no power to snatch this away. I phoned Fiona up that evening and as I was relaying my anxieties I felt sick and the awful butterfly feelings in my stomach returned. It was if we were going backwards, not forward. Needless to say, I had a few tears with John that evening. However over the next few days Julia began to improve and was well enough to enjoy an early birthday party with about twenty friends squeezed into the small lounge at the flat. About a week later we went to London.to see a Christmas show at the London Palladium in which Roy Castle gave one of his last stage appearances. It was disappointing that John had a prior engagement and couldn't come with us, but Julia and I had a real fun time together. We enjoyed the simple things of life: crossing London in a taxi; savouring the atmosphere in the theatre; and eating ice cream together. It was an evening to remember.

A few days later on Julia's actual 23rd birthday I popped in to see her and excitedly shouted up the stairs, "Hi Julia. Happy Birthday." Having run up the stairs two at a time, eager to surprise her with presents and goodies I was stopped in my tracks at the sight of her sitting on the bed crying. My elation was shattered by the words, "I don't feel well . . . . I am so angry . . . . I don't want to be ill again" Standing there awkwardly, I searched for words that would alleviate her pain. None came, so I gave her the next best thing - a hug. Adjusting to the news, I somehow found the words to reassure her

A Measure of Healing

that she would improve and tried to make light of the fact that she didn't feel well. I'm sure I sounded more convincing than I felt inside! Although inwardly my heart was heavy and I was really concerned, outwardly I kept bright so as to make something of her birthday for her. But it was hard going as Julia's utter frustration made her bad tempered. The following day was no better as she spent it in bed, and by the end of the week, arrangements to travel up to Leeds to see Fiona at the end of term had to be cancelled. Feeling as if she had flu, Julia became very weepy and fragile so I spent quite a lot of time round the flat cuddling her, reassuring and encouraging her and getting meals. No sooner had Fiona arrived home for her Christmas vacation than she went round to see Julia. The contrast between how she now found Julia and the time when she had last seen her, was too much for Fiona and she came home in tears. She was angry because she felt disillusioned, and Julia was angry because she felt let down by God. Surprisingly I didn't feel angry, but like John I was deeply disappointed.

I had anticipated that when Julia had been touched by God's healing grace, she would just go from strength to strength. Most of the people who had been dramatically healed at Sozo had made a good recovery from M.E., so we assumed this would happen for Julia. But as time went on I was beginning to recognise that Julia and I had different understandings and perceptions of healing. Somehow she had formed the beliefs:- *"Now God has healed me . . . . I must live in my healing,"* and *"If I have enough faith I will get better."* So the emphasis was on Julia striving to succeed in maintaining what God had given her, instead of resting and trusting in His grace. But part of her frustration was the fact that she couldn't live in her healing and hence felt a failure. We live in a society which says that if you don't achieve at something, you're a nobody. To some extent Julia already felt a failure in not achieving a normal healthy life, so when God gave her a gift of healing she was determined to succeed in being well.

I didn't subscribe to this theology of healing - I knew without any doubt that God had given her a measure of healing, but how this worked itself out was under God's control, not Julia's. In fact I used to feel quite uncomfortable when Julia talked about her healing as if it were a once and for all complete experience. I saw healing far more as a process - God had started something that He would finish. One day Julia urged me to phone a friend to say that she had been healed. "Have faith Mum that I'm healed," she insisted. "How can I when you are obviously still not well," I replied. Hereafter discussions about healing were occasionally the topic of conversation. I was always very careful to listen and respect Julia's point of view. The best way to support Julia was to give her the freedom to walk her own individual journey with the Lord and to allow her to come to her own decision about the theology of healing.

Within a week Julia had picked up again and came home for Christmas. On Christmas Eve she went out to a local pub with some of Fiona's friends - Fiona was very supportive and protective of her sister as it was the first time that Julia had been out socially for about two years. Julia used to laugh and say that she hadn't spoken to another man apart from her dad for well over a year! Although she smiled about this, I found it very poignant. Now going out to meet a mixed group of young people Julia understandably felt very nervous. However she enjoyed herself and was quite content to be quiet in the crowd, and sit and listen. After a quick rest back home, the girls met up with us at church for the midnight service. Although tired, Julia was holding herself together well, particularly as she had been asked to give her testimony as part of the sermon. Sitting listening to her story, I felt an immensely proud Mum. Being able to stand up and share her pain appeared effortless and the ease with which she spoke, flowed. I had a real sense of God being glorified in her life. On the way out of church I heard a young teenager turn to her Mother and say, "Cor, wasn't that girl brave . . . . I couldn't cope if I was ill like that . . . . isn't it amazing what God's done for her."

A Measure of Healing   113

With the passing of Christmas, Julia went off to Cardiff to celebrate the beginning of 1994 with Gail, Antoinette and other friends. She returned feeling infinitely better and it was very noticeable that she was much less tired and irritable. My head wasn't getting bitten off! Thinking positively about her future, Julia decided to have more independence so considered buying herself a car. Scanning the papers together, John and Julia found a suitable Ford Fiesta and excitedly went off to see it. On their return Julia was sparkling with joy as she told me the colour and amusingly described what it was like to drive. Giggling away she said, "My driving skills weren't too great! I stalled it - you ought to have seen the garage worker's face - he was not amused. Hey. . . . now I can go and visit friends - ooh . . . . I'm free." Consequently a few days later a blue Fiesta sat on the drive outside her flat. Little did she know that she would barely use it.

Not only had Julia hoped to have her own car one day, but another dream was to take part in a musical. She had missed this opportunity at school. Her teenage years were during the time of the teachers' strikes, when no extra-curricular activities were being organised. Earlier in our married life John and I had immense fun in taking part in musicals, and Julia was hoping for a similar experience. On a cold January morning she and her flat mate, Louise went off to Henley to audition for the chorus of a musical. Returning home full of excitement she gave us a demonstration of what they had got up to. Watching her twist and turn, as she tried to recreate the movements, I began to laugh with her. The more I laughed, the sillier and more outrageous her movements became until in the end we both ended up in a heap of giggles. John was looking on smiling, and I could see written across his face, 'What a daft pair." Being a dancer myself, I added to the atmosphere by mirroring some of the unconventional movements, which of course I over exaggerated - this made us giggle even more. What it was to be human and have some fun! About a week later Julia heard that she had been accepted for the musical. She was over the moon. To have been out of action for so long and now to see her dreams coming true was a real encouragement to her. However, sadly, as she began to deteriorate over the next few months owing to infections, this opportunity was never taken - her dreams were being shattered yet again.

A few days after the audition, Julia became ill with infected tonsils and had a course of antibiotics. She had hardly recovered from this infection when she went down with the usual swollen glands and muscle pains. Throughout February the pattern of having tonsillitis about every ten days or so established itself. As soon as she had finished one course of antibiotics and had a few relatively good days with no sore throat, she was back to suffering with tonsillitis again. Although this began to wear her down physically she was very positive and hopeful that this was just a passing phase. What she didn't tell me at the time, was that she was beginning to get muscle pain in her legs again. Fortunately she felt really close to God and was spending time on meditating on His word. The outcome of this was a daughter who was at peace with herself, and able to rise above her symptoms. By now she had also learnt to manage herself more appropriately, rather than push herself to extremes. It was difficult to understand why she kept slipping back when there appeared to be no rhyme or reason for this happening. A similar pattern continued into March, with another spell of tonsillitis. As time passed by, Julia became acutely aware that she wasn't well enough to go away with Louise over Easter, so had to cancel their holiday together. It was always very painful to have to cancel arrangements with friends as not only did she not want to let them down, but it also highlighted her loss.

However Fiona took her away for a couple of days to Bournemouth, but not before we had a heated discussion about taking the wheelchair. "If you use it, you are acting out being an ill patient," I said, trying to dissuade her from using it. I was obviously still very confused myself over Julia's healing as previously I had encouraged her to use it. "No, I'm not. I want to use it to conserve my energy,"

A Measure of Healing

she retorted. With hindsight I realised my attitude was wrong - I made a mistake by putting pressure on her and not listening to what she felt her body wanted to do. It's so easy for mothers to think they know best! But Julia stuck to her guns. She subsequently told me that she couldn't tell Fiona she didn't feel well enough to go out - this caused her too much guilt - so using the wheelchair was a necessity.

Seeing Julia relapse bought back the pain again for me: the loss of expectation; dashed hopes; concern for her future; fear of how this relapse might affect her; a sense of helplessness as a mother; and once more the anger began to creep out of the cupboard. The sense of heaviness and dread returned and I began to question why Julia was becoming unwell again. After all God had touched her, and He isn't a cruel and punishing God - He wouldn't take away something He had given her. I thought again about why some people don't get better . . . . some people enjoy illness; others remain ill because they don't want responsibility and are frightened of change; whilst others prefer to remain the helpless victim - but Julia didn't fit into any of these categories. Again I was having to come to terms with accepting the mystery of God's healing - He gives sometimes for a season, sometimes for the remainder of life. *Who has understood the mind of the Lord?'* (1)

One Sunday I was really encouraged by something I heard sung on the TV programme, "Songs of Praise". I caught the words,

I trace the rainbow thro' the rain,
And feel the promise is not vain
That morn shall tearless be. . . . (2)

Because I hadn't been really concentrating on the programme I didn't hear rest of the words of the song, but it didn't matter - the words that had caught my attention were a real encouragement to me. It was as if God was speaking directly into my situation, reassuring me of his promises by reminding me of the symbolic meaning of the rainbow.

Round about this time, I am not sure whether I became hypersensitive to other people's comments about how God had answered their prayers, or whether I was actually being bombarded by testimonies of God's goodness in answering prayer. What I was hearing were many people saying, "Oh, I prayed and God answered." *"Lucky for you",* I whispered under my breath! One friend said, "When I moved here, I asked God to give my children friends at school and happy teenage years, which he has done. Isn't He a great God?" It was on the tip of my tongue to reply, *"And what if your prayers hadn't been answered, would you still say that God was great?"* It was as if she was saying something like, aren't I clever, because I prayed, God answered and gave me my request - isn't He great! It sounded so superficial - yes of course when we pray God sometimes gives us the desires of our hearts, but when He says no to our requests He is still essentially a God of goodness and mercy because God is love. It is easy to believe in the goodness of God when all the evidence around demonstrates answered prayer, but it is quite another thing when prayers are left on the shelf. Suffering and unanswered prayers will always call into question the goodness of God, as lingering around is the suspicion that God cannot be trusted to have our best interests at heart. If God is good why then does He not help us escape from overwhelming times of sorrow and difficulties? After all, He has the power to prevent bad things happening.

In the story of Daniel's three Hebrew companions, Shadrach, Meshach, and Abednego, King Nebuchadnezzar was furious that they had refused to worship his idols, so he ordered them to be thrown into a blazing clay furnace. This is what they said, *"If we are thrown into the blazing furnace, the God we serve is able to save us from it, and he will rescue us from your hand, O King. But even if he does not . . . . . . we will not serve your gods or worship the image of gold you have set up."* (3). The words that challenged me in this reading were: *Even if he does not.* In effect the young men were saying, even if God does not exert his miracle-working power on our behalf, nevertheless our confidence in the love and goodness of God will not be destroyed. The Hebrews understood that God could

A Measure of Healing

intervene and save their lives, but He was not obligated to do it. Their faith didn't depend upon the outcome of their situation. Likewise I wanted my faith to be so strong that I was able to say, if God heals Julia - I believe He is a God of goodness. But even If God does not - I still believe He is essentially a God of goodness. Although I believed this in my head, I was some way off in completely believing it in my heart. But in meditating on this story I was able to say with a much deeper conviction, *"Even if God does not bring Julia to that place of healing and wholeness I desire for her, yet I will still believe that God is good."* Although I wasn't able to begin to understand why Julia was getting worse, I did believe that a sovereign purpose was at work. God never apologises for allowing tragedy and suffering to occur but He asks us to trust Him, and to believe that . . . *in all things God works for the good of those who love him.* (4)

It was hard looking on as a bystander and seeing all the old symptoms of M.E. come back to taunt Julia. Facing shattered hopes and seeing the crumbling of her plans again, increased my pain. A pain that was very personal; it seemed such a negative force at times and it felt such a waste. The pain of watching and waiting was very acute - it was isolating. No one can really understand another's pain and my sense of impotence was increased in the knowledge that Julia was also isolated in her own pain. Calvin Seerveld wrote, "Physical pain is very personal, locked inside the perimeter of your skin, so that even a deeply sympathetic person right next to you, *cannot* feel your pain." (5)

I found that I not only hurt, but the pain also invaded my very self, causing me to feel under attack. Consequently I tended to be quiet and hide in my shell. Sometimes Julia also used to withdraw to the safety of her shell - at other times she exploded on a short fuse. Perhaps one of the greatest displays of God's power is not for Him to remove the pain, but to keep us strong in the knowledge of His love throughout the trial. God is not silent. The comfort He offers is His presence - He was with me **in** my pain.

Being a coper I didn't readily talk about what I was going through, but a few people picked up the signs of my pain and asked me how I was. Sitting in a nurses' meeting, with Derek, our Senior Partner, I found myself with the other eight nurses discussing implementing changes. Just the association with the word 'changes' pressed my pain button - the changes that were going on at home in adjusting to having an ill daughter again. I struggled to hold back the tears and to keep my mind on the meeting, but it wasn't easy. Not wanting to draw attention to myself and thinking I had managed to cleverly camouflage my tears I was surprised when at the end of the meeting Derek called me into his consulting room.

"How are you, Chris?" he asked. "You were not your usual self in the meeting." "No, I'm not . . . ." and out tumbled all my disappointment, hurt and pain. By quietly listening in a non judgmental manner, he gave me permission and space to let it all spew out. It was releasing to verbalise the fact that I knew without any doubt that God had touched Julia with his healing grace, but for some unknown reason which I couldn't understand she was ill again. In spite of feeling confused as to what God was doing, and without consciously thinking about the words, I heard myself say, "Although I don't understand, yet will I trust Him". Verbalising this inner conviction was another significant step along the journey.

GRIEF

I grieve for my loss -
For what was but is no more
For what was to be but is not now
But I treasure those memories.

I grieve for my loss -
Where once there was laughter, now there is weeping
Where once there was happiness, now there is grief
Yet I treasure those memories.

I grieve for my loss -
Where once there was sharing, now there is loneliness
Where once there was friendship, now there is emptiness
Yet I treasure those memories.

Yet even as I grieve for my loss
There is comfort; there is peace
For despair becomes hope
When grieving with Christ Jesus

Julia

Chapter 8

A Slippery Monster

In distress, I sought the Lord (Psalm 77 : 2)

Sickness is one of the greatest disturbers of life. It enters unannounced, arresting all plans, ridiculing the idea of certainty and diminishing hope for the future. In the battle with illness there are many losses: loss of control, loss of identity; loss of friendship; and loss of certainty. I began to realise how much I had taken certainty and predictability for granted - it was predictable that I could go to work; do the shopping, see friends, go out together as a family . . . . . Now I was finding that what was once predictable for my daughter was becoming provisional. With Julia suffering with a chronic illness everything she did became dependent upon her condition. Even the ability to get up in the morning and have a shower and hair wash or not was dictated by her energy levels. Whenever she made plans Julia always tried to have a built in proviso, for she was no longer certain what her body would do and how she would feel. Many a time a planned outing or a friend's visit had to be cancelled as Julia's energy slipped away.

I accepted that this was how life was at that time, and in adapting to this uncertainty I made a conscious effort to learn to take it in my stride and not put Julia under unnecessary pressure, particularly not laying guilt on her that she couldn't do what had been arranged. "Never mind", I would to say, "It's disappointing that we can't go out as planned, but there'll be other opportunities". But Julia *did* mind. Having a sensitive nature, she felt guilty at letting us down as plans had to be aborted because she was not well, knowing that deep down it mattered to all of us that she couldn't join in life. Very occasionally Fiona used to get quite cross when I tried to make light of the fact Julia had to cancel an outing. Living for the moment, and enjoying life to the full, she reminded me that Julia *was* missing out on opportunities that she would never be able to recreate. Fiona was acutely aware of all the opportunities Julia had missed over the last four years. It mattered to her that her sister couldn't enjoy life in her twenties like other friends. Seeing Julia relapse after she had apparently been healed, struck a blow to her hopes, and feeling very disappointed and downhearted she returned to Leeds for her final term.

When one member of a family suffers, we all suffer. John and I were also feeling disappointed and confused and were finding it difficult to adjust to having an ill daughter again. Knowing that we couldn't change the situation, we discussed ways in which I could manage my role as a mother and carer in order that the inevitable stresses and strains didn't pull me down. One way was to let someone else take a cooked meal round to Julia's once a week - this would give me a break. This idea got off to a bit of a bumpy start as once or twice Julia was forgotten, then another meal taken round was greasy fish and chips - hardly food that an ill person would fancy! However once the system settled into a routine with Jo, a lady who lived round the corner from Julia, it worked really well. The benefits for Julia were not just a meal. Jo was another face and someone else to chat to, and over time a friendship was formed.

Another decision we made for respite, was for me to have at least a 24 hour break away every month. Although at this stage Julia was still living in the flat for most of the time, if she felt really ill she would come home - for anything from a few days to a week. Just seeing my daughter change again over a few months from a bubbly young lady, to a lifeless ill patient was incredibly painful. I felt that my heart had been broken - not divided in half - but fractured. With that came a sense that I had lost something. I couldn't identify what it was, but it was as if something had been broken inside me. Getting away from the situation would give me time to unravel some of my turmoil. So it was with a great sense of relief that I found myself driving along the country lanes, with the April blossom and

A Slippery Monster

spring flowers welcoming me into the countryside, en route to Highmoor Hall for a twenty-four hour stay.

Highmoor Hall is a Christian Centre, north of Reading, situated in the most beautiful grounds where there is provision for people to get away for quiet retreats. At the top of the old oak beamed house is a small room called 'The Hideaway'. Walking into the room I was struck by its simplicity, its warmth and welcoming presence. As well as a bed and easy chair, there was a desk by a window overlooking the garden and countryside. The view was was so peaceful. There was no other house or car to be seen, just horses grazing in the distant field and the yellows and greens of spring. I threw myself down on the bed and letting go of all my tension, I wept. The tears were not only an expression of my pain, but also of thankfulness that I was able to get away to somewhere so peaceful and just spend time in being. I relished having no demands, with the ability to come and go as I pleased, walking out into the garden and surrounding countryside. I was just by myself - me and God.

Like many others who find themselves facing a distressing time, I turned to the Psalms for comfort. The words of Psalm 77 resonated with my inner cries,

>*Will He never show His favour again?*
>*Has His unfailing love vanished for ever?*
>*Has His promise failed for all time?*
>*Has God forgotten to be merciful?*
>*Has He in anger withheld His compassion?* (1)

What I found so encouraging about the psalmist was that having been so honest he didn't end there. He went on to look beyond his present troubles, with God's bewildering inactivity, to draw new hope from what God had done in the past.

>'I will *remember the deeds of the Lord;*
>*Yes,* I will *remember your miracles of long ago.*
>I will *meditate on all your works*
>*And consider all your mighty deeds.'* (2)

(Highlighting mine)

This commitment and determination to say *"I will"* in the face of difficulties was a reminder to me to keep re-focusing on God's greatness.

I enjoyed reading other psalms where I could identify with the psalmists' expressions of their inner turmoil:- rage, loneliness, despair, fear, anger, and envy, to name but a few. Their honesty was a comfort. These psalms remind us that God does not abandon us when we make complaints concerning Him, and they teach us how to wrestle with uncomfortable feelings until they give way to hope. The psalmists do not indulge or wallow in their pain, nor do they deny or spiritualise it away - they enter into it and voice it with passion. Very often in Christian circles emotions such as anger or depression are stigmatised as inappropriate. But the psalms reveal not only a heart that questions God, but also a heart that yearns to know God better. What I found so challenging was the psalmists' resolve to go beyond their pain, and affirm God's never-failing love and kindness. David said, *"Scorn has broken my heart and has left me helpless; I looked for sympathy, but there was none, for comforters, but I found none. I am in pain and distress . . . . (BUT) I will praise God's name in song and glorify him with thanksgiving."*
(5) Finding himself in many difficult situations, David, unashamedly and persistently demanded that God help him. Likewise the Old Testament characters, Abraham, Moses, and Jeremiah argued with God on the basis of their helplessness. They knew that prayer did not mean talking and addressing God with smooth, eloquent words. For them, to talk to God meant to wrestle with Him - to take hold of God and argue with Him.

I decided to follow the pattern of the psalmist and wrote my own thoughts down.

"You say you are compassionate -
where is your compassion?
You reached out and healed people -

A Slippery Monster

don't you see Julia?
What's wrong with her?
Why do you bless others and not her?
Yes, you are standing there . . . . .
Looking on and strengthening us . . .
But not intervening.
I feel angry;
You wonderfully bless and intervene in other lives
But not Julia's.
YET, I will praise you
You are the Father of all creation
You created Julia in my womb
You have given her life and laughter.
You see all things from beginning to the end
Your ways aren't my ways
BUT you are my God, the King
And I will bless you and thank you
In everything."

My time at Highmoor was a great blessing and I enjoyed 'The Hideaway' so much that I have revisited it several times. Feeling nourished and refreshed I returned with vitality to face the months ahead. Supporting and caring for Julia was a privilege, as in her own way she was quite an inspiration to us. In May she wrote John and me a card saying:

"Dear Mum and Dad

Just a quick note, to encourage you both (you need it as well as me!), that you're doing well. I thank God for such loving and steadfast parents. All your practical help, especially gardening, and cooking Mum, as well as flowers and treats, has encouraged my spirits not to drop, (along with God's amazing peaceful reassurance and hope!).

You're very special parents and I am privileged to have you both. Keep going, smiling and teasing me. (Practical jokes are welcome if you can think of any!).

We'll keep battling together till the end - it can't be long now, can it?!
With all my love, Jules.

But he knows the way that I take; when he has tested me, I shall come forth as gold. Job 23:10.
What a promise! Wow!"

In encouraging each other, the difficult times seemed more surmountable. Moving through May and June the normal pattern for Julia continued - peaking and troughing. As she was bored with looking at the four walls in her flat, John and I took her down to stay with my sister, Andria. Being twins we had always been supportive to each other and Andria was always very glad to have Julia to stay to give me a break. We used to have long talks about M.E. and its effects upon Julia, but I don't think Andria could ever really grasp the nature of it. But then neither could I - it was like a slippery eel! One day I thought I had caught hold of it and understood it, the next day it had slipped out of my hands and I couldn't fathom it out. I think this was partly due to the fact that there was no pattern or consistency with the illness, apart from the aforementioned peaks and troughs.

Having enjoyed her time with my sister, Julia returned feeling she could now face her four walls again. But life wasn't that easy in the flat. Julia was struggling to come to terms with the fact that her flat mate, Louise, had met someone with whom she was falling madly in love. Julia was delighted for Louise and liked her boyfriend, but this isolated her further. An increasing loneliness was arising from losing all sense of having things in common with her flat mate. Sickness often puts a tension on relationships and as Louise appeared not to fully understand M.E. or the effects it had on Julia, their relationship became more strained. The previous Autumn when Julia was well, they had shared more things in common as they could do fun things together, like paint the lounge. But in feeling ill again, Julia wasn't able to invest the same time and energy into their relationship so it became more distant.

Because Julia didn't have something tangible, like a broken arm in a plaster cast, and because she spent most of her time resting, it was difficult for people to really understand what this illness was about. She became very sensitive to other people's sceptical remarks when they doubted her, and consequently at times felt she had to prove she was ill! Unhelpful comments often pushed Julia into a corner. When people offered a suggestion, not wanting to appear ungrateful or rude she felt she had to comply. She didn't have the inner strength to say no and stand her ground and go with what was best for her. This consequently led her at times into pushing herself beyond her energy levels. Feeling very vulnerable sometimes she used to perceive that others saw her as a fraud and selfish. Coping with chronic illness and the subsequent losses stirred up many overwhelming feelings for her. She talked to me about the powerlessness and the sense of defencelessness she felt and asked if she could talk to someone else, outside the family, who would be willing to listen and understand what was happening to her and how it felt. She didn't have the energy for an in-depth counselling session. She just wanted a listener to pop in every month for about half an hour. Isabel filled this need well and Julia found the times helpful. After about three visits Isabel suggested to Julia that she consider having Family Therapy with her husband, Jack, also a counsellor. Isabel thought this might be a helpful way to explore how the illness was affecting each one of us in the family.

Fiona was decidedly anti Family Therapy, and John was not keen either. I was quite open to give it a go - anything to help Julia and all of us to adapt to this difficult time. As a counsellor I had some limited experience in helping families and knew it could be of benefit. After some persuasion Fiona and John finally agreed and a date was set. Having graduated with a 2:1 degree from Leeds, Fiona was by now at home. She was still very reluctant about this form of therapy and when she went to collect Julia to bring her home for the appointment, she stormed out of the house saying, "I don't want to do this, I am only doing it for you and Julia." On arriving back at the house together, the focus was taken off the imminent session as Julia looked really shaken. Louise had unexpectedly fainted in the kitchen. Having had some nursing training Julia had coped with this well, but it had left her exhausted as she had expended all her energy. She really needed to go and lie down and rest, but there was no time as Isabel and Jack were due at any moment. Sitting and waiting in the lounge we chatted together. I don't think any of us felt unduly nervous, but I did detect a scowl on Fiona's face!

Isabel and Jack eventually arrived about half an hour late with barely an apology. That didn't go down too well with me - if they had let us know Julia could have had a rest for half an hour or so. The session was opened by Isabel inviting us to say five things about us as a family. So far so good I thought. Then as the session progressed, Jack and Isabel began to focus more and more on Julia. *"Hey that's not on,"* I thought. *"We're all here to talk about ourselves - it's not just about Julia."* I had expected that each of us in turn would have an opportunity of saying how we felt about Julia's illness and how we thought it was affecting our family. But we didn't. Jack said a few good, helpful things and then began to suggest that Julia was ill because she wanted to be the centre of attention. I was furious but felt powerless to stop the flow of what was happening. John told me afterwards that he also felt very angry and with hindsight wished he had stopped the session so as to protect Julia from unnecessary hurt and pain. We had always been so careful to protect Julia from people who were not helpful. I had met enough people, and read and seen TV programmes to know that many people with M.E. suffer at the hands of health professionals because they are misunderstood. I had always been grateful to God that Julia had never experienced this and now I was seeing it happen before my very eyes. She was more or less told that she was ill because she wanted the attention and we were told that as a family we were not open about talking

Julia setting out well and healthy to inter-rail round Europe, summer 1990

Fiona, John and Julia in Bournemouth, 1993

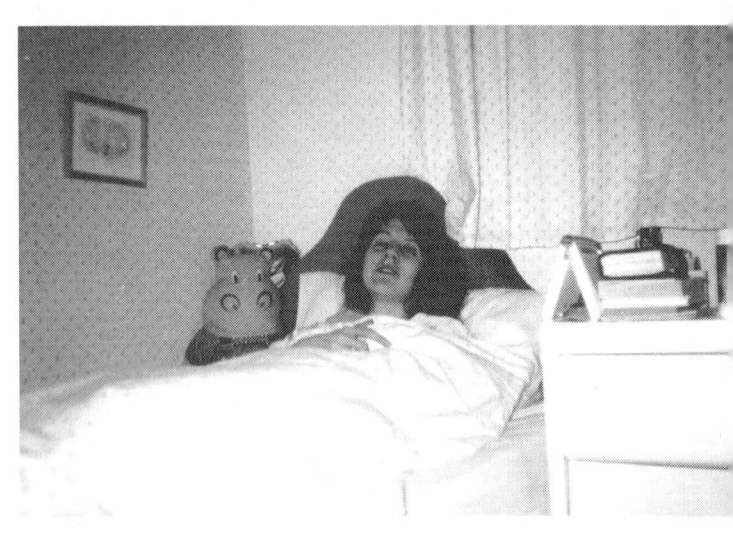

Julia when very ill, 1994

Geoff and Julia, Christmas Day 1996

Julia enjoying her nephews, Joshua and Ethan,
Christmas 2001

John, Chris, Julia, Geoff, Fiona, and Paul, wedding, October 1997

A Slippery Monster   129

about the situation. This was utter nonsense as nothing was said in the session that we hadn't already aired and talked about previously as a family. Jack wasn't listening - he had completely misjudged us. By now my blood was boiling, and it was with a great sigh of relief that the session ended. Julia's senses were assaulted and with her emotions stretching to snapping point she hastily went up to her bedroom - all I could hear were howling sobs.

Instinctively Fiona rushed up stairs to stave off the inevitable heartache, in trying to comfort her sister by giving her some moral support, but Julia would have none of it. With that Fiona came down stairs really upset and in tears. "I never wanted Family Therapy in the first place - now look what they have done to her. They've destroyed her, she is so distraught and thinks the illness is all her fault - she doesn't even want me in the room." With my arm round her shoulder I tried to comfort her - in her sense of anger and helplessness. Putting my own emotions aside I struggled to take hold of the situation and thought, *"what a mess"* - both daughters distraught, a husband pacing the kitchen white with anger and as for me - I was suppressing a mixture of anger, helplessness and guilt (after all I had all been in favour of the Family Therapy session.) After a couple minutes I said, "I'm going up stairs to see what I can do." Ignoring Fiona's comment, "Mum, it's no good . . . . she doesn't want to see any of us," I went.

"Go away . . . . Go away . . . . I'm nothing but trouble," was the cry that greeted me. Not really knowing how to respond I followed my instincts and ignoring her plea to go away, went and sat next to her on the bed. Along with her I also began to cry and shout,"How dare they say that to you . . . . you are not the only one angry . . . . we all are . . . . they completely misjudged us . .." I was so furious - I rarely get that angry. But just sitting alongside Julia, crying with her and agreeing that the whole thing had gone so very badly was very releasing for her and me. I didn't tell her to stop crying and shouting - I joined in with her! On reflection I caught a glimpse of how God must feel when he comes alongside us, sits with us, cries with us, shouts with us and never judges us. Slowly Julia calmed down. "I'm nothing but trouble," she quietly sobbed. Her fragile self esteem had been knocked. I challenged her. "You can either believe what Jack and Isabel have implied about you, or what your dad, sister, and I believe about you. Who are you going to believe?" Was she going to take on board what they had voiced - or what we thought about her? Was she going to believe people who barely knew her - or her family? And I reminded her that God didn't see her as trouble either, but as His precious daughter. Slowly the light began to dawn and the sobs died away. Leaving Julia on the bed, resting in peace, I returned downstairs to get the meal.

Sitting round the kitchen table about an hour or so later, we were all subdued, but nevertheless very supportive of one another. Talking honestly about our expectations of how the session might have been handled differently, and voicing thoughts from our own individual agendas, that we never had the opportunity to bring up in the session, we had our own family therapy - a time that was very positive. We all felt that we were heard and understood by each other without any judgments. Having looked at what had gone on, expressed our feelings about it and acknowledged what we had learnt we decided to try and leave it behind. This was quite hard for me as I was going to be working with Jack and his wife at a counselling training weekend in a few days time. Turning to God I asked for a heart that would flow out with gracious love to them both, and although at first I didn't find meeting up with them again easy, I was able to work with them without any barriers.

Standing back and looking at what was happening to my family life with very little control over the continuous ups and downs, I felt like a counter in the game of Snakes and Ladders. I am sure this was true for Julia too as it seemed that after her significant measure of healing, which had given her a swift race up a ladder, for some inexplicable reason a few squares later she landed on a snake, and slid down to the bottom again. The pattern had been repeated again and again over the years as if every time Julia climbed the ladder sooner or later she slid down a snake. Sometimes it seemed as if we were part of a cruel game. But however insecure I felt standing on the playing board of life, deep down I had confidence that God knew the number that would be thrown on the dice, and was therefore in control of where the counter landed. But how long was this game going to last?

DROWNING

Help, I'm drowning
Oh no ... please no,
I splutter and gasp
But as water gushes around my ears and I madly splash
I can hear so many different voices, and different instructions too:
'Kick your legs" ... "Try and float" ... "Swim" ...
"Don't panic" ..."Slow down" ... "Stay calm" ...
What should I do?
Whom do I believe?
The woman, the man, or the child?
This is a completely unfamiliar situation
Usually before I've had advice or training, or at least a warning ...

Help, I'm drowning!
Help, God ....
No one else's advice is much good
I need a secure lifeline, someone who can wisely pull me out:
The lifeline of your love never fails, never breaks, never falters;
Pull me out of these deep engulfing waters
Nearer to your heart
For only then can you teach me
Your lifesaving ways from the start.

Julia

Chapter 9

Why God do you allow Suffering?

Why do you hold back your hand? (Psalm 74:11)

With the arrival of the warmer summer months in 1994, there was an unspoken hope that the hotter weather would somehow help Julia to improve, but this wasn't the case. On her bad days she could hardly get out of bed where she lay hugging a hot water bottle, although on a good day, she was able to manage a short outing. Even going to a friend's wedding in July had to be carefully managed. We arranged to go up to the Midlands the night before and stay in a nearby bed and breakfast. But the wedding proved too much for her. She was sensitive to the lights and the noise, so leaving John and an embarrassed Fiona behind, I had to take Julia out during the ceremony in her wheelchair to the porch where we stayed and listened to the service. Here Julia could close her eyes, rest, and be less obtrusive.

As I stood in the porch I looked out through the ancient arched doorway, to the sunny scene beyond - the beautiful lush grass and the trees dancing in the breeze threw shadows on the path. The beauty of nature opened my eyes to God's presence. *"Lord, give Julia strength to walk her path of pain and suffering - please hold on to her,"* I inwardly cried.

Having already made arrangements for Julia to lie down at the reception in one of the bedrooms before the actual wedding breakfast began, she recovered enough to enjoy this part of the day. However the cost of expending so much energy exhausted her of course and for a few days after she was laid up in bed. Recognising that the effort of going to a wedding was too much for her she decided to to say no to other wedding invitations that year. Seeing her life become more and more constricted left her feeling very low and frustrated. To feel ill and very fatigued day in and day out was very debilitating. Again, it was as if her life was on hold.

Another significant event that highlighted the fact that Julia's life had been arrested by M.E., was the visit of her university friends, Anna, Caroline and Ango. Completing their four year course they had just graduated with their nursing degrees. Obviously Julia's disappointment was very deep - she hadn't been blessed with good health to get her degree or have a career she had always longed for. Yet I was touched with the grace and maturity Julia showed her friends. She was thrilled to hear their good news and was able to freely celebrate with them, even although she was hurting with her own loss.

With the passing of the summer months there was a new beginning for Fiona as she started a Postgraduate Certificate in Education in Cheltenham, whilst Julia's university friends were starting their first nursing jobs. In sharp contrast for Julia, there were no new beginnings. She was continuing to battle with intermittent sore throats and swollen glands and time ticked relentlessly by with no change. Seeing her sister's and friends' lives move on caused her to feel very low . "I'm going nowhere - how long is this going on for?" she used to cry.

How does a mother reply to this question of "How long?" There is no easy answer. How long is a piece of string? It was a question I was also struggling with and it was a comfort to find this impatient cry echoed in the Psalms: *How long, O Lord, how long?* (1); *How long, O Lord? Will you forget me forever?* (2); *How long will your anger smoulder against the prayers of your people?* (3) *How long? Will you hide yourself for ever?* (4) *How long will it be?* (5) The words, *How long?* display the audacity with which the psalmists wrestled with God on the basis of their relationship - a relationship which was based upon a deep conviction concerning His faithfulness. This phrase expresses the anguish of pain which goes

Why God do you allow Suffering   135

on and on with no end in sight. I couldn't offer Julia any trite answer in reply to her question of "How long?", but I could remind her and myself to choose to trust in God's unfailing love for us.

The other question that often accompanies the *How long?*, is the *Why, O Lord?* A question that people have agonised over for years and which has proved torturous to many in their faith. Seeing Julia first healed and then suffering again, I began asking the sixty-four thousand dollar question, *"If God is a God of love, why does He allow suffering?"* I knew there was no glib answer to this universal question but in pursuing possible answers it was important for me to explore my doubts. My first line of thought was to consider possible connections between illness and sin. When we go through a hard time we often ask the question, *"What have I done to deserve this?"* It's tempting to fear that we have done something wrong and that God has got it in for us. This was a common assumption that Job's friends subscribed to - that if you are suffering, there is sin in your life. Job had lost his home, his wealth, his family and his health because God had given Satan permission to abuse him. Having lost everything, he ended up covered from head to toe with boils, sitting on a heap of ashes. When his friends saw Job's condition they were so shocked that for seven days and nights they were speechless. (6) Then Job shared his feelings with his three friends. Even though God had declared Job to be blameless they assaulted him in a cycle of attacks and defences, "You deserve what has happened because of what you have done." Job replied, "I'm sorry, I don't know what I've done!" and they would say, "Yes, you *do* know." In contrast to this Old Testament train of thought, in the New Testament Jesus rejects the idea that suffering is a punishment for sin. In the story of a blind man, the disciples asked Jesus, *"Rabbi, who sinned, this man or his parents, that he was born blind?"* *"Neither this man nor his parents sinned,"* said Jesus, *"but this happened so that the work of God might be displayed in his life."* (7) This reply frees many people from the burden of believing that their physical suffering is a result of God's punishment. When we fall into behaviour that is contrary to God's ways, such as abusing our bodies with alcohol, the ramification may be the physical condition of cirrhosis. This is a consequence of sin, not a punishment for sin. Therefore there is not always a direct link between suffering and sin.

The second question I explored was, *"Is suffering consistent with God's love?"* It is not easy to believe that God is a father of love, when tragedy arrives on our doorstep. Rabbi Harold Kushner wrote the book I mentioned in an earlier chapter, *When Bad Things Happen to Good People*, after watching his son die of a terrible disease which speeds up the ageing process. The young man looked more like ninety when he died at the young age of only nineteen years. Kushner argued that God is a God of love and is therefore distressed when bad things happen to us, but He is limited in his power to prevent them.

This is not a Christian belief. The Bible very clearly states that God is omnipotent; He is all powerful; He can do anything he chooses. He chose to give us freedom - a choice to deviate from God's divine will. This is illustrated in the story of Adam and Eve who used their freedom to rebel against God rather than trust Him. Since then the whole universe has been thrown into chaos and disorder. Therefore the presence of tragedies, pain and suffering in our world does not contradict God's love - it is the price of our freedom.

Some people have the concept that suffering is the direct opposite of love, and that the Christian belief in a loving God is inconsistent with the presence of suffering in the world. But at the heart of any Christian understanding of suffering is the cross. In the suffering and death of Jesus Christ on the cross we catch a glimpse of God's amazing love. God revealing Himself through human flesh - Christ, dying for me. *For God so loved the world that He gave his one and only Son, that whoever believes in Him shall not perish but have eternal life.* (8) God the Father suffered the agony of seeing His Son, Jesus, mocked, spat upon and rejected, and then crucified in an undignified way on the cross. Why? *This is how God showed his love among us: He sent his one and only Son into the world that we might live through him . . . . he loved us and sent his Son as an atoning sacrifice for our sins.* (9) The cross shows the love and compassion of our God for all those who suffer, as He suffers along with His people. Although there is suffering, God remains a God of love.

Having explored the question, *"Why Lord, do you allow suffering?"* I realised that I had come to the point where I needed to move on. In order to accept the fact that I shall never be able to understand human suffering from God's perspective I needed to suspend judgment on what God was doing. "Faith does not know why, but it knows why it trusts God who knows why. What God is doing maybe mystery, but *who God is,* is not." (10) Faith is not demanding. There is a world of difference between trusting God for a miracle , which is the kind of faith which is demanding, and trusting in God, which is the way of true faith. Having stood still for a while, ruminating and cogitating on the *why* of suffering I came to the place of accepting that it is a mystery that only God understands. The simple truth is that God defies all human logic. Reading Paul Malte's booklet, *Why Does God Allow Suffering?*, summed up my thoughts:-

> "The Bible itself never offers very easy answers to suffering, or to sufferers. Even in Job, the classic book on suffering, the problem of evil is never explained away. But, Job, does learn to live with suffering - and with the Lord Creator. Deep in his soul - not his mind - Job discovers the peace which transcends all human understanding. Jesus - who claims to be God's representative among men - never unties the intellectual problem of God's goodness and God's power. He simply acts to demonstrate the Father's goodness and His power channelled personally to people. Jesus does not heal all the lepers in Palestine, exorcise all unclean spirits, make

whole all marriages, give people the inner attitude, the courage and joy, to handle suffering. He does nothing to ward off His own death, and He becomes the victim of human hostility. He suffers both the anguish of physical death and the hell of alienation from God. By suffering with us He suffers for us. He suffers so that our suffering might be transformed and transcended into triumph. Christians have no tidy answers to suffering, no easy ten principles for happy sufferers. They only have attitudes for meeting it, handles for overcoming it, outlooks for transcending it." (11)

During the autumn months of 1994 there were no significant changes. Julia continued to come home every so often when she felt too ill to cope by herself in the flat. With her twenty fourth birthday looming in mid December, John and I arranged a very rare outing for us all - we booked a table to take her and her friend, Cathy, out for a meal. In order to store up enough energy to manage this, Julia came home for a few days beforehand so that she could fully rest. Planning for one of her rare outings, the formula went something like this: an outing = a few days resting beforehand to conserve energy plus three to seven days resting afterwards to recover. Unfortunately John went down with gastric flu on her birthday so obviously couldn't go out, which was a great disappointment to us all. The three of us were sitting in the lounge late that afternoon, wondering whom we could invite at the last minute to go in his place. "Let's ask Geoff," was Julia's suggestion. Geoff was a member of our congregation whom we had invited several times for Sunday lunch and on one of these visits he had briefly met Julia. After that meeting I asked him whether he would pop in occasionally to see Julia, as she was very lonely having lost her only friend, Gail, who had moved away. Hence he had occasionally visited Julia from time to time, so it was easy for her to pick up the phone to invite him to take John's place. So before long there was Geoff, a tall, dark, handsome man in his late twenties, standing on our doorstep with a birthday card for Julia, ready to join us for a very enjoyable evening out. The four of us were very relaxed with each other. In fact we were quite frivolous at times and it was good to see Julia really laugh and join in the fun with Cathy and Geoff. When we returned home, Geoff made the comment to John, "You can be ill any time John, and I'll take your place!"

Running true to form in the pattern that we had come to know, Julia felt very fatigued after this evening out and was very tetchy. While Julia was still at home with us Andria visited a few days later. I always enjoyed seeing my sister and her lively company was a welcome distraction from looking after Julia and John with his gastric flu. But even with my sister around, Julia wasn't herself. She was very irritable and weepy and I felt as if I were treading on eggshells. If I said the wrong thing, I anticipated that she would blow her top. Fortunately we didn't come to blows, and in spite of being still very off colour, she returned to the flat so as to be able to entertain her university friends, Anna, Carolyn and Ango for her birthday. It was important for Julia to hang on to what little independence she had, as she wanted to entertain them in her own way in her own place. They were making a special effort to visit her, and Julia didn't want to disappoint them by calling it off because she didn't feel well. Having prepared all the food at home, I took it round to the flat and was met by the usual joyous greetings from her friends. It was interesting to hear how their new jobs were going and catch up with their news. I left the three of them chatting inanely in the lounge, with Julia having gone to rest on the bed for a while. They were very good and understanding of Julia and their energy and enthusiasm for life gave a lightness to the celebrations. Julia enjoyed the evening with what little energy she had, but within a few days she crashed.

This time it wasn't with the usual swollen glands, but gastric flu. Bringing her home again I found her so weak that she could hardly crawl to the bathroom. Her pale lifeless face was such a sad picture. Trying to accommodate her need to rush to the toilet, we put a lounger in the bathroom for her where she stayed for the next twenty four hours. Fortunately our bathroom was large enough to make that possible. The pain of seeing Julia so ill again felt overwhelming. Tears of sorrow flowed easily and my whole body ached with anguish as I felt crushed by a sense of helplessness.

It felt as if I was standing on the banks of a fast flowing river, watching my daughter being swept downstream, buffeted in swirling water. As the strong current carried her round the corner beyond my vision, I had no idea what would happen to her. Would she be swept to the safety of the river banks? Would she find something to hang on to? Would she be swept out to sea? Or would she drown? I felt helpless - all I could do was stand and watch and pray.

Having spent the night sleeping in the bathroom, Julia began to recover and was thrilled to welcome Fiona home a few days before Christmas. But Fiona found the adjustment from a busy student lifestyle to an environment which was nurturing an ill sister, very difficult. Although Julia had recovered from the gastric upset, she was left so fatigued that all she could do was chat to Fiona for about half an hour a few times a day. Within a day of being home, Fiona was bored. She missed being able to do things with her sister. I felt the unspoken tension between them: Julia because she felt guilty at not being well and angry with herself that she couldn't be the well sister that Fiona longed for; and Fiona because she felt frustrated and disappointed that Julia was ill again. Both of them were battling to come to terms with their loss of expectations. Fiona was very open and honest in speaking to me about her own inner turmoil and I always tried to make time for her when she was home. Seeing both of them struggling in their own way, and being there for them emotionally, was very draining. Fortunately John was there for me as he quietly stood in the background, giving me the emotional support I needed.

Christmas day was difficult for all of us. John, Fiona and I wanted

Why God do you allow Suffering 141

so much to include Julia but she was too fatigued really to join in. The whole day was such an effort for her. Apart from managing to sit up for Christmas lunch, and playing Trivial Pursuit for half an hour in the evening she just lay lifelessly on a lounger in the lounge. We all sensed that Julia was very low and fed up with her situation - she was like a volcano waiting to erupt. The volcano spilt out its lava at bedtime! Having to help undress her as she was too fatigued to do this for herself was the final straw. Weeping tears of sorrow and despair, she cried, " I can't do anything . . . . . what hope have I for the future? There is a blank page for 1995, and I can't write anything on it" And then a few sobs later, "All I can do is write a few words in a cards of encouragement to others - Mum, that's *all I can do* - I can't do anything else with my life." The agony of seeing Julia so despairing bought tears to my eyes, then before I knew what was happening Fiona had quietly slipped into the room and was crying with us, comforting Julia. Wondering what was going on John also appeared and the four of us ended up crying and hugging each other. What a way to celebrate Christmas Day! Then to make matters worse Julia's hot water bottle leaked all over her bed - that felt like the last straw for me. I couldn't rise above it and make some throw away flippant remark and laugh - I felt utterly drained. Having settled Julia into a clean bed, we all prayed together as usual. But I found it such an effort. I had to muster all my energy together to be determined to say, *"I will . . . . thank you for this special day and thank you for your love for each one of us."*

Happily Boxing Day was better. I think that the emotional outburst for Julia the previous evening had alleviated some of her pain as she certainly seemed brighter and had the resources to cope better. In the evening we were joined by Gail, Antoinette and two other young friends. I was relieved that the atmosphere was lighter, and particularly for Fiona who could enjoy the company of other healthy young people. We played some games and although Julia didn't join in, she was able to watch and laugh with us. In the patches when Julia felt well enough, she enjoyed being with people in this way, even though she was too fatigued to join in the games and conversation. Sometimes this was misinterpreted and Julia wrote the following poem expressing the fact that her silence was an enforced survival technique rather than a deliberate withdrawal.

MY SILENCE

"The chatter of friendly voices buzzes in my ears
Light-hearted chit-chat, amusing scenes
Sprinkled with high-pitched laughter and shrieks of delight,
Bringing smiles to each face
Late into the night.

Surrounded by the friends I know well, I remain quiet
In the midst of conversation I sit in silence -
But it's the silence of tranquillity - I'm happy just to observe,
To watch, to listen, and
Laugh at the absurd!

I'm sorry my silence upsets you; it isn't meant to offend;
It's not lack of interest, unfriendliness, moodiness or cause for alarm;
With M.E., I'm exhausted, lacking energy even to talk -
I can't join in conversation,
Remember details or thoughts.

So please don't get annoyed with me, irritated or cross,
I'm content to sit and listen - I will, I must!
Yes, at times I get frustrated with my silence in company,
But once I'm well my chatter
Will be non-stop - you'll see!"

Why God do you allow Suffering

Although Julia went back to the flat in January 1995, I didn't feel that she was well enough to be left by herself. Knowing how lonely she used to feel I thought it was helpful to spend hours by herself, but she wanted to be there. Julia was very weepy and I felt she was beginning to show signs of falling apart - she couldn't get things together. Popping in most days I became increasingly concerned for her, and considered that she was now too ill to be left without a daily visit. In fact some days I went round two or three times. Sometimes she didn't have the energy to undress herself and get to bed, so I would quickly cycle round on my bike and spend time with her at the end of the day. In the midst of all this, Julia had put up pictures, words of scripture and poems on the walls and bedside table around where she lay so that she could gaze at them. Expressing herself in poetry when she had the energy, was very therapeutic for her, and she found this creative way of communicating a great source of comfort.

> "May the peace of God run in and thro' you
> Like gentle streams flowing over you
> Quietening all fears
> Quietening all worries
> Releasing the tears
> Drowning the torment
> May God's peace dwell inside you
> Giving inner reassurance to guide you"   *Julia*

In January I had been asked to speak at an evangelistic Ladies' Supper at Yateley on the subject of "Times of trials and suffering". Basing this on my own testimony, I ended up by saying that it wasn't a happy-ever-after success story as God hadn't brought us through the suffering yet, but He had held on to us. I was really encouraged by the response, particularly when a letter from the organiser arrived saying:

"Your frank testimony of suffering and the journey through pain has opened many people to a new aspect of God at work in all situations. I was so pleased that Shirley said that it was a success story for I am sure that this is how the Lord views your situation and response."

Perhaps all the heartache was being used by the Lord! It was out of this encouragement that the desire to write such a book as this was first conceived.

This wasn't the only speaking engagement round about this time as in February I had already committed myself to being away for three weekends on the trot to speak at different conferences. I was concerned that Julia wasn't well enough to look after herself but she was adamant that I shouldn't change my plans for her. Knowing that I wouldn't feel at peace if I left her without any support, I only went away for twenty four hours for two of the conferences, and arranged for friends to pop in. Fiona came home to look after her for the other weekend. John was also able to go round and watch TV with her, but obviously he couldn't help with her personal care.

In February Julia had a two week break for respite care in Burrswood - a Christian centre for medical and spiritual care. During this time I could relax knowing that Julia was being well cared for with twenty four hour nursing care. I thoroughly enjoyed the freedom from the responsibility of caring: I was free to choose what I did with my time; I wasn't keeping an ear out for the phone, expecting a call round to the flat at any time; and I could spend more time with John. Whilst she was away about ten friends gathered together with John and me and we spent an evening praying for her. By now I was finding it difficult to pray for her healing. I think this was probably due to the fact that I had prayed and fasted for this for years, only to be disappointed, and I couldn't face further disappointment. My prayer had changed to, *"Grant me a willing spirit, to sustain me"*. (12) and *"Please give us grace sufficient for the day"*. I left others to pray for her healing!

Why God do you allow Suffering

Visiting Burrswood halfway through Julia's time there, Fiona and I found her looking better, less drained and fuller in the face with a quiet radiancy about her. As she had spent most of the time in her room, we took her downstairs in the wheelchair for a change of scenery. We visited the book shop, and then went into the chapel. It was very small and intimate. As the three of us sat there quietly, soaking in the presence of God, Fiona began to sing. She is a very gifted singer and was in the worship group at her church. Her beautiful clear voice rang out with the words:

> *"Faithful One, so unchanging.*
> *Ageless one, You're my rock of peace,*
> *Lord of all I depend on You.*
> *I call out to You again and again.*
> *You are my rock in times of trouble*
> *You lift me up when I fall down*
> *All through the storm*
> *Your love is the anchor*
> *My hope is in You alone."* (13)

By the time Fiona had sung these words several times none of us had a dry eye. These words spoke so profoundly into our situation, giving us comfort and hope. In the chapel that afternoon the three of us had one of those rare experiences of God's loving presence that are so special we couldn't put it into words even if we tried. During the remainder of our time in the chapel I noted that something else new was beginning to happen. We found ourselves thanking God for the little things that Julia could do: she had sight to enjoy the beautiful views of the surrounding countryside; she had hands to sew creatively; she had ears to listen to music. So much in life we take for granted - we wanted to stop looking at Julia's life and seeing what she couldn't do, and start seeing all the things she could do. When we came to leaving Julia that evening, Fiona and I came away feeling very uplifted and inspired.

When I collected Julia a week later, she continued to look better and at peace with herself. When I prayed with her that, "God would water what had been *sown* at Burrswood:" her reply was, "That would ruin it - I've *sewn* a patchwork pillow!" It was encouraging to see her sense of humour returning and we had a good laugh together. But she still wasn't at all well so was living at home. We were giving her all the comfort and support we could, and when John returned from a conference, having not seen her for about three weeks, he just sat and hugged her for long periods.

By March of that year, the relationship between Louise and Julia had become more strained and Louise had given her notice. I could understand her decision to move out because it could not have been easy living with a flatmate so unwell. A few evenings before she left, they had had a disagreement and I received a very panicky phone call from Julia saying she couldn't breathe. When I arrived Julia was very shaky and upset having had a panic attack. The tension in the house was unbearable: Louise was in the lounge with her fiance and Julia was in her bedroom. I was furious - although I didn't blame Louise for the argument, I am sure they were both as bad as one another, I was cross that she had no idea how vulnerable Julia was with so little energy. To my horror, before I could stop myself, I said to Louise, "I'd like to see how you would cope if you were in Julia's shoes". I didn't handle the situation well, and to some extent I blew it that evening! However when we were leaving, God gave me the grace to go into the lounge, shake Louise's hand, look her in the eyes and wish her all the best for her future. Bringing Julia home in these circumstances was so painful - I didn't know what to do with myself. Having settled Julia, I paced the floor for the best part of the night, feeling a mixture of anger and guilt, and unable to pray coherently. All I could do was to cry out to God and remind myself of the words of the song, *"All through the storm, your love is the anchor, my hope is in You alone"*.

I HEAL YOUR WOUNDS

Crying in the deep hurt and agonising pain
I wonder where God is in the midst of this change -
The buried inner wounds wrenched open, tattered, bleeding
Can I face the painful past and receive God's healing?
I muster all my courage, which is seconds drains away
Help me, God, please help me - there must be some other way.

Slowly my eyes are opened to my own inadequacy -
A helplessness which brings new strength; hope lives again in me
A reassuring love now blunts the harsh knife-edge of pain
Comforting me as aching wounds begin to throb again:
Jesus whispers, 'Give me your broken heart to heal;
Give to me the gaping wounds my blood alone can seal,
And don't despise or minimise the scars that will remain
They mark the work I've done in you - a record of your gain
My life shines through those scars you bear; they're beautiful to see
Bringing honour to the Father and glory still to me'.

Julia

Chapter 10

Relinquishing Ownership

Give ear to my words, O Lord, consider my sighing (Psalm 5:1)

Still feeling upset about the episode at the flat the previous night , I dragged myself through the next day, struggling to forgive myself for my hasty words. However I needed to get myself together because I was taking Julia to Peniel Church in Brentwood the following day. We had heard about this church through networking with other M.E. Christians as many people had been completely restored to health through their ministry. As at Sozo, the people at Peniel are a very loving fellowship and they had arranged for Julia and me to stay for the weekend in a flat next to the church. Arriving at the flat late on the Friday afternoon we were overwhelmed by their generosity and love expressed not only in the accommodation which was very snug and homely, but also in the well-stocked fridge and cupboards. We both had a sense of God's bountiful blessings for us, which particularly enabled me to leave behind the guilt which I had been struggling with.

In the service that evening, Julia received another measure of healing. I think this time we were both conscious that we should not get over-excited. From our past experience we were only too aware that we could not assume or presume that any measure of healing granted by God would necessarily progress into complete healing. Obviously our hope was that Julia would continue to get stronger and stronger, but we didn't know what was around the corner and consequently we both felt a little cautious and apprehensive. After a relatively good night's sleep, we awoke the next morning to sunshine pouring through the pretty flowered curtains. We were blessed with a beautiful day with a cloudless, deep blue sky. Gazing up into the sky I reflected on that fact that there is no limit to God's faithfulness, which like the sky stretching into outer space, just goes on and on. I was reminded of the words, *Your faithfulness reaches to the skies.* (1) We both sat in bed talking about all our blessings before meandering into the kitchen for a drink. Julia savoured having the energy to do simple things:- taking a shower; sitting having breakfast in the lounge overlooking the church's well-kept gardens. We packed a picnic lunch and walked to the lake in the church grounds and sat, basking in the sun, absorbing the beauty of God's creation. Later in the afternoon, after a rest, we went into Brentwood. We didn't go mad, but just spent a short time wandering around the shops. Being able to do this without a wheelchair gave us both a sense of freedom. We were a mother and daughter going about our everyday life, doing normal things. What a joy!

Apart from telling John and Fiona what had happened, we shared the Brentwood experience with only a very few people. I don't think any of us could bear the thought that we might tell people, only to find at a later date that we were then having to say that Julia had deteriorated again. We had found from our previous experience that people don't really understand, and this further adds to our sense of isolation. Julia settled happily back into the flat and increased her activities with a daily 20 minute round trip to Asda. My birthday followed a few days later and on answering the doorbell, to my surprise I found Julia standing on the doorstep with a great beam on her face, holding out a bouquet of flowers for me. She had walked the half mile from her flat to our house, something she hadn't done for over a year. The thrill of seeing her there bought tears to my eyes. Throwing my arms round her I exclaimed, "This is the best birthday present I could ever have."

Although Julia's energy levels still fluctuated, she now had more good days than bad. For the first time in fifteen months she was well enough to go to church with us on Good Friday, and we were also able to enjoy other family outings such as a walk and a picnic by the Thames. We had a wonderful time. I was quietly optimistic that Julia would continue to grow stronger and stronger as she was taking things at a sensible pace. There was no throwing herself back into life at breakneck speed as she had done before. She was itching to drive her car again, knowing that she had hardly driven it since it had been bought, and it had been sitting in the garage for over a year, But she took it slowly and John took her out first for a short drive just to help her regain her confidence. Having a very logical and practical mind, she quickly felt at ease with a short drive on a quiet road, but she wasn't really well enough yet to ferry herself around. At the end of April she went down with another virus for about five days, but had recovered sufficiently to join Fiona and myself as we drove down early one morning in May to the New Forest.

Fiona was going for an interview at a secondary school for a teacher's post in psychology. Having dropped Fiona off at the school, Julia and I went deeper into the New Forest where we just sat and soaked up the sunshine and beautiful scenery. We really enjoyed the leisurely day together, having a picnic lunch and stopping off at a pine shop on the way back to the school. Julia was particularly interested in looking at pine furniture as she was considering buying her own bedroom furniture for the flat. Feeling better, she wanted to start creating her own home and furnish it herself. Deep in the various brochures we had acquired, we sat in the school car park when suddenly we became aware of a knock on the window, Fiona's cheerful face appeared. Flinging the car door open and before she had time to speak, we bombarded her with questions. "How did you get on? . . . . How many other candidates? . . . . What was the head like?" With a shriek of delight, she answered, "I've got it . . . . guess what . . . . there was only me for the interview!"

Not only were we thrilled that she been offered a job, but even more delighted with its location. We had all been praying for a job within easy travelling distance of Reading, as Fiona wanted to be nearer home, particularly to be able to support Julia. There were very few teaching psychology posts advertised, so to have found a job about one and a half hour's drive away was great news and something to celebrate, particularly as it was in such a beautiful part of the country. I have many happy memories of going to the New Forest as a child, and it was an area that I loved. The school was not only on the edge of the New Forest, but also near the coast. It wasn't long before my imagination played frivolously with the idea of visiting Fiona and going for long walks. John and I both loved walking across the colourful heathland in the Forest and along the coast, and I could foresee many more visits to this area. God couldn't have given Fiona a more suitable place to live! I couldn't help but think what a topsy-turvy world we live in. It was difficult to understand why Fiona always seemed to fall on her feet without any effort, whilst Julia always had to struggle.

Although Julia still had times when her symptoms returned, overall she slowly improved and enjoyed the visits of her friends for a couple of hours once a week. When Fiona came home for May half term, we enjoyed an afternoon clothes' shopping with Julia - something we hadn't done together for years. It was wonderful too that Julia was well enough to come out to a really good restaurant, something else we hadn't done for ages. We were very encouraged that Julia's ability to cope with outings was becoming more dependable, and a couple of weeks later we set off for Cheltenham to celebrate Fiona's 23rd birthday. Collecting Fiona en route, we spent the day in the country. The four of us set out together for a walk, but Julia soon had enough so returned to sit in the car and enjoy the scenery whilst the three of us continued walking over the hills. On our way back to Cheltenham we stopped off for a meal, returning to Reading about 10 pm. The excursion had been memorable for all of us, but particularly for Fiona, as we had all been able to celebrate her birthday doing something special for her. It was amazing that Julia had managed such a long day and for once didn't go down with extreme fatigue a few days later. She was noticeably improving.

This improvement was maintained over the next few weeks and with a great sense of excitement I soon found myself driving Julia to watch the tennis at Wimbledon. We had two tickets for Court No 1. We set off from home chatting away, but didn't keep this up for long as Julia was soon asleep - she still felt very tired all the time. I was a little anxious about how we would get from the car park to the courts, as Julia still couldn't walk very far, but I needn't have worried. After parking in a disabled space (Julia had an orange disabled sticker) we found a taxi was waiting nearby and with no energy lost we soon arrived at the courts. Sitting watching the play, Julia kept on having to remind herself that it wasn't a dream - it really was happening. Yes, she was back into life again and just doing normal things at Wimbledon like having strawberries and cream gave us both enormous pleasure. We felt as if Julia had been released from being a hostage in her four walls and the freedom that others took for granted was relished by the pair of us. Just being there amongst so many people was a tremendous experience. But Julia still needed to take life carefully so for part of the afternoon she took time out to rest. Finding a quiet spot which was out of the way of the hustling crowd, Julia sat on the concrete, leaning against a wall for support, listening to gentle relaxing music through her Walkman - she looked a picture of contentment. By late afternoon we decided to head for home so as to miss the rush hour and Julia slept most of the way back. Again, she managed this outing without becoming too tired over the following days.

With another week speeding by, Julia started making arrangements for a barbecue in the garden at the flat. She had invited a number of friends, including Geoff who was now appearing more often on the scene. Since he had first gone out with us on Julia's birthday the previous year, he had occasionally popped round to see her but more often had chatted on the phone with her. He was the first to arrive, holding a large punnet of strawberries in each hand - he knew that these were Julia's favourite fruit! Whilst I prepared the food, Geoff was a great help in getting the barbecue going. Having done all I could and being redundant, I left, knowing that I could leave Julia and her guests in Geoff's capable hands. The evening was a great success, but Julia suffered the old repercussions over the next few days.

Our forthcoming holiday in Fuerteventura gave me some anxiety. I was a little concerned about leaving Julia in the flat with none of us around as Fiona was still in Cheltenham finishing off her term. However Geoff lived close by and said he would pop in to see that she was OK, so that set my mind at rest. Whilst we were away, Geoff did more than pop in to see Julia. He took her to an open air concert where they picnicked together. Romance was in the air! They obviously enjoyed each other's company and felt very relaxed together so it wasn't surprising when we returned from holiday to hear that they were officially going out with each other. John and I were naturally delighted with this news, not only because we thought Geoff was so good for Julia - he seemed instinctively to understand where she was, and never put pressure on her - but to see Julia being well enough to enjoy a relationship was a great joy to us. She had missed out so much on life in her twenties, perhaps at long last things were picking up again.

With the passing of time Julia became very tired and weepy. It was hard to know how much she was exhausted by the emotional stress of going out with someone new, and how much she was wearing herself out with just chatting to friends. Antoinette visited for a day and they had such fun together talking and catching up on news that I don't think Julia thought of stopping! It seemed unnatural for her to put the brakes on when she was enjoying herself. In spite of feeling emotionally fragile over the summer months she kept going; enjoying a weekend away with Geoff and his parents, before going away with Fiona to a small cottage in the Cotswolds for a few days.

With both girls back in Reading in a scorching, hot August, Fiona drove Julia to a nearby lake, where they enjoyed sitting in the shade having a picnic lunch, gazing out over the water studying the antics of the ducks. Unfortunately Julia still didn't have the concentration to drive her car, but Fiona enjoyed using it! On one of their picnics by the lake I cycled straight from work to join them. Leaving Julia curled up on a rug, Fiona and I went off for a walk. "Mum, Julia seems really tired; I don't think she's as good as she was." My heart missed a beat - hearing Fiona voice her concern touched a raw nerve in me. I had become quite accustomed to ignoring the ups and downs of M.E. - but always at the back of my mind was the fear that Julia could relapse. The thought of this stirred up feelings of anxiety, but I knew there was nothing I could do. Breaking my train of thought Fiona said, "Let's pray as we walk along," so this we did reminding ourselves of Isaiah's words, *"You will keep him in perfect peace, whose imagination stops at God."* (2)

Fortunately Fiona's and my fears that Julia might be deteriorating were unfounded, but on the other hand she didn't improve either. With careful planning Julia and Geoff went up to the Midlands for a wedding. They drove up the day before, and by taking time out to rest at various times throughout the day Julia managed her energy levels so as to enjoy the wedding. Because Geoff was then going on holiday with friends, John and I drove up to collect Julia after the reception. When I saw Julia and Geoff walking towards the car, I caught my breath. They made a stunning couple with Geoff's dark good looks, and Julia looking radiantly attractive. She was wearing a new long, flowing dress with pink flowers on a navy background and had ditched her glasses for contact lenses. This was another rare glimpse of Julia being well enough to enjoy doing what other normal youngsters do. I could see the changes in her - she looked taller, more confident and seemed so much more relaxed. The parts of Julia that had been suffocated and buried under the illness were beginning to burst forth again. But this memorable day had a sting in its tail as Julia wasn't well for the following week. It seemed as if she was walking a tightrope - if she did a bit too much she became ill again. But what was a bit too much? She didn't know that until she had overdone it!

With September quickly upon us, once again we said goodbye to Fiona as she launched out into her first job. Since Fiona needed a car, Julia let her have the blue Fiesta as she hadn't been well enough to use it, Julia looked for an automatic, thinking this might require less concentration and thus be easier to drive. A few days after Fiona left, Julia went to Burrswood for another two week break. It was a time of great blessing for her and this was reflected in a card she sent me:

"Dear Mum

This is to tell you that you are very precious to me. More and more I appreciate all you do for me, (and you have a husband to look after!). I'm so grateful. Thank you for all you do. Every time you give, my heart sighs contentedly with gratitude and I am sorry for the times when it doesn't resound from my mouth. At times I forget you need encouragement in everyday things too, I brush over your human frailty and expect you to do everything. I suppose I perceive you as Super Mum! - it certainly feels like it sometimes when you're whizzing around smiling, helping, and sharing. But Mum I want to tell you again I love you for being you - my special friend.

I see those times when you're heavy-hearted, frustrated and upset - your eyes silently speak. Next time you feel like that when I'm unwell, be reminded of God's promise, *Do not fear . . . . I will strengthen you and help you.* (3) Let him help you. Lift your eyes from the chilly mists and dark shadows on the earthly horizon to the soft clouds of comfort, rising bubbles of joy, and gaze at the still, blue sky. I pray He will fill every ounce of you with His tender love, deeper and richer than before. Our Father is wonderful. Lovingly he wants to pour His blessing out abundantly more and more. Keep going - it's not my health that dictates our friendship, but our love.

Love Julia"

Her time at Burrswood was very positive, particularly as for the first time in years she delighted in a very gentle swim, in the hydrotherapy pool. However the excitement of enjoying simple leisure activities was soon knocked on the head as having returned home, Julia became unwell - this time with an ear infection. It was so discouraging to see her have barely a few weeks on her feet, only to go down with a virus or infection. No wonder she was not making any strides forward! Whilst she appeared to be entrenched on a plateau again I was struggling with all the usual feelings associated with loss.

Fortunately I had arranged a weekend break from caring, by attending a CiCP leaders conference. This was a time for me to get away from the situation and recharge my batteries. The agenda for the conference was to seek God's heart for the future of CiCP, which first involved the relinquishing of its ownership into God's hands. With this theme very much in the forefront of my thoughts, going to bed on the Saturday night, I was reminded of Jesus' words, *"If anyone would come after me, he must deny himself and take up his cross and follow me. For whoever wants to save his life will lose it, but whoever loses his life for me will find it."* (4) As I began to reflect on this verse, I heard God's quiet voice questioning my attitude: was I really willing to lay down my demand for a healthy daughter? As far as I was aware I thought I had handed ownership of Julia to Him, but I was being challenged at a much deeper level. God was asking me to lay down all my rights. "In the face of loss, we will demand our rights, even if we have none, because we feel we are being unfairly treated." (5) Rights - this is part of the spirit of our age with Consumer Rights, Welfare Rights, Patient Rights, Animal Rights, Human Rights, and Civil Rights, to name but a few. Having been brought up in a culture that has a degree of legitimacy in demanding rights, I realised that this attitude had affected me. To some extent I was still demanding from God my right to have a daughter who was able to live a normal life. But how could I think

Relinquishing Ownership

like this? I was ashamed as I discovered the depth of my selfishness, demandingness and self-centredness. I had no rights - I deserved nothing - all that I had was a free gift from God by His grace.

Responding to what God was showing me, I began to identify all the rights that I was consciously holding on to, by putting each one on a post-it note. I wrote:

"I give up my rights to see Julia:
- *well, and grow into her full potential;*
- *have fun, laugh and enjoy life;*
- *be independent and drive a car;*
- *be able to fly abroad and have a holiday;*
- *enjoy walking in the sunshine,*
- *married with children;*
- *have a career in nursing".*

This was painful work, but I knew I had to push on and face the dark areas of my self-centredness. Feeling convicted in the core of my being I moved on to write out all my selfish desires - each one on a separate post-it.

"I want to be :
- *free from responsibilities in caring, so that I can do what I want with my time;*
- *free from dealing with the emotional pain of sadness, anger, guilt, despair, helplessness and hopelessness;*
- *free from the struggle to hang on to God and trust His promises;*
- *free to spend more time with John and be able to go away together;*
- *free to be a normal family;*
- *free to have time to see the wider family and build relationships;*
- *free to be me - full of lightness and laughter, rather than heavy with pain".*

Holding all these post-its in my hand, I knelt on the floor and confessed my shortcomings to God. Then lifting up my hands I surrendered all my demands to Him - reading out the post-its one by one and laying them down on the floor - I was transferring ownership of my life and Julia's back to God. *"Our lives are yours,"* I sobbed, *"do with them what you want."*

I felt I was jumping over one of the most important and difficult hurdles in coming to terms with my shattered dreams. Unless I was able to settle once and for all the issue of who owned the right to our lives, I would never be able to live with life's disappointments. God alone, the creator of the universe and maker of man, has the right to do what He wants. *Our God is in heaven; he does whatever pleases him.* (6) In all the lessons one can learn from Job, the fact that God does not explain to Job why he is suffering, remains a mystery. Yet Job ended up accepting that he had no right to his life, *'No plan of yours can be thwarted.'* (7) "To surrender all your rights to Another might appear to be a sign of weakness, but that kind of weakness is the weakness Christ displayed when He submitted all His rights, even to death on the cross, knowing that the seeming weakness provided God with an opportunity to reveal His divine strength." (8).

I was reminded of a beautiful but anonymous meditation on *rights* that Fiona Castle found very comforting, as she watched her husband Roy, die of cancer:

"He had no rights:
  No right to a soft bed, and a well-laid table;
  No right to a home of his own, a place where his own pleasure might be sought;
  No right to choose pleasant, congenial companions, those who could understand him and sympathise with him;
  No right to shrink away from contact with sin, to pull his garments closer around him and walk in cleaner paths;

Relinquishing Ownership

No right to be understood and appreciated; no not by those on whom he had poured out a double portion of his life;
No right even never to be forsaken by his Father, the one who meant more than all to him.

His only right was to endure shame, spitting, blows, to take his place as a sinner at the dock; to bear my sins in anguish on the cross.
He had not rights.
And I?
A right to the comforts of life? No but a right to the love of God for my pillow.
A right to physical safety? No, but a right to the security of being in his will.
A right to love and sympathy from those around me? No, but a right to the friendship of the one who understands me better than I do myself.
A right to be a leader among men? No, but a right to be led by the one to whom I have given my all, led as a little child, with its hand in the hand of its father.
A right to a home, and dear ones? No, not necessarily; but a right to dwell in the heart of God.
A right to myself? No, but oh, I have a right to Christ.

All that he takes I will give;
All that he gives I will take;
He, my only right! He, the one right before which all other rights fade into nothingness.
I have full right to him: Oh, may he have full right to me!"
(9)

I can't say that I felt amazingly different after the weekend away, but I did have a greater sense of peace. Every time my thoughts wandered down the 'I demand' avenue, I reminded myself that I had no rights, for everything that I had was an undeserved gift. No sooner had I returned home than John went away for the next fortnight to help on a mission in Cardiff. I joined him for 48 hours and had great fun getting involved in some of the activities, including a mime on a busy street in the pouring rain! One of the younger members of the team approached me to ask if I would help her create a dance to a new song by Graham Kendrick. We looked at the words together.

For the joys and for the sorrows
The best and worst of times,
For this moment, for tomorrow,
For all that lies behind;
Fears that crowd around me,
For the failure of my plans,
For the dreams of all I hope to be,
The truth of what I am.

For the tears that flow in secret,
In the broken times,
For the moments of elation,
Or the troubled mind;
For all the disappointments,
Or the sting of old regrets -
All my prayers and longing,
That seem unanswered yet:

For the weakness of my body,
The burdens of each day,
For the nights of doubt and worry,
When sleep has fled away;
Needing reassurance,
And the will to start again -
A steely-eyed endurance;
The strength to fight and win:

For this I have Jesus,
For this I have Jesus,
For this I have Jesus,
I have Jesus. (10)

These words were such an accurate expression of where I was, that by the time we got to the 2nd verse, *For the tears that flow in secret*, I just broke down and cried. This song was a real comfort to me as it reminded me that Jesus understands all my feelings, the joys and sorrows, the troubled mind and disappointments, the shattered dreams and the failure of my plans - *For this I have Jesus*. This song was inspired by the preaching of Charles Price who told the story of an elderly friend of his who always said, "For this I have Jesus - it was his catch phrase, and he used it on every occasion, and for everything that happened to him, good or bad!" (11) The words not only encapsulated my inner turmoil, but I also found them very powerful because they incited me to have a steely-eyed endurance - and boy, did I need it! I didn't always feel that I could keep going, but *for this I have Jesus*.

In October Julia had an appointment in Essex to see an occupational therapist (OT) who worked with Dr Findley, a consultant neurologist, whom Julia had seen a year or so earlier about her M.E. As a result of their work, a National M.E. Centre had been set up in that area. The OT advised Julia about the importance of pacing herself in order to stop the peaking and troughing, and offered other practical ways to conserve her energy. It was suggested that she follow a rest and activity programme - and rest meant rest! This was relaxing, closing the eyes and doing nothing, although quiet, restful music was allowed. During these rest periods there was to be no stimulation at all, as we were told all the senses use up energy. She suggested that Julia built in six rest periods throughout the day each lasting from half an hour to one hour, depending on the time of day.

Interestingly, the Holy Spirit had shown Julia over the past eight months to have a complete rest time, just listening to instrumental music, followed by an activity time. In the early years, like many other people who suffer with M.E., we had innocently thought that watching TV, or reading a book was resting, as they were non-active. We had not understood that the visual stimulation of TV, or the concentration required to read, used up energy. In her activity times Julia could shower, get dressed, have a meal, go for a walk and be creative or read etc. We accepted that this programme was not a cure, but more a way of managing the illness. Leaving the occupational therapy department I couldn't help feeling very relieved that at long last someone had given us some practical help. Here we were into the sixth year of M.E. affecting Julia's life so profoundly, yet no one previously had offered us any constructive guidelines for pacing her life.

Keeping to the timetable was very hard for Julia at first as she found it quite legalistic and binding. One day I was late in taking her meal round to the flat and she phoned asking, "Where are you?". She was angry that I had messed up her daily schedule as she had been waiting for me to come during her activity time. When I eventually arrived with the meal there was something of an atmosphere between us because I also felt angry that Julia was not more flexible. Sitting down with her I talked through the issues - the programme was a helpful framework, but it wasn't a life or death matter if she didn't strictly adhere to it as it was a helpful guide to pacing herself, not a remedy for her illness. Her recovery didn't depend upon her getting it 100% right. We had been told that Julia could still dip even following the programme, but she was less likely to. After I had talked things through with Julia, she slowly became more flexible in adapting to a new way of living.

The distance that Julia walked on a daily basis was slowly increasing as she was following the suggested regime of increasing the distance by about ten paces, every fourteen days or more. This was very slow

Relinquishing Ownership 163

progress but there was a pay off as when Fiona came home for half term she saw a definite improvement and one day Julia actually said she felt fine. Feeling stronger to cope with more situations she asked me to take her to Brighton to a conference at which John Wimber and Mahesh Chavda were speaking. My first reaction was that I didn't really want to go as I didn't want to have the emotional strain of looking after her - although she was better than she had been, she still wasn't entirely independent. But reminding myself *"For this I have Jesus"*, we set off for Brighton one cold November day to stay in a self contained flat for a few days.

Once there I really enjoyed the conference and met several old friends whom I hadn't seen for years, which was a great joy. Julia managed to sit through some of the sessions on a sun bed - fortunately she didn't feel isolated as there were a few others on sun beds as well, including our friend Val, who also had M.E. During one lunch time break I had left Julia in the main hall and was speaking with an old nursing friend whom I hadn't seen for over 20 years, when the fire bell went off. We were told to exit the conference centre as soon as possible. My immediate reaction was concern for Julia - would she be able to cope in the crowds by herself? I wasn't allowed back in the hall to find her. Searching for her familiar face amongst the hundreds of others outside the conference centre caused my stomach to turn over as I wondered what sort of effect this would have upon her. Would she panic? When I eventually found her she looked very pale and shaken, and I was so relieved to find her still able to smile with relief. Apparently floods of tears streamed down her cheeks as she made her way to the exit, surrounded by crowds of people - she felt anxious, as she had no energy reserves for the unexpected - but she had coped.

Knowing Julia needed to sit quietly and recover, we had no choice but to walk to the nearest hotel, as it was too cold to sit on the steps outside the centre. This episode reminded me of how vulnerable Julia still was, but at least she could manage to walk short distances and as we sat sipping coffee in the hotel we laughed about our escapade. Julia was noticeably growing in confidence as one morning she made her own way down to the conference centre by taxi, which was something she couldn't have done a few months earlier. Fiona and a few friends drove over from Ringwood for the final evening of the conference. Arriving late, we didn't see them until the end of the evening, when I was introduced to Fiona's friends, one of whom was Paul. He greeted me with a warm smile and welcoming arms - I couldn't help but think that he was a fine young bachelor! I whispered to Fiona, "he's dishy". "Oh Mum, trust you - I hardly know him"! and with that Fiona was off with her friends to make the homeward journey. The next morning Julia and I had a short walk along the beach, before returning to Reading, having been challenged and stimulated by the speakers, and feeling much more refreshed and full of renewed energy.

Although Julia was tired, the following week she was enthusiastic to continue to set small goals to become more independent. By now she had a red automatic Fiesta and wanted to start driving again. The OT had given her a very simple regime, advising that at first Julia sat in the car daily for a week, just to familiarise herself with all the pedals and gadgets again, then to drive the car up and down the drive for another few weeks, before taking it out onto a very quiet road for about a 100 yard drive. In other words, as in everything else, Julia had to build up very slowly to driving the car again. So over the next couple of weeks Julia worked on this and John took her up to the top of her road where she drove a very short distance. Julia was obviously delighted and had a growing sense of achievement but unfortunately it was very short lived as she became ill with yet another virus which put her out of action. This not only put a stop to her driving for the time being, but also meant she had to miss her cousin's wedding. Once again John, Fiona and I put on brave faces as we went to this special occasion, but inwardly we felt part of us was missing as we were very conscious that Julia was not with us. But for once Julia didn't feel down that she was missing out on the

Relinquishing Ownership

fun, as Geoff was a happy distraction.

That Christmas of 1995 was the best for many a year, as we weren't overshadowed by illness and we had a great deal of fun. Having returned from the midnight service the girls came and sat on our bed and we all opened our stockings together. Wrapping paper was hastily ripped away and tossed everywhere and our squeals of delight went on till about 2 am. How wonderful it was just to be spontaneous and do simple things together! On Christmas day it was Fiona we left behind, so that we could spend a couple of hours in the evening with Geoff and his parents. Although Fiona said she was tired, I sensed that she was finding it quite hard to cope with the fact that Julia had a boyfriend. Bubbling underneath the surface was a degree of sibling jealousy. For once Julia was able to enjoy something Fiona didn't have in her life! The remainder of the holiday weeks passed smoothly with no difficult moments, with Julia managing her rests and activity times. Moving into January 1996 small progress was maintained and Julia began to drive the car occasionally.

However, although all looked well on the outside and Julia's physical progress was encouraging, things were not quite so good in her inner world. Before Christmas I had found myself listening to her tears of pain over the fact that she felt rejected by people who had hitherto given her support, but for some reason had not continued. Supporting people who are chronically sick is time consuming, and what we were finding was that very few people are able to sustain a long term commitment. Coupled with this sense of rejection, someone had said something to her which had rocked her confidence in herself, and she became quite weepy over simple things. This continued in the New Year and once again we saw that Julia didn't have reserves of energy. Physically she was improving as she was able to walk from the flat to our house on one or two occasions, but emotionally she was vulnerable. There didn't seem to be any major trigger for this as her relationship with Geoff was going well, but another virus in March didn't help. This time round, she was too ill to stay in the flat and came home for about seven days to be nursed at home. Even Alison, her doctor, said that she had never seen her so low, so her medication was changed.

Adjusting to this setback caused my tears to return as I felt a knife twisting in my aching heart. Although I was trusting God in the situation, the pain didn't go away. It felt as if John and I were standing with Julia on a station platform, waiting to catch the next train to London. We had our cases with us as we were expectantly waiting to go on a journey. But one train after another sped through the station. None of them stopped to pick us up and we were left feeling bereft, and forgotten. That is how I felt - God was passing us by, and we were left waiting, whilst others got on with their lives. Yet at the same time I also knew that God was with us in the situation - what a paradox! As one day merged insignificantly into another I detected signs that Julia was beginning to fall apart. Recognising this for herself, she began to panic as she feared losing all the independence that she had recently gained. "I don't want to go backwards," she would cry. Seeing Julia in this place gave me a few sleepless nights as well, and it was so hard going, that it seemed as if I was wading through water which was up to my chest, with no banks in sight. The only thing that kept me plodding forward was moving towards a cross in the distance. This is where I needed steely-eyed endurance. The cross reminded me of God's love for us - He hadn't deserted us; He was with us in the situation. Focusing on the Easter story with the anguish and crucifixion of Jesus, which then moved on to the resurrection power and joy of the risen Lord renewed my hope.

With this Easter hope in our hearts eight of us went away to a cottage in the Cotswolds over the Easter holidays in 1996. Besides John and I, were Geoff and Julia, Fiona with her two friends, Jane and Sarah, and perhaps the most interesting addition to the party - Paul. He was the dishy bachelor I had already been introduced to at

Relinquishing Ownership

Brighton! Singing together in the same worship group, Fiona liked him a lot and had mustered up enough courage to invite him to come away with us. Much to her surprise and joy, he had agreed to come down for a few days. Little did he know where that would lead him! It was very amusing to watch Fiona and Paul trying very hard to keep their emotions in check, when it was obvious to all of us that they liked each other! Walking across the fields, Sarah teased them both by encouraging them to walk through a kissing gate together, but Paul would have none of this and firmly kept to the back of the group! The two young men shared a room and they both sat up talking one night until the early hours. Geoff encouraged Paul to ask Fiona out as it was obvious they were very much attracted to each other. And so it was that they became a couple.

We were all thrilled with this outcome as they seemed made for each other. The sad aspect of the holiday was that Julia had become so fatigued that she could hardly go out and when she did she was forced to use the wheelchair again. Fortunately the cottage had a wonderful log fire, so we would leave Julia and Geoff enjoying this during the day, whilst the rest of us went out walking. In the evenings we relaxed together by playing games, accompanied by much hilarity.

Returning from this enjoyable and eventful week away, Fiona went back to Ringwood and Julia came home for a few days to recover from the journey. It was very clear to me that Julia wasn't in a very good place - and when I saw her having to crawl out of the bath onto the floor, the agony of seeing her relapse hit me. All our dreams were being shattered and our hopes dashed yet again. But God knew what He was doing, and I was able to quietly say, *"Into my Father's hands I place her."*

Totally relinquishing Julia into God's hands wasn't easy. When God asks us to let go of our children, He is perfecting our ability to trust Him with that which is most precious to us. Abraham saw his surrender of Isaac as an act of worship. Relinquishing is about letting go of our expectations for our children and acknowledging God's ownership. Having given our children our best, it is important we move on, and "let go and let God". This poem illustrates this:

"It's Your Move, Daughter . . . ."

I gave you life
> but I cannot live it for you.

I can teach you things
> but I cannot make you learn.

I can give you directions
> but I cannot always be there to lead you.

I can allow you freedom
> but I cannot account for it.

I can take you to church
> but I cannot make you believe.

I can teach you right from wrong
> but I cannot always decide for you.

I can buy you beautiful clothes
> but I cannot make you lovely inside.

I can offer you advice
> but I cannot accept it for you.

I can give you love
> but I cannot force it upon you.

I can teach you to be a friend
> but I cannot make you one.

I can teach you to share
> but I cannot make you unselfish.

I can teach you to respect
> but I can't force you to show honour.

I can grieve about your report card
> but I cannot doubt your teachers.

I can advise you about friends
> but I cannot choose them for you.

I can teach you about sex
> but I cannot keep you pure.

I can tell you the facts of life
> but I can't build your reputation.

I can tell you about drink
> but I can't say NO for you.

I can warn you about drugs
> but I can't prevent you from using them

I can tell you about lofty goals
> but I can't achieve them for you.

I can let you baby sit
> but I can't be responsible for your actions.

I can teach you kindness
> but I can't force you to be gracious.

I can warn you about sins
> but I cannot make you walk with God.

I can teach you about Jesus
> but I cannot make HIM your Saviour.

I can teach you to OBEY
> but I cannot make Jesus Your Lord.

I can tell you how to live
> but I cannot give you Eternal Life"

(Author unknown).

I always feel like adding another couple of lines to this poem:-
> "I can comfort you in your pain
>> but I cannot make you better."

KNOWING HIM

I know God is my peace
I know God is my joy
And I know that self-pity's a devilish toy
I know that guilt is a self-centred ploy
And calming peace and lifting hope are far better to employ.

I know God is my hope
I know God is my faith
And I know that health and healing are not mine to dictate
But when should I shout and demand
And when should I plead and wait?

It's easy to ask, but hard to believe and harder still to wait.
For God says he'll give the desires of my heart
And answer whatever I ask; - for my part
I know God accepts me and loves me and I
Acknowledge I'm under his all-seeing eye -

In faith then I accept His will, my eyes on my Father's face
In time, I trust, I'll feel Him touch me with his healing grace.

Julia

Chapter 11

The Dark Waiting Room

I wait for the Lord, my soul waits (Psalm 130:5)

On our return from the holiday in the Cotswold, Julia came home for a while to recover from the return journey. One afternoon ten minutes or so after I started speaking to Julia I was shocked to hear her say, "Mum, I've had enough - I'm exhausted." Her voice was faint and thin and she was curled up on her bed, with lifeless eyes and icy cold hands hugging a hot water bottle to her chest. Her face was ashen and there was a pale, waxen look to her skin. I held her close and just sat silently with her for a while. I found it hard to take in that I was losing something of my daughter again - her energy was draining away. It felt as if she was being robbed quietly and silently by a thief in the night. Bottling up all my feelings I gave her a kiss and slipped out of her room.

Downstairs John said something quite innocent to me, but I exploded. "For goodness sake . . . .why don't you just go ahead and do it! Don't ask me." John stood there, with his blue eyes staring incredulously at me. "What have I just said to upset you?" "Well, if you don't know I am not going to tell you," I unfairly threw back at him. "Christine, what's the matter? This isn't like you." And with that he came and put his comforting arms round me and the dam burst, releasing all my tears and pain. "I'm sorry, it was nothing to do with you. It's me . . . . I'm feeling under stress the whole time. I'm so upset about Julia." Looking into his face, I could see tears well up in his eyes also. Spontaneously we threw our arms round each other and held each other close, knowing that words couldn't express what we both felt.

Although Julia felt so poorly she insisted on moving back to the flat as it was smaller and so much easier for her to walk. Kathryn an energetic young lady had moved in the previous December, so Julia was not entirely alone. I continued to pop in most days, taking cooked meals around in the car, and often going in at lunch time as well as late afternoon and around bedtime. Geoff also visited several times a week. As Julia was so fatigued she limited all visitors to about a quarter of an hour so as to conserve enough energy for her short daily walk, and in order to have time and energy to give Geoff. I went back to having to give her baths and wash her hair - it was always a bad sign when she asked me to do this. I knew the strain was beginning to tell on me as I began waking in the small hours with a tightness in my chest and palpitations and early in the morning with butterflies in my stomach, wondering what the day would bring. I found comfort in the words of a song based on Lamentations (1)

> *The steadfast love of the Lord never ceases,*
> *His mercies never come to an end;*
> *they are new every morning,*
> *new every morning;*
> *great is Thy faithfulness, O Lord,*
> *great is Thy faithfulness.* (2)

With John away at a conference over the May Bank holiday, I knew that I needed to get away for a break. After preaching at the Sunday morning service I went down to join Fiona and Paul, my sister, Andria and her husband Brian, for lunch in the New Forest. It was so good to get away and I immediately felt the benefit of a change. I borrowed Fiona's bike and enjoying glorious sunshine, Andria, Brian and I cycled along the beautiful winding roads in the forest. We stopped off for a cream tea and sitting relaxing I found myself laughing with Andria over something very silly and small. Next to our table was a young toddler in a pushchair who was innocently making faces at her food. This just set us off, and it was so good to enjoy a lighthearted moment - I hadn't laughed for weeks. The day away was a real tonic for me. Having enjoyed such a wonderful, refreshing day, I swung the car onto the motorway and headed for home. Feeling stronger I was ready to take up the reins of caring again. Fiona had given me a card and present for Julia, and as I had almost to pass Julia's front door on my way home, I decided to stop off and give it to her. She would be encouraged to receive something from her sister. Feeling full of energy I ran up the stairs, two at a time, shouting, "Hello." But there was a deathly silence.

Walking into the lounge I found Julia sitting on the settee with tears streaming down her face, and Geoff comforting and holding her. Trying to sensitively tone down my exuberance I asked, "What's the matter?" In between sobs she cried, "I'm not sleeping . . . . I'm so tired that I don't know what to do with myself." Feeling lost for words I didn't know how best to reply, so I quietly sat on the floor gently resting my hand on her tired body. After a while I asked if the sleeping tablets were helping - she said they didn't seem to be making any difference. I felt totally helpless as I couldn't say or do anything to change the situation. Seeing anxiety written all over Geoff's face added more sorrow. Poor chap - what was he going through? He had hardly seen Julia well.

I became increasingly concerned about Julia. Disappointed at seeing herself deteriorate again she started to brood over what was no longer possible and began to withdraw and shut herself off. Signs of depression were beginning to surface, with negative thoughts of self-condemnation. Popping in to see her one day I was met with a very irrational comment, "You won't like me." She felt so frustrated with having such little energy and so angry with herself for being ill she couldn't accept that others would like her. I recognised that for the first time I couldn't connect with my daughter. Feeling very concerned I went to see Alison, who was always ready to listen, and asked her to visit Julia to check she was OK. After the visit Alison reassured me, "Julia isn't mentally ill if that's what you are worried about - she's just very fatigued." "Thank you, that's what I needed to hear", I replied. But in my heart of hearts I knew things weren't quite right - mothers are usually accurate about their gut reactions.

With Fiona home for another wedding, I told her of my concern, so she went round to see for herself how Julia was. On her return she said that she had found Julia quite rational and they had both decided between them that I had the problem! It was me that had become an over-anxious mother! I was starting to think that myself. Was I beginning to get things our of perspective? But deep down I didn't think that was true. John tended to side with the girls and I was left feeling totally isolated. It felt as if I was knocking my head against a brick wall - it seemed that no one was believing me.

Not only was I seeing my dreams hit the wall, with the ensuing disappointment dragging my spirits down, but now I was battling to survive in a dark and arid desert where people weren't listening to me. My faith seemed "reduced to a mere point of dry, stubborn conviction set amidst a mass of clamouring objections and doubts." (3) I longed for a rational explanation of what was going on, but even that would not be enough to soothe my emotions. What I needed was a friend who would listen to me and help me sort out my confusion, and one who would remind me of God's faithfulness when I couldn't see it on my own. Picking up the phone I spoke to Mary and blurted out the hurt I felt as no one was hearing my concerns about Julia. I was grateful that she listened, and like a true friend she came round the next day. Sitting in the sunny garden I poured out my heart to her. As another mother, she heard my cry, and although she couldn't offer any easy answers, at least I felt someone had understood me. She also reassured me that God was in the situation and that He would faithfully hang on to us.

As the days rolled into weeks, there was no change in the situation, but the strain was beginning to have an impact upon me. I started to think that perhaps *I* had a problem - people were telling me that Julia was just fatigued, but I thought more than that was going on. Was I becoming a neurotic mother? How could I tell what was what?

Consequently I was losing confidence in myself and becoming angry that no one was taking me seriously. One Sunday evening after church I said to John that I had to know whether I was making things out to be worse than they were and suggested that we went to see Mary, and her husband Derek, who was the senior doctor at the practice. I trusted Derek's wisdom and his honesty with me. We knew them well enough to phone them in an emergency, as I was beginning to think that if I didn't get my head sorted out soon I would lose it. Fortunately they were in. Spilling the story out I asked Derek if he thought that I was overreacting. He immediately put my mind at rest and reassured me that, from what he heard, he, like me, would be concerned. My motherly instincts were right - what a relief! It would have been unethical to discuss Julia's medical treatment because she wasn't his patient, so although the situation did not change, I felt more equipped to handle it as I began to believe in myself again. There was nothing I could do, apart from pray that Julia would accept the fact that she was becoming clinically depressed.

Reflecting on this waiting room experience Julia has since said, "When there was no progress over a long period of time, it was easy to slip into thinking, 'God is denying me healing because I'm not worthy of it'. As a result I become confused and I wanted to give up fighting. But I have since learnt that 'Delay is not denial'. When God allows a delay in answering prayer, He is not denying His children His presence in their situation."

Towards the end of May 1996 Fiona phoned to say she and Paul wanted to come down and see us within the next 48 hours. We had our suspicions - were they going to get engaged? It was difficult to arrange a time as John and I were so busy being away at different conferences that the only time we could manage to see them was on the Sunday evening. Arriving with big grins on their faces they sat in the lounge with us passing the time with very superficial talk. Eventually John asked Paul whether he had anything special to ask.

... We were right! They were planning to get married the following summer.. . . .

Popping a bottle of champagne (which John had just happened to put in the fridge earlier!) we celebrated with great joy. But in the back of my mind I couldn't help wonder how Julia would react to the news. I didn't know then that Fiona had already told her. Knowing Julia, I knew on the one hand she would be delighted because she liked Paul, but on the other hand I wondered how much she was hurting that her sister had got engaged before her. Julia had intimated to me that her relationship with Geoff was serious and long-term and has subsequently told me that she and Geoff had already talked about getting engaged before Fiona ever met Paul. So when her sister announced her engagement Julia felt angry that she had been pipped to the post yet again. Sibling rivalry was around! Julia also felt that she herself had failed in not taking the opportunity to do something before her sister.

Life continued with Julia showing signs of extreme fatigue and depression, but she denied that she was depressed. "I am low because I am so tired," she would say. Although she was on antidepressants they didn't seem to be helping her, and she appeared to be resistant to increasing the dose. I became so exasperated by this, that in the early hours of one morning I sat at my computer and wrote her a letter, part of which I reproduce here:-

> "Dear Julia
> I find this very difficult to write, but I am risking doing it because I feel that I must put some facts before you. If I don't, you might always say, "Mum, why didn't you tell me?". So here are some general facts and information - it is your choice what you do with it - I will not mention this letter again unless you bring up the subject.
>
> You have asked several times, "What am I doing to

myself?". You acknowledge that emotionally you are very fragile - anxious, fearful, angry at times, guilty, sad, weepy, want to give up on life, and not sleeping, - these are all signs of depression. Depression is not always about wanting to commit suicide, it is about people being emotionally fragile. You have said that you feel agitated, and I know that your thoughts sometime run away with themselves. This may sound very dramatic - but it isn't.

You have a choice to
1 - accept the fact that you are suffering with some degree of depression, and explore how you can help yourself
or
2 - stay where you are in the hope that things will get better.

We will always love you and your Dad and I will never stop fighting for you. How you decide to react to this letter is up to you.

Love Mum"

(On reading the draft of this book, Julia saw the full text of the letter for the first time and remarked that she would have found it more constructive if I had offered to help her to achieve small and specific tasks, rather than think about the choices).

In the light of the morning I reflected on what I had written. Coming to the conclusion that committing my muddled thoughts to paper had been something of a therapy for me, I decided that the letter might not be so helpful for Julia. Instead I just wrote her a card with a very simplified version of the above. But Julia continued to concern me, and although I was looking forward to the holiday we had booked and to getting a break, I was anxious about how Julia would cope. She was still very fatigued and would phone me late at night feeling very anxious. "Mum, will you just pray with me, I am feeling very frightened." Sometimes I responded by going round to the flat; at other times I reassured her over the phone. I began to dread a distressed voice on the other end of the line as I couldn't accurately assess how she was, and sometimes my imagination played games with me. However one phone call I was surprised to receive was Julia saying that she and Geoff were coming round to see us before we went away on holiday. I was a little bewildered by this as Julia was more or less housebound, but thought it was probably something to do with her trying to get some respite at Burrswood whilst we were away. She accepted that in our absence she wasn't well enough to look after herself, so she needed some care. We discussed together the possibility of John and me cancelling our holiday, but she wouldn't contemplate this. "You need a break, Mum," came her undemanding comment.

With my mind on our impending holiday and concern to get a room booked at Burrswood, I greeted Julia and Geoff with the usual warm welcome. In spite of looking drawn and peaky, Julia looked radiant and Geoff's face shone with his cheery smile. I should have smelt a rat, but I didn't! They didn't beat about the bush; they had come round to announce their engagement. Naturally, I was thrilled. The news was not unexpected, but the timing was. It took the wind out of my sails. My immediate reaction was one of joy, until I asked if they had any plans for a wedding date. "Yes . . . . This year . . . . December 26th. We have booked the church." I felt I went into free fall, with my stomach jumping into my mouth. *"That's crazy,"* I wanted to shout, *"You're not well enough."* But somehow I managed to override this thought, and said, "That's a very special time of year, but do you realise how stressful it will be on top of your birthdays and Christmas?" "Oh, we'll manage," they said.

Looking across at John, I could see that he was delighted for them both, but was struggling to come to terms with a Christmas wedding. I decided to make no more comments about their actual wedding, but focused on how thrilled we were that they had become engaged.

The Dark Waiting Room

Reeling from this news I decided to put the thought of a winter wedding on hold whilst John and I went away the next day for a Greek holiday.

Before flying out of the country I managed to get hold of Fiona and ask her what she thought of the the news. She was delighted. As if sensing that I was a little anxious about the plans, she said, "Julia can't wait for ever to get better, before she gets married. There is never going to be a right time for her at the moment. She's met someone she loves and he loves her for who she is, and it's important for her to move on in life". Knowing that Fiona was young like Julia and thus more able to see the situation from Julia's perspective, I really valued her comments. "Yes, you're right, Fiona. Thanks for helping me to see things more clearly."

Whilst John and I were away relaxing and sunning ourselves in Greece, arrangements for Julia's admission into Burrswood were finalised so friends drove her there. Feeling very fatigued and ill, she spent most of her time on the bed in her room. She had deteriorated to such an extent that in her activity times, all she could do was manage to eat a meal, watch a little TV, or have a conversation for about five to ten minutes. After discussion with the resident doctor, Julia's medication was changed, in the hope that she would begin to sleep better. Returning from Greece it was a bit of a shock to find that she could only manage a five minute talk on the phone to us, and we were concerned to find Geoff feeling low and discouraged. This wasn't surprising. Having just become engaged, he naturally wanted to enjoy the company of his fianc e, and Julia obviously wanted to be with him. But this wasn't to be. This monster of M.E. had come between them, and we were all hurting.

When I went to collect Julia from Burrswood I was stunned by how ill she looked yet again. Driving her home she was as white as a sheet. Suffering with pain in her back and with her energy spent, tears silently moistened her cheeks. I didn't dare take my eyes off the road, as I knew if I allowed myself to focus too much on Julia I would crumble. Tucking her into bed at home with us that evening, I again reassured her of our love and the fact that we would never stop supporting her. Then I reminded her that God was holding her in His hands, and that He would bring her through. To which she replied weakly, "Yes, I know, but how long have I to wait?" As hard as it was, I replied honestly, "I don't know," and with that Julia turned her face away with tears trickling down her cheeks. During the dark times of her waiting, Julia wrote a poem addressing the question,

HOW LONG?

Lord, I long for a healthy body again,
> How long will I have to wait till then?

I often wish that I knew the date
> There is a hope but when will I catch the bait?

I long to run for miles and walk for hours
To leap and catch the ball,
> To be included with them all.

I long to visit endless mates,
> To listen and debate.

To chat and make a din
> - you'll know when I am in!

I long to bubble with excitement,
> Over a holiday or an outing.

To decide on the spur of the moment
> No hours of rest or cancellations.

I even long to wake up joyfully
> To plan the days ahead of me.

To have no crippling limitations
> To stick to my arrangements.

I long to weep with tears of happiness

> Not silent tears of sadness.
> For boundless energy, an active body
> Not this listless, pathetic and useless body.
>
> Lord, all I ask is that you heal me
> Please just listen to my plea.
> Lord, I know that one day I'll be well
> That's my hope - I cling to thee.
> Julia

The day after Julia's return from Burrswood, John, Geoff and I went off to Fiona and Paul's engagement party. It was tough leaving Julia behind, but even more difficult for Geoff to meet all our relatives without his fiance by his side. But there was no way that Julia was well enough to go. She was exhausted after the journey from Burrswood and spent the next few days curled up on her bed, too ill even to get dressed. She didn't want to see people as she was always quietly resting and the only time she appeared was for about quarter of an hour, for a meal twice a day. However I did sometimes go in and just sit with her and turn the pages of a large book of landscape illustrations based on the Psalms. The beauty of God's creation took her beyond her four walls and she found these pictures a comfort. That was the measure of all she could do - lie and gaze at pictures.

When Alison visited she remarked how ill Julia was looking, as her skin was breaking down with septic spots, particularly on her back. But having spots all over her face was not a pretty sight either. On a positive note, Julia wanted to celebrate the first anniversary of going out with Geoff, so with my help she managed to get dressed, and I cooked them a special meal so that they could enjoy it together. Fiona and Paul arrived a few days later en route to yet another wedding, and Fiona was disturbed to see Julia so ill. Julia only had enough energy to see her for about ten minutes in the morning and over lunch time, so very little conversation was exchanged. Because

Fiona had Paul with her, I think something of the pain she felt for her sister was lost in her new and exciting relationship. I was relieved that Fiona had other distractions and thus didn't feel the intensity of what was going on at home.

Caring for Julia became more and more stressful as she continued to deteriorate. She was increasingly shutting herself away from the world - withdrawing from us all, including Geoff. Her bedroom curtains were closed to shut out the bright midday summer sunlight that hurt her eyes. It was difficult to know how much of this was due to M.E., how much to depression. Once again her medication was changed. Looking on I couldn't help but wonder how I might cope with feeling so fatigued with flu-like symptoms day in and day out, not knowing how long it would go on for. Waiting wasn't easy. I had no control over the time when Julia would start to recover. I felt as if I was stuck in a room, with all the blinds closed, waiting for the first sign to announce the longed for improvement.

Waiting room experiences aren't always comfortable and they are often not by choice either. If a patient at our surgery is stuck in the waiting room because the doctor is running late, he is preoccupied with one thing - hearing the buzzer call his number up. He doesn't want to stay there for ever; he wants to move on and see the doctor. Sitting in the dark waiting room of suffering felt suffocating at times and I didn't want to stay there any longer than I had to. But once again I was faced with a choice. I could either sit there resigned and give up hope; or kick and scream; or run away; or willingly choose to trust in God's sovereignty and use the experience as a springboard for growth. Meditating on the words, *Wait for the Lord; be strong and take heart and wait for the Lord* (4) was a source of strength.

It was also good to remind myself that many godly men and women who are upheld as models of faith in Scripture found themselves stuck in a dark waiting room. Abraham had to wait until he was one hundred years old, before Sarah was blessed with a child. Moses had to wait for forty years, wandering in the wilderness; then for another forty years he waited for the Lord to deliver His people. Joseph, who was sold by his brothers, was imprisoned by false accusation and spent years waiting in prison, before he was eventually made second-in-charge of Egypt. Elizabeth, the wife of Zechariah was plagued by the curse of barrenness, yet she was *upright in the sight of God.* (5) She waited quietly in her suffering, which was particularly difficult as in her day childlessness was believed to be a sign of God's judgment. Her waiting room experience ended when she became the mother of John the Baptist, but the one who spoke to me most of all was Hannah.

Hannah was a childless woman in a society which viewed bearing a son as a woman's glory. Her waiting was made more painful as her husband's second wife, Peninnah, constantly and petulantly provoked her. "No babies yet! Perhaps next time!" For years Hannah wept before the Lord, finally making a promise that if God gave her a son, she would give him back before the ark of the covenant in Shiloh. Her waiting eventually came to an end with the birth of Samuel. Hannah's story not only spoke to me about waiting, but also reinforced my desire to be a godly mother - to be like Hannah in seeing my children as gifts from God intended to be given back to Him. I had already relinquished ownership of Julia to God, but now, in this dark waiting room, where I hadn't been before, I was fearful of where the depression might take Julia. I prayed that, like these famous characters who had been tried and tested in their waiting, but had all hung on to God, we might do the same, and be able to say as Job said, *When he has tested me, I shall come forth as gold.*(6).

There was no easy formula to waiting on God. There were times when it seemed that my faith was being stretched to its limit like a piece of elastic. For me, waiting on the Lord was not a matter of sitting back, but of aggressively taking hold of choosing to place Julia and my desires into His hands. Sitting in the dark waiting room, was not just about allowing God to work things out His way -

it was also about accepting that He would do this in His time. I genuinely desired to trust God, but I struggled with His timing. Although I knew in my head that the Lord's timing is perfect and always for His glory, the road between my head and my heart was somewhat blocked! I found a way of handling this waiting room experience by using my imagination. Every morning I would visualise carrying Julia up the steps to where Jesus was seated, and laying her in His arms. Knowing that He was well able to take care of her, I would then deliberately turn my back on them both and walk back down the steps. Choosing to place Julia into the Lord's hands and rest in the knowledge of His ability to work things out His way and in His time, released in me a greater sense of peace.

Unfortunately Julia was not able to let go and trust herself to God. She was too frightened and wanted to be in control. My heart strings were pulled tighter as she continued to slide down the slippery slope. *"Surely she has to hit the bottom soon and turn the corner,"* I would argue with myself. Continuing to stand by her, yet feeling utterly helpless Geoff was becoming subdued and quieter. With a strong Christian faith, he said that he knew God had a future for him and Julia together, and that he would wait for her to get better. In the light of how ill Julia had become the Christmas wedding was never mentioned again. We supported him as best as we could; welcoming him into the house whenever he wanted to visit Julia; giving him meals; and allowing him space to talk. Fiona and Paul visited again, but the visit left Fiona even more upset and she was in tears. I was becoming uncommunicative and sometimes John, in his pain would become angry. We were all deeply hurt. Mary was standing on the sidelines as encouraging as ever. I really appreciated the little ways that she showed she cared. One day I found a candle on the doorstep with a note from her saying that the candle was an expression of light in the darkness. Another time I found on the doormat a card of a sunrise. Mary had written on it, "The darkest hour always precedes the dawn. " What a blessing she was to me.

During one sleepless night, when I felt all my emotions were hemming me in, and there seemed to be no glint of light, I put down my thoughts and feelings on paper:-

> *"Lord, my heart feels sick - so does my head. I am battling to hold on to your presence and not feel despair - but it feels so heavy, sad and I still can't believe what is going on. It seems like a nightmare - where are you God? On the one hand it feels as if you have forsaken us - yet I know you haven't. Why are you so silent? We are all hurting in the waiting.*
>
> *Aren't we good enough for our prayers to be answered? I sometimes feel that I have not come up to the mark - if I had, you would answer prayer. I know this is a wrong perspective, but I long to have a glimpse that you are with us - that there is some hope and that in this season of suffering you will soon give us a sign that it is ending.*
>
> *But no, it is all quiet. As Geoff says, it's like a brick wall when we pray. Yet I still love you and I know you love me. Please give me a willing spirit to sustain me."*

With Fiona, Paul and Geoff away camping at New Wine, a summer conference, Julia was becoming more entrenched in her room. Not wanting to be disturbed at all, she no longer managed a bath or a hair wash and had no energy to eat. When I suggested that she was depressed, she retorted, "Mum, you are being negative. I am so fatigued that I can't do anything.". Insisting that her door was shut, because it would then be quieter, she just lay in bed all day. The only time she got up was to go to the toilet. What a sad sight she looked with her tall, thin frame bent over, as she weakly tottered along the landing. The nights of insomnia lingered on like an unwanted guest and I would often sit with Julia in the quiet of the night, but during the day she invariably asked to be left by herself.

She was still pushing us all away. I couldn't sit back and watch her deteriorate any longer as she seemed to be crumbling at a frightening speed. "John, we've got to do something," I urgently said one Friday morning. "If we don't, there is no knowing where she will end up". I was in a fighting mood! "Call Alison out," John suggested. "I can't, she's away on her summer holidays." "Well, what else can we do?" "Ask for an emergency appointment at the surgery and go and see Derek." I didn't ask Julia what she thought - she wasn't well enough to make any decisions - I had to take the situation out of her hands.

Sitting in my counselling room at the surgery with John, waiting for Derek to join us seemed very unreal. Fortunately we didn't have to explain everything from the beginning as he remembered our earlier conversation. As we talked together it became clear that Derek needed to see Julia, to make a clinical judgment. But I was in a dilemma. If I told Julia that Derek was visiting she would probably say she hadn't asked to see him as he wasn't her doctor, so we decided that the best action was for him to call unannounced that evening. I didn't like doing this behind Julia's back. We had always had an open and honest relationship and I felt I was deceiving her by not telling her what was going on. Yet, she really wasn't well enough to make any rational decisions.

On Derek's arrival I went upstairs and knocked on Julia's door. Not waiting for an answer I went in and sat alongside Julia who was curled up in bed, and quietly said, "Dad and I have become so concerned about you, that in Alison's absence we have asked Derek to come and see you. He is downstairs". A spark of anger crossed her blank, vacant face, as she retorted, "You can't do that. Mum, why didn't you tell me?" "I didn't ask you first, as I thought you would probably say, no. We are doing this because we can't sit back and see you deteriorate any more. I don't think you are aware how ill you are." Looking incredulously at me, she said, "I can't believe you have set this all up." "I've hated doing it this way, but I couldn't see any other way forward - so will you see him?" After a pregnant pause, she agreed, "But only if you stay with me."

"Hello Julia, I hear you are not at all well," were Derek's opening words, and his relaxed bedside manner soon put her at ease. After a while I was able to slip out leaving doctor and patient to continue in private. No sooner had my feet touched the hallway, than Fiona arrived home from New Wine. Full of her usual energy and vigour she burst forth with, "Hi Mum - I've had a fantastic time". Taking one look at my face worn with anguish, she then said, "What's going on?". As I filled her in on the situation, I saw her joyous bubble pop, and her face became drawn as pain for her sister gave way to tears. It was as if her whole body language was crying out with the words, *"When will it ever end?"* How hard it was as a mother to see both my daughters hurting so much. If only I could have waved a magic wand - but I couldn't.

All Derek would say when he had finished seeing Julia was that she was very ill, and that he was increasing the dosage of her medication and starting her on something else to help her sleep. I went back upstairs and was met with, "I'm cross that you called Derek out." "Yes, I expect you are, but we are only doing this for your own good". And with that, Fiona quickly appeared on the scene. Trying to be her cheery self, she was obviously struggling to know what to say to Julia and only managed a very stilted, "Hello". The atmosphere was rather strained, and after exchanging a few sentences with her sister Julia asked to be left alone as she felt exhausted. I think deep down Julia accepted that her dad and I had intervened because we genuinely loved her and felt we had to do something, as she never mentioned this episode again.

With Julia so ill, John and I became very tense and irritable with each other. The atmosphere in the home was heavy and sombre as we were conscious of Julia lying in bed 24 hours a day; with no energy to do anything, and with no spark of life. When Alison returned from holiday the following week and visited Julia, she was shocked to see how quickly she had deteriorated. Then Julia became even weaker as she suffered a sore throat and fever. There was nothing we could do but sit, pray, and wait for the tide to turn.

I WANT TO GIVE UP

I've been on this journey before
There's no glitzy limousine , no miracle cure
I know where it leads - the path is cruel and tough . . .
I want to give up.
I want someone else - someone who wins battles -
to do all the fighting:
my one weapon, energy, is all used up.
I want someone else - someone with endless stamina -
to do all the trying
for me the effort is just too much.
I want someone else - someone who's hungry -
to enjoy the food I eat:
for me it's just like medicine.
I want someone else - someone attractive -
proudly to wear my clothes:
on me they hang, the colours too bright.
I can handle the pain;
It's life continuing busily without me I can't handle:
I'm sorry - I want to give up.

Julia

Chapter 12

Fighting Despair

Why have you forgotten me? (Psalm 42:9)

During the long hours and days of waiting for Julia to improve, it felt as if a heavy blanket enveloped me like a shroud. It seemed to be my constant companion, affecting my every thought, feeling and action. I was tired and lethargic as the emotional battles left me sapped of all energy. It was as if a radio station was turned up to ear-shattering levels saying things like, 'If you just learn the lesson God is trying to teach you in this situation, then Julia will begin to improve. If you were a better person God would hear your prayers.' Fighting off these words was exhausting. I had stopped making demands on God about how and when things should happen and in my desperation all I could do was cry out to Him to carry us through. Deep inside I felt naked and broken. *'Whatever you want Lord . . . . . . glorify yourself.'*

Recognising how emotionally exhausted John and I had become, yet knowing how ill Julia was, we felt very ambivalent about getting away for a prearranged few days break to friends in Devon in late summer of 1996. Not surprisingly the quality of my life had suffered in my role of caring for Julia's needs. Having been a dancer in my younger years, I was used to pushing against the pain and wearing a plastic smile as the show must go on , and to some extent I went into automatic pilot with my face feeling like a mask - smiling outside but crying inside. But now I was aware of the importance to stop pushing myself to keep going, and look after myself, taking note of my needs. I longed for a break to get away from the strain and tension - to leave the heaviness behind.

As mothers it is so easy to lose ourselves in giving to the needs of the rest of the family, and never recognise that we also have needs. I

Fighting Despair

have counselled many mothers who struggle with feelings of guilt as soon as their needs are mentioned. It's as if they believe that as a mother they should be super woman and always be there to meet the demands of the family. They live under the tyranny of the *oughts* - I ought to do this and I ought to do that. To admit they have needs, would be paramount to saying they had failed in their task to look after others. But as mums we ignore our needs at our own peril - we are more likely to suffer from burn-out, stress symptoms and deep resentment, which may well tip us into depression if they are unaddressed. I didn't want to go down that road, so having spoken to Geoff and Julia we decided to get away for a couple of days leaving Geoff to care for Julia.

Enjoying the change of environment and sea air, I began to find my energy return and with no demands on either of us, John and I were able to relax and laugh together again - something we hadn't done for many a month. The break was over all too quickly and as we stepped outside into the sunlight saying our goodbyes, I couldn't help wondering how we would find Julia. Whilst we had been away, there had been no change and Geoff had spent much of his time basking in the sunshine, in between getting meals. Occasionally he would sit with Julia for a short while, but she still didn't have the energy to see people. In fact she chose not to see me when I returned - perhaps she was angry and felt rejected that I had gone away, and now was rejecting me. I don't know - but what I do know is that I wasn't as strong as I thought I was walking back into the situation - all the pain came flooding back. However later that evening she apologised. Choosing to make no comment about her behaviour, I was soon filling her in about what we had done whilst away. I felt a little uncomfortable about telling her too much as the conversation was all one sided. Julia hadn't anything to talk about - her life mostly consisted of lying in bed without the energy to do anything at all.

However, during the following weeks we were encouraged with

some very small signs of improvement. It took about a month before exhaustion allowed Julia to totter out of her bedroom under her own steam when one day I found her sitting quietly in Fiona's bedroom for a change of scenery - she hadn't left her bedroom for months, apart from going to the toilet. Another day she spoke for a few minutes about her engagement. But perhaps the thing that tugged our heart strings most of all, was the fact that when John left the house to go out one day, Julia walked to the landing window and waved to him. He just wept with joy to see his daughter well enough to do this. Although John didn't openly share his emotions as easily as I did, he had nevertheless been deeply upset at seeing Julia so ill. Being very much a person who likes to feel in control, he had grown in adapting to the changing circumstances and was very understanding of Julia. He would spend time just sitting with her, holding her hand, keeping her company in the loneliness of her suffering, Having given her something of himself, he would quietly slip out of the room, and come and find me saying despairingly, "Poor Julia, is there nothing we can do?" and we would invariably hug each other for comfort in our helplessness. As a result of John's tangible expression of love to Julia, their relationship grew much closer.

With so much inevitable focus on Julia I was aware that it would be very easy for Fiona to feel forgotten and marginalised. It was very important to spend time with her and not overlook her needs. Consequently when she was home I tried to arrange special outings, when as a mother and daughter we could get away together and enjoy our relationship. With her forthcoming wedding just a year away we decided to spend a day up in London looking for a wedding dress. This was a very refreshing diversion from the heaviness at home, and we had a wonderful time. I was so grateful that one of my daughters was well enough to enjoy doing things with. After the inevitable cup of coffee, we went straight to a big store where Fiona found the wedding dress of her dreams. A lump stuck in my throat as she tried it on - she looked so beautiful. "I think this is it, Mum,"

Fighting Despair

she said. But because it was the first one she saw, we decided to ask the store to put it aside. Having traipsed round Oxford Street and Knightsbridge we found nothing to beat it, so returned at the end of the day to buy the dress. Fiona wanted to try it on once more so that we could take some photos to show Julia, as we intended to leave the dress at the store until the wedding. Whilst encased in the dressing room, we couldn't help overhearing another bride talk about how tight her wedding dress was, and her need to lose weight. Poor girl - she was getting married in a few weeks time! Fiona and I looked at each other and quietly giggled together as our imaginations ran riot! We were by now so tired that we just slipped into silly mood and anything would have made us laugh. It had been a very productive day:- a wedding dress and samples of material for bridesmaids' dresses.

On our return I wondered how Julia would respond to hearing what we had got up to. In fact even though she was probably hurting inside, she appeared to cope well and came and sat on the top of the stairs for half an a hour listening to Fiona give her a run down of the day's events. Little glimpses of Julia like this were still very rare. Occasionally her face would lighten up with a smile and the brief sound of her laughter would encourage us, but then there were also the dark despondent days when she found it hard to face life as she had lost all hope that she would ever get better. On one of Alison's visits John and I asked her , "Will the Julia we know ever be back?" "I'm sure in time she will get better," was the encouraging reply. Fiona was also feeling this loss as she said, "It's as if my sister has died". All we could do was to lean on God.

This concept of leaning on God is beautifully illustrated in the most precious of love-songs, the Song of Solomon. *Who is this coming up from the desert leaning on her lover?* (1) This is a very intimate picture - it suggests an attitude of complete dependency and reliance, of total trust and assured faith in the one being leaned upon. It also portrays a picture of someone completely at peace with themselves, content not to be totally self-sufficient, without any strength and unable to support themselves. In our helplessness as we lean closer and harder upon the Lord, His love holds us firm. It is His strength made perfect in weakness, not our persistence, that helps us to emerge from the desert. As we leant on Him, It would be His sustaining power that would bring us out of the darkness.

With Julia so ill, it was decided to try and get NHS funding to send her to Oldchurch Hospital in Essex, under her consultant, Professor Findley. They had a small four bedded unit for M.E. sufferers and three years previously Dr Findley had wanted to admit Julia, but at that stage there was no NHS funding available. Now all the stops were being pulled out to fight for it again. When one of the secretaries told me that news had just come through that funding had been granted, I was so relieved that the tears poured forth again. I was under no illusion that the hospital could offer a cure, but it would ease the pressure on us, and hopefully help Julia to move forward. We had been under the impression that Julia would be admitted within weeks, but in the middle of September we heard that for some reason her name had not even been put on the waiting list. This was a major disappointment. When we were asked if we could continue to look after her until October, or even maybe November, John's comment was an emphatic 'no' we couldn't manage until November. My remark was, "I think we can if we have to." All I could do was to trust that God would give us all the strength we needed. Just as well we couldn't look down the road and see that we had to wait several more agonising months before she eventually went in to hospital in the New Year.

In these dark days when Julia was ill enough to be in hospital, but still waiting for a bed, I was caring for her at home. Our experience was that "tomorrow" would be just another day that drifted away from us as one day merged into another. It would have been so encouraging to me emotionally if someone had acknowledged just how ill she was, and that I was doing OK with the caring. But nobody did. I felt isolated and lonely at first, until some practical and medical help was forthcoming:- Alison, Julia's doctor, as supportive as ever, called twice a week, and the district nurse came the other three days. She was a young woman of similar age to Julia so this was another friendly contact from outside the family. Her bathing of Julia on days when she could manage it, lifted the whole issue out of the mother-daughter arena. Even so, a bath often left Julia totally exhausted - this was the sum total of what she could do.

As hour succeeded hour, and day gave way to day, Autumn passed and still it felt as if we were enshrouded in thick fog. When Fiona and Paul visited in October Fiona was so distressed to see her sister still so ill that we ended up in tears, yet again! Julia continued to have more bad days than good days with no major signs of improvement. Occasionally she managed to get dressed, but most of her time was spent in bed. The pain was never-ending. Julia was so ill, but there was nothing more we could do. I felt impotent and it was difficult not to let this feeling of helplessness slip into hopelessness. This was made worse by hearing that the hospital could not offer Julia a bed until the following March. All I could do was to accept that only God could move this mountain, and I would whisper, *"Have mercy, O Lord. Whatever .... whenever."* I felt I couldn't face the future as all the *what ifs* came tumbling out, so I very much lived in the present. I tried to take one day at a time, but several days seemed to attack me at once! Getting away for a 24 hour break once a month became increasingly important, as it was so easy to get discouraged. Despair had become my companion.

The one antidote to despair is hope. Hope is the light at the end of the tunnel, when all around is dark. Without any light to focus on, darkness can be so disorientating that we can become mentally unbalanced, as this story about the actress, Billie Whitelaw demonstrates. On the BBC programme, *In the Psychiatrist's Chair*, she talked about the traumatic experience of acting in *Not I*, as the entire theatre was blacked out, with even the Exit signs covered.

There was not one glimmer of light anywhere to be seen and Billie was completely covered in black clothing, with only her mouth showing through. Sitting on a chair in the middle of the stage in this environment of total darkness, Billie became totally disorientated. She lost all sense of where she was, and began to feel that she was spinning round and falling over and although sitting on a chair, she had the weird sensation of tumbling through the empty darkness. With nothing to focus on, she had no hope of orientating herself so asked for a small, single light to be placed at the back of the auditorium. Focusing on that light enabled her to complete the performance. But the effect on her was so disturbing that she has had to receive medical help since this experience.

Sometimes our darkness can cause us, like Billie Whitelaw, to feel so disorientated that we think we are tumbling down a bottomless pit. The adversity of life can leave us so devastated that hope is buried in the black pit of pain. Often at this point we experience the battle with despair - our hearts deadened to the idea that we will ever be helped or rescued, accompanied by a refusal to struggle and fight. Just as Billie found that focusing on a light gave her bearings, so focusing on Jesus, the Light of the World, gives us a sense of hope in our despair. Christian hope is built on the bedrock of God's love, and reminds us that out of Jesus' death came the glorious resurrection. The resurrection offers hope. However dark life is, it is important to focus on the fact that God is faithful and will never let us go. One day our pain will end and something more glorious will emerge.

Hope is a word about our tomorrows, whereas very often suffering seems to be the word for our todays. Paul, writing to the Romans, advocates a joyous and triumphant life, *We also rejoice in our sufferings, because we know that suffering produces perseverance; perseverance, character; and character, hope. And hope does not disappoint us, because God has poured out his love into our hearts by the Holy Spirit, whom he has given us.* (2) We can experience joy in our suffering because we know that God will bring something good out of pain just as a mother endures the pain of childbirth, because she knows suffering will give birth to a precious new life. Paul traces the process that suffering will bring - starting with pain and ending with hope. Learning to hope in God will save us from trying to anchor our souls in self or the things of this world. As we put our hope in God, His Spirit will flood our hearts with a sense of His love, and this gives us the ability to stand firm in the presence of suffering.

During these months of heartache, my thoughts frequently turned to the role model I find in Jesus. When He was in difficulties and faced suffering, He didn't make a song and dance about it, *He was led like a lamb to the slaughter, and as a sheep before his shearers is silent, so he did not open his mouth.* (3) I didn't want to be a stoic, but neither did I want to open my mouth and shout about my situation to all and sundry, like a Town Crier shouting out to get people's attention. Consequently I didn't say very much, and quietly walked the tight rope, trying to balance my feelings of despondency with confidence in God's faithfulness. In the writings of John of the Cross, he also echoes this principle. "When anything disagreeable happens to you, remember Christ crucified and keep silent. It is impossible to make progress except by working and suffering courageously, always in silence." (4)

As mothers walking the path of suffering, it may be helpful at times to stop and view the landscape and identify where other people are. To me it felt as if I was in a hot, dry, desert where the sand and rock stretched out monotonously to the horizon. Occasionally there were just very little green shoots to be seen. In the distance I could see Julia wilting in the heat of the day, and in her hand was a piece of paper. As I drew near, I could discern the words from the Song of Songs, *Arise, my darling, my beautiful one, and come with me. See! The winter is past; the rains are over and gone. Flowers appear on the earth; the season of singing has come, the cooing of doves is heard in our land. The fig tree forms its early fruit; the blossoming vines spread their fragrance. Arise, come, my darling; my beautiful one, come with me.* (5) A wonderful promise about the first signs of spring appearing. A friend also gave this scripture to Julia, which was a tremendous source of encouragement and comfort as she felt God was saying that the worst was over, and that He would bring her out into a place of growth. *The winter is past* also spoke into the situation of another mother, a friend of mine, called Jill.

Jill was struggling to find hope in the midst of despair in her anguish over her daughter. Here is her story::

"Our eldest daughter Jane was born with cerebral palsy that resulted in severe learning difficulties. In spite of her limitations she grew to be a confident and mature twenty year old, and was able to work part-time and interact socially. We were delighted with her progress.

Against this backdrop a series of incidents involving sexual assault by another adult with learning difficulties occurred and its impact upon Jane was to alter our lives dramatically over the next five years, resulting in me virtually having to give up work to care for her.

Jane first signalled her distress by acute anxiety and withdrawal from normal activities and as the whole picture emerged she became very depressed, regressing to a state of fear, false guilt and paranoia accompanied by outbursts of anger. The lowest point came when Jane had to be admitted to a Psychiatric Assessment Unit because her behavioural problems were so severe. It seemed that things could get no worse and there was little hope on the horizon as there were no resources available in our area for someone with Learning Difficulties.

As a mother I encountered pain at a level that I had never

Fighting Despair

experienced before as it felt as though a sword had pierced my heart. It seemed that the more we prayed the worse Jane got and at times my rage at God would break out. Where was He in all this? Why had He allowed it to happen? Couldn't He at least stop the pain! No easy answers followed but as I took my emotions to God I began to feel a sense of reality. I found that at my lowest points He was often speaking very clearly and I needed to learn to listen - despite my overwhelming feelings.

Hosea spoke powerfully to me: *'Therefore, behold I will allure her - bring her into the wilderness and speak kindly to her. Then I will give her vineyards from there and the valley of Achor as a door of hope.'* (6) **Hope** for me was what I desperately needed - it seemed non-existent in the circumstances. Out of my despair I began praying that God would indeed open 'doors of hope' to encourage and sustain me through this seemingly endless trial.

The doors that opened were many and varied; they did not always mean a change in the circumstances or in Jane's[2] health, but I began to trust God 'even if' things did not change: a deepening confidence in God Himself sustained me. I began to understand Joseph's experience, recounted in Genesis, where his trials seemed to go from bad to worse yet he proved that, *'God can make you fulfilled in the land of your suffering.'* (7)

Some of the many 'doors of hope' opened to me were encouragement and support from friends, pictures from God that helped me understand what was happening, Bible verses and, perhaps the most precious, the discovery of God Himself

---

[2] Jane has improved tremendously and has now moved into her own home shared with three other young women with learning difficulties. She is becoming happier and rebuilding her confidence in both social and work situations. Her anxiety levels still run high at times for which she continues to need medication.

and the depth of His compassion, mercy and love for me. I remember having a picture of shattered glass - symbolising my broken mother heart - and seeing Jesus with tears in His eyes picking up the pieces and with bleeding hands transforming them into a crown of diamonds which he placed on my head. To me this meant that He felt the depth of my mothering pain and, in ways I still cannot fully understand, was transforming it into something precious and of value - the pain would not be wasted."

I could identify with Jill's thoughts and feelings, particularly her sense of despair as on some days my own despair seemed so overwhelming that I felt under a thick cloud. I was struggling to live with the tension of deferred hope. There was a temptation to think that it was better not to hope, than to hope and be disappointed. The words in Proverbs, *Hope deferred makes the heart sick,* (8) brought new understanding to me and this gave me a determination to go on fighting and struggling, because I knew if I didn't I could become ill. Facing reality, that to hope is to become vulnerable to pain, I was learning to live with the pain of deferred longings, rather than take the easier path of freezing all my desires. I was well aware that in carrying so much emotional pain I was prey to depression. In order to fight this, I not only cried out to God and reminded myself of scripture, but also told myself that *"It won't last for ever"*. I was learning to take one step at a time, and rejoiced when I had got through the day as it bought me closer to the time when there would be an end to all the pain. *"That's another day closer to seeing Julia recover,"* was my thought. Fortunately my low, black days were intermittent and didn't last for too long. A counselling friend of mine said she thought I didn't slip into a reactive depression because I could be honest about where I was and cry out my pain. I think I must have cried out at least enough tears to float a liner!

Somehow in God's strength we were making it through and discovering the truth of the verse which assures us that, *God will never let you down; he'll never let you be pushed past your limit; he'll always be there to help you come through it.* (9) It was with a great sense of relief that arrangements were made for Julia to go into Burrswood in December. This was just as much for a change of scenery for Julia, as a break for John and me. It was healthy for all of us. With John away, Mary drove Julia and me to Burrswood. Once we had settled Julia, Mary and I excitedly belted ourselves up in our car seats and set off to find somewhere to have a meal - a celebration of my freedom from caring. Having no responsibilities for a couple of weeks, I enjoyed going down to stay for a weekend with my sister, Andria, and relished the time of just doing things for myself and spending more time with John.

Two weeks later as I drove Julia back from Burrswood, she seemed to be at peace with herself and was excited to be home. We sat chatting away in the kitchen and I was surprised that she managed half an hour sitting up with apparent ease. After a few days at home she decided to go back to her flat for a week. I was very unsure about this as she was still very ill. However the freedom to decide for herself was one of the few luxuries she had left, and I wasn't going to take it away from her. God reminded me that as an eagle pushes out her young from the nest in order to help them fly, Julia was being nudged back into her flat. Then when the eagle's young begin to flounder the mother swoops down and catches them on her back before returning to the nest with them. God wanted me to be ready to catch Julia when she floundered again and bring her back home. So Geoff moved her back to the flat and although Julia was peaking and troughing, she and Geoff laughed a lot over her birthday weekend in December. It was good to see her sense of fun returning. However a couple of days later she deteriorated again and could hardly crawl out of bed. So back home she came and when I saw her having to crawl up our stairs as she didn't have the energy to walk, I again felt I was on the roller-coaster of discouragement. The thought of having her home really ill over Christmas gave way to another torrent of tears. Turning to Mary to offload my emotions, I sobbed down the phone, "Mary, I am finding it so hard to face reality that we are going to have Julia ill again, for yet another Christmas."

Encouragingly Christmas 1996 was not as bad as I thought it might be. I found preaching at the midnight Christmas Eve service quite liberating and over the next few days there were a lot of enjoyable distractions:- Geoff was around for all of the holiday period; Fiona and Paul joined us on Boxing day for a few days, spending one evening with all Fiona's friends in the house; and John and I had the opportunity to catch up with our friends. Although Julia was only well enough to join us for short periods of time, the atmosphere was light and we had many a laugh and played mad games together. Geoff and Paul got on really well and would spur each other on to see who could scoff down the most of my chocolate cake! My future sons-in-law enjoyed my cooking and even now always clamour for my cakes!

Moving into January 1997 we had all returned to the demands of our work, leaving Julia feeling very low, "my life is going nowhere." She was getting bored with the routine of her activity and rest periods - although managing her day like this had certainly helped her to creep forward. Over the past four months she had grown strong enough to get dressed every day, and had more energy and confidence to cope with seeing a few friends again. Although they were very small improvements, at least they were in the right direction. One morning in January the longed and hoped-for phone call from the hospital in Essex came, offering Julia a bed that day. Julia's immediate reaction was, "I can't go . . . . I'm not ready . . . . it's too sudden - I've no time to adjust that's it happening today . . . . I will be on my own with strangers." "But Julia, if you turn this down, you will have to wait much longer again. We don't have to get there until 8 pm this evening - you can see Geoff and say your 'goodbyes' before we travel after rush hour." After a quick phone call to Geoff, the decision was made. She would go.

Fighting Despair

Because of the winter bed crisis, the four M.E. beds in the 6-bed unit had been used for emergencies and Julia's bed was the first one to be released back to its proper use. Thus Julia found herself sharing this unit with five other men - one on continuous oxygen and another who snored horrendously! At one point a very seriously ill young man was placed in the bed next to hers which added to her stress levels as she couldn't avoid hearing some of the very distressing conversations. This was all rather a daunting experience! Fortunately the regime for M.E. patients was to keep the curtains closed round their beds during their rest periods and when they didn't want to be disturbed, so Julia found herself at first hiding behind her curtains for most of the day! Her first week was a settling in period with various tests; the second week was assessments by a multidisciplinary team, and in the last week a programme would be worked out for her. Because Julia had already been adopting a recovery programme, there were no major changes. The team gained her confidence as they completely accepted her with gentleness where she was, and encouraged her by never questioning or condemning her for what she could or couldn't do. Just working freely in the here and now was very therapeutic.

With Julia in hospital John and I got away for a weekend break in the Forest of Dean. We both found it easy to forget the fact that Julia was in hospital, but Geoff and Fiona were finding this thought quite hard to cope with. Half way through her stay there, Geoff and I visited Julia to find her more settled, but longing to come home. Like many NHS staff, their resources were stretched and hence they were too busy to be consistent in their care. There was some helpful advice to put into practice, but on the whole Julia continued very much with the programme she had been managing at home. The greatest help the M.E. team gave, was to build Julia's confidence by encouraging and affirming her that she was managing herself well and doing everything right and reminding her that recovery would not take place overnight, but take considerable time.

When John and I collected her she was relieved to come home as she felt worn out with the constant hustle and bustle of hospital life. Ironically she came out feeling worse than when she went in as she was suffering with swollen glands and sore throat. I felt quite angry about this as she hadn't suffered with swollen glands for several months. But this was soon forgotten as the next day I went off to speak at a conference on "A Place of Rest". The time away was very helpful for me to reflect on what God was doing in all of our lives as a family and to thank Him for all our blessings. In my absence Fiona had come home to help look after Julia, and when I returned I was overjoyed to catch a glimpse of normality. Having heard my car arrive home, the two girls stood at the landing window smiling down at me and shouting, "Hurrah, she's back!" My eyes filled with tears as I entered the house and was greeted with such an atmosphere of joy. Fiona seemed to be her free and happy self, Julia was more communicative, and John was more relaxed. Although Julia still had to spend the greater part of most days in bed she was much brighter. In our different ways we all encouraged her to keep going as we all believed that eventually she would make it back into life again. Fiona said it was the best she had seen her sister for about a year - "She's more like her old self," was the comment. With plans for Fiona's wedding a frequent a topic of conversation over the following weeks, Julia became really excited with the final choice of bridesmaid's dresses - she was planning to walk down the aisle behind her sister! The sociable, fun loving Julia was slowly beginning to surface again.

Towards the end of February Julia's friend, Antoinette, made arrangements to come and visit her for a day. Since they hadn't seen each other for about a year, they had a joyous reunion. After catching up with each other for a while, Antoinette left Julia to have a rest, and joined me for coffee. Sitting round the kitchen table talking together, I noted what an attractive young lady she was with beautiful ebony coloured skin, and the most striking eyes. Suddenly I became aware of these saucer-shaped, brown eyes penetrating my

Fighting Despair

gaze as she looked intensely at me. Quite out of the blue she said, "Chris, I have something serious to talk to you about. You're life has been affected enough with looking after Julia. I have a suggestion to make." The wind was taken out of my sails - what did she mean?

THE PERFECT ROSE

A delicate beautiful rose formed as a precious gift
Pure white, without blemish or spot
Perfectly created in all its splendour
Every petal unfurled in glory . . .
But a petal bruises as the rain lashes down
Another and another as the cruel wind buffets and batters
One final blow and the rose lies crushed
Petals scattered on the ground

The rose and its beauty are no more
The storm fades; stillness falls
A gentle breeze stirs; sweet fragrance fills the air -
The crushed petals release a heavenly scent -
The aroma of Christ which never ends.

Julia

Chapter 13

Blessings

Our daughters will be like pillars carved to adorn a palace
(Psalm 144:12)

Antoinette explained, "As I was entering Julia's bedroom this morning, I sensed that God was telling me to offer to take her back to the flat and look after her there." Hardly daring to believe what I was hearing, I looked away from those big, brown serious eyes - as if looking away would bring home to me that this was only a dream. But I began to realise that it wasn't my imagination playing games, as Antoinette continued, "We are all called to be part of the family of God, and as a sister in Christ to Julia I have a responsibility to relieve you and John, and spend some time in caring for her. You have done your share." This was completely unexpected. I was so taken back at hearing such a generous offer of love, that I burst into tears. "Are you sure? Do you know what you are saying?" "Yes," came the calculated reply, "God has spoken to me."

It transpired that Antoinette was fully involved in a large London church which was encouraging the congregation to move out in acts of faith, in obedience to God. Undergirding this focus was an emphasis on the support of intercessors - to ask God to move what seemed immovable mountains. Antoinette had been open to God about how she was to respond to this challenge, and when she had walked into Julia's room that morning, she had heard the quiet voice of God calling her to serve Him in this way. The thought had not crossed her mind before. It wouldn't be too difficult for her to come and care for Julia for several months as she was in between changing jobs. John, like me, was deeply touched by this offer, and when Antoinette talked to Geoff about it, he was also of the opinion that this was an amazing blessing from God. It was agreed that Antoinette would not mention anything to Julia that day as she wanted first to go back and talk things through with people in her church and make sure she had the prayer backing for such a venture. Having decided to tell no one else until the plans were finalised, I phoned Fiona and told her to pray for Antoinette as she had a very important decision to make. Call it godly intuition, or whatever, Fiona guessed what was going on! But Julia didn't and was quite surprised when Antoinette returned again the following week. With Julia still in bed and wondering what was going on, I left Antoinette with her to break the news. Eventually I was invited to join them and one look at Julia said it all. With her face sparkling with joy, she excitedly said, "This is amazing - what a blessing from God." It was agreed that Antoinette would move into the flat a few weeks later to clean it, followed by Julia just before Easter.

I felt totally humbled that God had chosen to walk into our lives in such a manner. After all the years and months of feeling isolated and overlooked, it was if God was saying, " I've not forgotten you." What a poignant and tangible way He expressed this to us - never in my wildest dreams had I thought something like this would happen. My heart was overflowing with thankfulness.

Over the next few weeks Julia continued to pick up very, very slowly, but when she had done just a bit too much, she became low and weepy again. She couldn't do much more physically than, with help, have a bath most days and the occasional hair wash, but she had more energy to be interested in other people's lives. As far as possible, Julia wanted to be fully involved in the preparations for Fiona's wedding and was excited to be the first to see my outfit for the wedding. This was a long, lemon and lime green soft flowing dress, with a matching lemon jacket and hat. However she then wore herself out trying to describe it to Fiona over the phone! With the impending return to the flat she had to pace herself very carefully as she gathered her things together to move back. It seemed incredible that she had been confined to her bedroom for the best part of the last ten months and had only come downstairs for the first time at Christmas. On the downward journey she would bump down the stairs on her bottom, and Geoff would then carry her back up. This was invariably with a 'piggy back'; sometimes they laughed so much at the indignity of this that it was touch and go whether Geoff could make it to the top before he dropped her! As Julia's limbs became stronger with the passing of time, she was able to crawl up the stairs on all fours.

With Julia now being cared for by Antoinette at the flat I felt incredibly light and free - I no longer had a carer's responsibilities. So it was a bit of a shock to find myself fighting to hold back the tears when leading the Easter Day service. We had just sung the words,

> *Over sin he has conquered:*
> *Hallelujah! He has conquered..*
> *Over death victorious:*
> *Hallelujah! victorious.*
> *Over sickness He has triumphed:*
> *Hallelujah! He has triumphed.*
> *Jesus reigns over all* (1)

Rejoicing in the wonderful Easter story which demonstrates the power of the resurrection over death, I was left struggling with an inner tension. Believing that this same power is available today, I was left feeling sad that God had not triumphed over the sickness in Julia's life here on earth. I almost felt guilty for feeling like this, as it wasn't as if God hadn't demonstrated His power and love in bringing Antoinette into our lives.

Reflecting on the resurrection of Christ I recognised that although suffering remains a painful presence in our world, it has lost its sting. Christ identified himself with our suffering humanity, and died so that we could somehow become like Him. The suffering and death of Christ on the cross, opened up the way for us to enjoy a new relationship with God and the powerful resurrection was a promise of our new life to come. Although we remain captives in a world of suffering today, we can rejoice in the sure and certain hope that there is a new horizon, beyond which we will find ourselves in a new world where there will be an end to all suffering and tears. There is a not-yet element to the final victory of Christ over death and suffering. It was this hope that had kept me going through the years. In *A Journey Through Suffering*, Alister McGrath brings out another aspect of Christ's victory over suffering:

> "There is a day-to-day, moment-by-moment victory, which Christ died to make possible. Each time we suffer, we are being offered an opportunity to claim a small victory over suffering. How? By not allowing it to intimidate us. By not allowing it to succeed in breaking our trust in God. But more than that: we can allow God to speak to us through that suffering. We can allow him to transform us, and to show us new depths of relationships with him, and with others." (2)

It was with the resurrection joy in my heart that John and I went round to the flat to join Julia, Geoff and Antoinette for Easter Day lunch. It was a beautiful, clear spring day and we had a most enjoyable, relaxed time together and Julia was able to sit up for about one and a half hours. The girls appeared to be getting on with each other and Antoinette was taking seriously her responsibilities in caring for Julia. Being joyfully redundant, I left them to get on with their lives together and would pop in only once a week or so. Just being free from having to take meals round gave me a new sense of independence in the ability to get on with my life. As the warmer weather with rising temperatures marked the first signs of summer, Julia's ability to sit outside, heralded the first glimpse of independence. An electric stair lift had been fitted to allow Julia the freedom to go downstairs when she wanted and sit outside on a little wall by the front door. This was no distance for her to walk, and sometimes when she knew I was due to visit, she would be sitting on the wall waiting for me. It was such a delight for me to see her sitting there to welcome me. Her face beamed from ear to ear as her expression said, " Look, I'm well enough to do this now." As she grew stronger over the summer months, occasionally an ice cream van would stop outside the flat, and she would enjoy the independence of buying herself an ice cream and sitting on the wall savouring it. To many people this would be a very insignificant event, but to us it was a considerable step forward. Although progress was still very slow, overall, new ground was being covered.

On the whole, the relationship between Julia and Antoinette had worked well. However Julia sensed that Antoinette was disappointed that despite all the intercessory prayer backing from her church in London, there had been no major healing. In the early days of June, Antoinette began to talk to me about leaving. Feeling immensely grateful to her for all that she had done I couldn't help but feel wobbly about the timing of this. Julia was still not well enough to look after herself and I didn't want her to have the stress of living by herself again, with Fiona's wedding only two months away, so I was honest with Antoinette and said that I thought the best time for her to leave would perhaps be at the end of July, just before the wedding, so that Julia had no major changes to cope with. We prayed that the time would be ripe whenever she decided to go, and I asked God to give me grace to accept whatever the outcome, and trust Him in it. A few days later Antoinette came and told me that she had decided to leave at the end of June. I felt at peace about this, and Julia graciously accepted the impending loss of her friend and carer. Acknowledging their thankfulness to Antoinette for all that she had done, Geoff and Julia marked her farewell with a candlelit dinner at the flat. Antoinette had joined us for a season of our lives, and I will always be grateful to her for the love and compassion she had given us all, particularly Julia. She was a very special person.

When one significant person leaves one's life, it is hard to trust God for another particular person to fill the hole, so we began praying for another flat mate. In the meantime Julia remained alone in the flat, and although she coped in some ways, in other ways she was lonely and found it difficult to stop and rest with no one else around. Geoff did what he could, popping in before school and then going round to make the evening meal. Very slowly Julia began to walk outside - at first just along the drive, and then increasing the distance every seven to fourteen days. Some days I used to accompany her on this activity, and at other times on a warm summer's evening she and Geoff would walk into her colourful garden which was exploding with flowers. As she grew in confidence and strength, her independence grew too and occasionally she took a walk outside by herself. We were optimistic that by August she would be able to manage 40-50 metres - the length of the aisle she wished to walk down as a bridesmaid at her sister's wedding.

Another small step Julia achieved was a one-off short car journey to Geoff's house, which was fortunately only an eight minute drive away. Three weeks before Fiona's wedding, they invited us round for a meal and gave us some news that left me completely speechless. Out of the blue Julia said, "This may come as a surprise to you, but we are planning to get married on October 25 this year." I was so shocked that I felt paralysed. I couldn't say anything or take anything else in. With my thoughts rapidly speeding round the race track of my mind, I tried to comprehend the ramifications of this decision especially as we were up to our eyes with Fiona's wedding. I imagined a quiet, low key affair so I was even more stunned when I heard them say they wanted a big wedding, inviting all the people who had supported them over the years! Struggling to regain my equilibrium, I didn't burst into tears, but got up from my chair and went round to give them both a big hug. As a mother all my anxieties rose within me. I wanted to stop them from making such a major decision and say, *"But Julia, you are only just beginning to recover - the stress of a wedding and moving house could set you back months again. If you want to get married then, why at least don't you have a quiet, low key wedding?"* But I knew it was not the time to immediately tell them my honest reaction, I didn't want to spoil their news. As if knowing that I would find their plans difficult to take in, Julia continued, "But mum, we have to get married during

Geoff's school holidays and knowing that we don't want a Christmas wedding, we would have to wait until next Easter, and we don't want to do that. Neither of us want to spend another winter apart, especially with Geoff having to travel to and fro in the dark to visit me, and with me living all alone." "Fine, you must do what you want to do," I tried to say convincingly. Continuing in their excitement, Geoff said, "We've made some plans already. The church is booked and we've booked an old vintage car." With that, they pulled out a brochure, pointing to the car they had chosen. I couldn't take it in - they could have chosen a sky blue pink car for all I knew! All I could think of was the implications of this astounding news. There were only three weeks to Fiona's wedding, then another eleven weeks to Julia's. The timescale would have been demanding enough with two healthy daughters, but knowing that Julia would need so much extra support made the prospect even more mind boggling. *"Lord, we're going to need all the strength and grace to cope with this one,"* I whispered to God.

Feeling not only numbed and shocked, but also very fearful and troubled, I couldn't sleep that night so I turned to God and asked Him to show me whether I was being unnecessarily apprehensive. It was as if He gave me the reassurance that He was in control and I was filled with a peace that enabled me to face all the stresses and strains that lay ahead. John's reaction to the news was very positive although like me he wondered how wise the timing was. However Fiona gave me her usual reassurance that her sister wasn't doing anything daft, reminding me that, "No time will be the right time for them with Julia not well, they've just got to go for it as best as they can."

We all decided that apart from Geoff's parents, the news would be kept secret until after Fiona's wedding, as we didn't want to detract from her special day. The only two things we planned to organise over the next few weeks before Fiona's August wedding, were somewhere for the reception and buying Julia's wedding dress.

Geoff, John and I went round looking at suitable places for the reception, but at such short notice it was difficult to find a place to match our requirements. It had to be within easy travelling distance as Julia often felt nauseated even with short car journeys; and because she couldn't use stairs everything had to be on the ground floor, including a room for her to lie down and rest in. To our delight we happened to find a very suitable place in Sonning (just outside Reading) which was free until 6 pm. This suited us well as Julia wasn't well enough to have an evening function, and we thought a deadline was a good thing as it meant she couldn't wear herself out with too long a day. The staff were also very accommodating in meeting our requirements. They made arrangements to screen off a corner of the reception room that wouldn't be used, and to lay a mattress on the floor for her use. We were all thrilled as we couldn't have found a more suitable place and although Julia hadn't seen it, we reassured her that she would really like it.

Now came the job of finding a wedding dress. Unfortunately I put Julia under some unnecessary stress, as I thought it was a good idea to go to a shop which hires them out, and ask to borrow some dresses over the weekend for Julia to try on. Perhaps I was too persuasive in encouraging Julia to agree to this idea, as she didn't mention that she had seen a wedding dress she really liked in a magazine. Arriving at the flat with five wedding dresses over my arm, I was concerned to find Julia looking very pale and tired so we decided to try them on with at least a 30 minute interval so as to give her a rest in between. By the time we got to the fourth dress on the Sunday afternoon I was beginning to feel anxious as I could see she was becoming exhausted and I detected that she was getting stressed not only with the effort of trying them on, but by the fact that none of them were really what she wanted. Then she showed me the dress of her dreams in a wedding magazine. Returning home I said to John, "This is the very thing I was worried about - she's exhausting herself just in thinking about what she wants and in trying dresses on." But there was nothing I could do.

Our next line of action was to phone all the local stockists for the dress she really liked in the magazine, explaining to them Julia's position and asking if I could bring the dress home for her to try on. Soon John and I found ourselves driving off to Marlow for that dream dress. Having put a small deposit on it, we were able to bring it home late on the Saturday, to be returned on the Monday. Again, we were so grateful for people being so accommodating to our situation. Fortunately the dress turned out to be all that Julia hoped it would be and John, the proud father, took it back to the shop on the Monday and ordered a new one. Phew! I heaved a sigh of relief. Now I could forget about Julia's wedding and turn my thoughts to Fiona's.

With two weeks to go, Fiona came home to pack up all her belongings. Not wanting to miss out, Julia also came home for the weekend and it was so good to hear the house ringing with squeals of delight and laughter as they discovered forgotten memorabilia from the past. It was such a blessing to have our last weekend together as a family filled with such joy and happiness. As we waved Fiona off in a car packed tight with boxes, John and I shared a precious moment together knowing that we were closing the chapter on having a single daughter - the next time she came home would be as a married woman.

Fiona had decided to get married in the church in Ferndown, Dorset, where she and Paul worshipped. At first she was concerned whether I would be upset, but I was quite content to go along with what they wanted. We were blessed with different people in their church offering us accommodation, which meant that Julia and Geoff could travel down eight days before the wedding to give plenty of time for Julia to recover from the journey. However she had recovered enough by the next day to surprise Fiona at her hen party, popping in for an hour, early evening, before the rest of them went out for a meal.

I drove down to Ferndown on the Wednesday before the wedding to be involved in the final preparations. Dropping in to see Julia and Geoff, it was clear that Julia was becoming rather anxious about how she would cope with the big day as she was very fatigued. I talked her through her anxieties, reassuring her that we weren't putting any expectations on her, just having her there was a bonus for us. If she couldn't walk down the aisle then Geoff could push her in the wheelchair, and that would be fine. But I knew of her inner longing to walk behind her sister - she didn't want to let her down. Leaving Julia I felt rather strained and anxious myself about how well she would manage the next couple of days of waiting for the big day to arrive.

In contrast, Fiona was a bundle of energy and joy and had no obvious anxieties about her wedding day! Running around in the car that afternoon doing lots of small errands with Fiona directing me here, there and everywhere, I began to bring up my concerns about how Julia would cope with Saturday. With an irritated sigh, which I rarely get from Fiona, she changed the subject. I got the message - she didn't want to know what was happening to Julia. Fair enough, this was her wedding and she didn't want any distractions. So I made a conscious decision not to mention the topic again. Instead I took my concerns to the Lord and He comforted me with the promise, *Cast your cares on the Lord and he will sustain you; he will never let the righteous fall.* (3)

With the last few days before any wedding there are always hiccups and I received a phone call from Geoff saying Julia was panicking. "Can you come over and talk to her", was his urgent request. There was a miscommunication between the girls over Julia's visit to the church to familiarise herself with it and when she practised walking up and back down the aisle she suddenly felt fatigued and faint and thought she had overdone it. Feeling very fearful she panicked that she would not have enough energy for the wedding. Driving over in the car I had butterflies in my stomach, not knowing how I would find Julia. I found her very anxious and somewhat cross with me, "You and Fiona underestimated the length of the aisle - it is much, much longer than you told me." Apologising profusely I tried to calm her down by saying that I was sure she would be all right on the day and would be able to manage just walking one way, and that the waiting was the hardest part. After a while she began to relax and we were able to laugh together. I always knew when Julia was relaxed as I could say or do something daft that would make her laugh. After praying together I left to return to Fiona and Paul.

The Friday was a hectic day as I was involved in some of the flower arranging so I spent most of the day working away in the cool of the church. Outside it was blisteringly hot as we were having a heat wave - we hoped that it would last for another day! Late afternoon, once I had finished the flowers, I made a quick to visit to Julia. I found her still anxious and nervous but fortunately not as panicky as the previous day. But wedding nerves were surfacing with Fiona and Paul! They weren't exactly having an easy time as things were quite tense between them.

Waking up to another glorious, hot morning, I had a sense that God was going to bless the day and that everything would run smoothly. Fiona appeared calm, and when I drove the hairdresser over to do Julia's hair, I found her nervous but in control. Little did I know that Julia had woken with a thumping migraine and every time she lifted her head it throbbed, spinning wildly! Geoff prayed and sat quietly with her as she rested in bed - telling herself not to panic as there were still four hours to go. As she focussed on getting ready in small stages, the headache slowly receded. Finally, on a scorching hot day, we all gathered together in the church porch. With her proud father beside the bride, Fiona looked radiant in an off the shoulder dress with a boned bodice, decorated with pearls and Julia was sitting in her wheelchair, looking very attractive in a purple dress.

As a mother I felt relieved and delighted that Julia had made it. My parting words were, "Enjoy yourselves, girls," and with that the wedding spun into action.

We enjoyed a wonderful day - everything went smoothly. To see Julia walk down the aisle as a bridesmaid was all that we had hoped for. It didn't matter that she didn't join the wedding party in the vestry or walk back down the aisle, nor the fact that she quietly and sensitively disappeared periodically for a rest before finally slipping away after half an hour at the reception when she became sapped of all her energy. She has subsequently told us that because we were all so laid back and relaxed she didn't feel anxious and under pressure, so was free to do what she could and thus enjoy the day. For the first time she felt as if John, Fiona and I accepted her where she was and said, "You even laughed as I was carried down the church steps - with everyone looking on; for once you didn't wince with embarrassment!"

Fiona and Paul made a delightful couple and were very at ease with each other and with the day. In the evening we had great fun with a lively barn dance and having waved Fiona and Paul off in their car covered with shaving cream and the usual balloons at around 10 pm, we went on dancing until nearly midnight. Not surprisingly John and I were exhausted the next day. Fortunately with the heat wave continuing we were able to go off and laze on the nearby sandy beach and catch up on ourselves.

With Fiona and Paul away on honeymoon in Ireland, Julia and Geoff stayed in their bungalow for the following week to give Julia time to recover. The effect of the wedding with such a huge demand upon her resources laid her flat out for several days and when she returned to Reading the cost was still evident as she had very little energy to do anything.

But looking on the bright side of things, God was blessing us in other ways. Julia had a new South African flat mate, Theresa, a very gentle young lady who was very willing to help practically where she could when not at work. She had moved in a few days before Julia went down for the wedding, so when Julia returned there was someone in the flat for company. Theresa and Julia quickly established a very close friendship and were both very supportive to each other, with Theresa offering to be involved in Julia's wedding in any way she could help. God had again provided just the right person for Julia.

With ten weeks to finalise the plans and preparations I knew time was tight. So Julia and I made a list of all the big decisions she had to make: bridesmaid's dress, invitations, bouquets, flowers, and wedding dress fitting, etc. and we made a plan to tackle one of these major items every week. There were no spare weeks, as we had at least ten major tasks on our list

At the end of August Fiona came home so that together we could look for a veil for Julia and for her bridesmaid's dress. Fortunately we found a dress in a deep wine colour that not only suited Fiona's auburn colouring, but was also one of Julia's and Geoff's favourite colours. Plans were coming together and although Julia continued to feel very exhausted, we were on track. In the midst of all these preparations John and I went off to Israel for ten days as we were leading a tour there for the first time.

It wasn't ideal disappearing only four weeks before the wedding, but we had no choice as arrangements for this holiday had been made at the beginning of the year. Leaving my concerns for Julia behind, we had a wonderful time, only to hear on our return that Julia had felt so fatigued whilst we were away she had got quite low, and was now suffering with a cold and swollen glands again. My immediate reaction was to feel upset and angry as I questioned, *"Are they pushing things too far in getting married this October?"* My second reaction was to take my feelings to God and as I was praying, these words from Isaiah came to me, *I am he who will sustain you. I have made you and I will carry you.* (4) It was as if God was saying that He would not only sustain and carry me through all the preparations, but that would also be true for Julia.

We lost a couple of weeks in our preparations as Julia was too ill to do anything and had to cut back on her involvement as she just didn't have the energy. As she began to pick up again time was running out - we had planned to leave the final week with no major decisions or outings. However in the event I had to take her to the florist to finalise the bouquets the Monday before the wedding. We were sailing a bit close to the wind! Visiting the florist two weeks before by myself for an initial enquiry I had a niggling apprehension about whether the florist was good enough for what Julia wanted, and when Julia visited her on the Monday she also had doubts. But I was so emotionally exhausted in supporting Julia through all the preparations and having to do so much myself, I couldn't face chasing round for another florist within four days of the wedding. Also I didn't think that it was a good idea to put Julia under this sort of stress. However it was a decision we would regret.

The remainder of the final week sped by uneventfully, with Julia taking a back seat and resting as much as possible. Like any bride to be, this proved to be very difficult as her emotions swung from excitement to anxiety, with "nerves jumping around inside of me!" Geoff had slowly been taking some of her furniture and belongings over to his place and he had done enough in the house to make it possible for Julia to move in. As it was an old terraced house he had put in a new bathroom upstairs, and whilst they were away on honeymoon the stair lift was to be moved from the flat to their new home. But for the moment the stair lift was needed in the flat as Julia remained there until the wedding. In addition to all the other arrangements, we had given considerable thought to the question of how Julia could best manage her wedding day, and we had therefore scheduled rest times into the overall plan.

The day before the wedding I was tied up for most of the afternoon and early evening with flower arranging again so only briefly popped in to see Julia. To keep her mind focused, she had set herself a small task of wrapping up a 'thank you' gift for one of the ushers and I went round to help her with this. Everything seemed to be under control and although understandably nervous, she seemed to have the energy to chat quite freely. Fiona arrived late afternoon and stayed at the flat. It was a great help for me to know that Fiona was looking after Julia as she was very understanding and supportive of her sister, and together with Theresa I knew they would be fine.

Waking in the early hours of the following morning, my thoughts turned to the nagging fear that had been at the back of my mind through all the wedding preparations - that on her wedding day, Julia would wake up feeling really ill with headache and swollen glands. Facing my fears, I recognised that the worse scenario would be that she might be too ill to walk down the aisle, and once officially married she might have to disappear, leaving us all to carry on with the celebrations without the bride! In order to overcome my natural anxieties I had to keep reminding myself that God had promised to sustain and carry her, and that He was in control. Holding on to this gave me some peace, and my anxiety diminished as the morning unfolded. Around 8 am I cycled round to pop a card through Julia's door, and to my surprise the girls called out to me - they were waving from the window as they munched banana and custard for breakfast! *"Well, so far so good"* I said to myself as I cycled back down the path, and when I received a phone call from Fiona at about 9.30 am saying that everything their end was going smoothly, and that Julia was coping and was OK I felt a weight lift off my shoulders. *"Thank you, Lord,"* I whispered.

Although the day had got off to a good start we had a major hassle over the bouquets - our doubts about the florist were realised. The bouquets were not as we had asked for or expected and when Julia saw them she burst into tears. *"We could have done without this emotional crisis,"* I thought. Julia loved flowers, but her disappointment with them was evident. At least Julia's bouquet was better than the bridesmaid's, which quite frankly I felt embarrassed about - it was nothing. In fact Fiona discreetly lost the bouquet as soon as she could! Julia's flowers had not been wired into a handle as requested, and with so little strength she was upset with the difficulty she had in holding them. With very little time to spare I found myself driving down into Reading town in the middle of a busy Saturday morning, to ask for a wired handle to be fitted. One could sense the mood of disappointment and anxiety amongst the girls and I tried very hard to lighten the atmosphere and say, "Come on, we can't do anything about the flowers now. People will be looking at how beautiful you look, not at the flowers - it's not the end of the world." Inwardly however I could have kicked myself that we hadn't gone with our intuition and found another florist. However, there was no point in crying over spilt milk!

Having carefully planned the timetable for the morning, Julia began to fall behind schedule as her hair took over an hour, instead of the anticipated twenty minutes. She looked very attractive with her hair rolled up, with little rosebuds placed here and there, but after having this done she felt so exhausted she needed to lie down and rest. During this rest time I quickly drove home to change into my outfit - a mauve, blue three piece suit with a large rimmed hat (which I forgot to check in the mirror that it was at the right angle!), and rejoined the beautician and Fiona as we sat around waiting for Julia to recover. Time ticked by. Quarter to one passed . . . . Ten to one passed . . . . . and the wedding was at 1 pm! I didn't want to hassle Julia as I knew she might become anxious and panicky and then not enjoy the day - after all this was a huge day for someone who was so ill and rarely goes out - so I just said to her, "It's your day, people can wait." But it was the father of the bride who became increasingly anxious as we waited, and he had to summon all his patience to keep quiet so as to avoid upsetting the bride. Julia was getting married at our home church and therefore we knew there were no other weddings that day. Eventually she emerged and without appearing to hurry her, we tried to speed things up. Fiona had already left for the church, and we told her to reassure Geoff, resplendent in morning dress, that Julia *was* coming, but that she would be late!

Arriving about twenty minutes late, on a sunny Autumn day, the bride entered church with her Dad whispering reassuring words, " You look beautiful, ... you'll make it down the aisle, lean on me." As I turned to watch her float down the aisle in a beautiful cream brocade dress with an elegant train, I realised that, like me, many friends in the congregation who knew of Julia's struggle, were moved to tears - they were streaming down my face. She had made it - what a relief. During the first hymn Julia very nearly fainted, but as she caught a glimpse of the congregation out of the corner of her eye, she felt "a wave of love which lifted me up and carried me throughout the rest of the day." It was a very touching service with Julia and Geoff sitting throughout, and the church packed with people. One could sense the love and support people were giving Julia as she took this step forward into marriage and for Geoff as he promised to care for his new wife. During the signing of the register, Fiona and Paul sang some worship songs that were so beautiful as they harmonised together, again there was many a tear in people's eyes. Seeing Julia and Geoff walk back down the aisle as a radiant married couple, I glanced across at John. Our eyes met and unspoken words of joy and relief were exchanged.

With the service over, it was arranged that Julia would go to the vestry in her wheelchair to have a rest before the official photographs were taken in the church. Whilst this was going on, all the church guests were invited into the church hall where there was a finger buffet and wedding cake. Members of our congregation had organised a wonderful spread and it was a good way of filling the time in between the service and the main reception, particularly as Julia had to rest for much of the time. (However the rests never happened as time was running out!). In the midst of speaking to friends, someone told me that Julia wanted to see me. Wondering what was going on, I knocked on the door of the vestry to find Julia and Geoff sitting and relaxing, laughing away. "What's up?" I asked, quite relieved to see that it was nothing serious. "Mum, my bra wasn't done up properly. As I walked up the aisle I felt this ping" "So we had a lopsided bride waltzing down the aisle then!" Having fixed her up, I left them both enjoying the quiet of the moment together.

The day continued to run smoothly but by the time we arrived at the reception we were way behind schedule. I was promptly told by the staff that everyone had to sit down for their meal immediately as we were late! This caused a few problems as we hadn't yet had any formal photos taken in the grounds - we managed to negotiate a five minute photo call. The other major factor was that Julia was due for another rest. This had to be abandoned. However, half way through the meal, she and Geoff disappeared behind the screen giving time out again for Julia to lie down as she was overcome with exhaustion. It was unusual to have a wedding breakfast without the bride and groom, but it didn't worry me. Some people accepted this, but a few couldn't understand why Julia didn't have the energy to talk to guests - but that was their problem! The happy couple appeared again for the speeches, but not surprisingly Julia was becoming really exhausted, so when it came to the cutting of the cake, Jackie, Geoff's mum, and myself were invited to cut it on their behalf. Seeing Julia rapidly waning in energy, I encouraged her to start thinking about changing whilst she still had some strength left and with that Fiona took her off in the wheelchair.

As we waved the happy couple off on honeymoon, which was only a ten minute drive away, I felt very thrilled with the day's events and proud that my daughter had managed it so well. My overriding feeling was one of thankfulness to God - Julia's marriage was the miracle that had happened in the midst of the illness. Although God had not restored her yet to health, He had, against the odds, given her a wonderful caring husband. I don't honestly know how I would have coped with the pain of seeing Fiona happily married, and Julia being left behind to face a life of pain and loneliness. Fortunately I didn't have to face this, God in His mercy had richly blessed us as a family, particularly Julia.

A PRECIOUS LIFE

Father I see your hands stretched out towards me
Open, held together as if you ask something of me,
Something I can place in your hands - but what?
Nothing rises within me, though many things come to mind.
But your hands are held out - so gently, so silently, so poignantly
This is not the time nor the moment to pile on the mound of little things.
Your hands look so worn from many years of caring, loving, guiding,
Yet strong and firm as if they could effortlessly carry anything.
As I see these hands reaching out steadily before me
Tears well up in my eyes at their vulnerability
Not demanding . . . just waiting, so patiently . . .
Vulnerable . . . I may never put my hands in yours, like a trustful child
Father I see your hands stretched out towards me
Yearning to lift me, to love me and tenderly mould me.
In the silence of the moment I weep -
All I can place in them is my trust for my life,
My trust in your timing, your freedom,
For all that lies ahead I cannot see;
Father now my fragile, precious life cradled
In your loving hands for me.
Julia

Chapter 14

Hidden Treasure

Ascribe to the Lord the glory due to his name (Psalm 29:2)

With Julia and Geoff happily away on honeymoon, arrangements were made for the stair lift and an intercom system to be installed in their house. The intercom was placed in the lounge and also in their bedroom, making it easy for Julia to speak to anyone who might ring the doorbell. Whilst I spring-cleaned the house, friends decorated the rooms with flowers and balloons to greet their arrival home.

Once home and unpacked, they phoned to say how much they had enjoyed their time away. Not surprisingly Julia was exhausted during their honeymoon but they made it special in little ways: Geoff took her in the wheelchair along the nearby embankment of the River Thames; they enjoyed fireworks in the garden, with Julia watching from the window. I was conscious that as newly-weds settling into a new life together, they needed time and space to adjust. I didn't want to intrude as Geoff had now taken on the responsibilities as the main carer. However I thought it was important to talk through with them, their expectations of my role, and for me to say what support I could offer them. It was decided that every Wednesday I would go round at lunch time and spend the afternoon with Julia, taking them a meal I had already cooked. This would give Geoff a day's break from cooking. The other task of which I relieved Geoff was all the ironing - fortunately I found this quite relaxing and would work through the pile whilst Julia had a rest. Another offer came from Dorothy, a friend from church, who ended up doing their weekly shop as she worked in a large superstore. This was another great help - so all in all we were giving them practical support in areas where it was most needed.

The months running up to Christmas were uneventful as Julia gradually adjusted to a larger house and thoroughly enjoyed making

Hidden Treasure 229

it home for them both. Julia came up with creative interior design ideas and found it immensely fulfilling watching Geoff do the DIY jobs with the occasional helping hand from her as she found herself having a go for five minutes or so. As a married couple they seemed to be blissfully happy and adjusting well. They entertained John and me one evening to a delicious meal and we had a really enjoyable time, accompanied with much laughter. It was really special for us, her parents, to see Julia walk to the front door with Geoff and wave us goodbye - the picture of them standing together looking so happy was a memory we treasured.

Entering another new year (1998) it wasn't long before the dark clouds began to gather again. By March Julia was beginning to show signs of deteriorating, becoming very fatigued, and although she paced herself sensibly, by April she was looking really wan and ill. As the weeks silently slipped by, her energy quietly and unobtrusively leaked away from her. I was beginning to identify a measure of depression returning as her thought patterns became distorted. Standing helpless and watching all this going on brought back something of the old pain and inner tension. We had seen Julia improve and then deteriorate so many times before it felt as if I was back on that roller-coaster of emotions. For instance, when Geoff invited himself and Julia over for a Sunday lunch I was so excited to welcome them, particularly as Julia hadn't visited us for several months, that I eagerly cooked a special meal for them. But my enthusiasm was shattered when Geoff phoned up to say Julia was too ill to even get out of bed.

When our hopes and expectations for our children are dashed over and over again, inevitably disappointment follows and our emotions often feel as if they are taking a roller-coaster trip. We climb the steep hill of anticipation and are just beginning to relax and enjoy the beautiful view, when, without any warning we plunge downhill at a speed that forces every breath out of our body. Then we are thrown around at high speed as we hit the twisting and turning track. With so much centrifugal force threatening to throw us overboard, we hold on tight to the handles. Screaming with terror on a ride we cannot control, we feel it will never end. It seemed to me that I had been on this roller-coaster ride so many times before, that in its familiarity the horror was slowly losing its power. Although I still felt the stomach-launching bumps as I careered downhill feeling out of control, I was learning to relax and hold on to God.

I am sure Julia must have felt she was on an equally crazy roller coaster ride. Over the past eight years there had been times when she had slowly and painstakingly climbed up the side of a steep hill, only to find herself losing the energy to hold on to her footing, so slipping and falling down the hill again, losing all the ground gained. When she hit the bottom, and saw how far she had fallen, discouragement set in. In one dark moment she said, "It's not worth trying to climb up the hill again, only to fall back down it." Seeing herself deteriorate once more, Julia became quite low. Feeling too fatigued to see anyone, she kept me at arm's length so that she and Geoff could work through things together and learn to lean on each other in new ways. Consequently I had not seen her for ten days.

Standing in the surgery reception area one morning waiting for a patient to arrive, I couldn't help hearing a telephone message come through from Geoff, asking to speak to Alison. I tried to argue with myself that this was probably not serious, until I saw Alison walk out of the surgery carrying Julia's notes. Knowing that it was unprofessional to cross confidential boundaries and ask what was going on, I was left with a nagging anxiety. This was not allayed when I phoned Geoff a couple of days later to ask about Julia, only to be told, "She's just very tired and fatigued." I felt so frustrated that was all he would say, I knew she was more than just fatigued. Perhaps they were trying to work things out in their own way and had not wanted to concern me. In talking subsequently about this situation they voiced the fact that as my concern became evident in again seeing my daughter relapse, this in turn triggered off a greater

Hidden Treasure

anxiety in Julia. So what had appeared to me as Geoff's unwillingness to give me the whole picture, was in fact just his way of trying to protect Julia from further anxiety. The other factor they mentioned was that it would have been helpful to them if I had gone round and sat and talked with them about my fears and concerns, so they had an opportunity to say what was really going on. It's easy to be wise in retrospect!

John and I stayed over the half term with Fiona and Paul and inevitably our concern for Julia became the topic of conversation. Together we decided that Paul should phone Geoff to ask how things were as he would probably open up more to him than to any of us. Geoff admitted that things were not easy and he sounded weary with the strain. John and I were in a dilemma. Not wanting to interfere, but recognising that Geoff was feeling the stress of caring for Julia, we decided to call in unannounced with some flowers, on our way home. We found Geoff anxious and as we talked, he slowly began to open up. He appreciated us calling round, and although we didn't see Julia as she was in bed feeling too fatigued to see anyone, Geoff suggested I pop in the next day.

Often I felt as if I was walking a tightrope of not knowing how much to say to Julia and Geoff, when to keep quiet and when to voice my concerns. I didn't want to interfere, and wanted to adhere to the mother-in-law rule - only give advice when asked! At times I found it quite perplexing to know how to hold the tension with the boundary between being a mother and counsellor. Occasionally through counsellor's eyes I could see things happening , yet chose to keep quiet for I am a mum to my daughter, not a counsellor. This was a difficult balance which I am sure I didn't always get right. The girls sometimes teased me about being in counsellor mode!

Arriving to see Julia the next day, I was shocked to see her sitting curled up on the floor looking very drawn, pale and weepy. I sat on the floor with her, as we tried to have something of a conversation together. But it wasn't easy. Julia cried, "I'm frustrated that I can't do anything. If I accept where I am and face reality, I then end up feeling angry with what I have lost. But I haven't the energy to deal with this anger so end up feeling frustrated all over again. Then because I haven't the energy to deal with anything, all my thoughts tumble out of control like laundry tossed around in a tumble dryer. I'm trapped." It was very sad to see her like that - no wonder Geoff was needing a listening ear. As I came away I cried tears of sadness - however I was optimistic as this time it was recognised much quicker that Julia was on a pathway heading for depression and her medication was changed.

The following week I became more involved again in her care. The district nurse continued to bath her once a week, and I went in to bath her at other times, which was encouraging as there were some little signs that she was improving. But she still didn't have the energy even to join us for John's sixtieth birthday celebrations. This was a strange evening. On the one hand we were all enjoying partying, yet we were very conscious that Julia was not with us. The pain of this for me certainly took some of the joy out of the evening, and to see Geoff by himself without his new wife by his side, further twisted the knife.

But the pain didn't stop there; the knife was driven in further with the events of the next day. Fiona and Paul were staying with us, so I cooked Sunday lunch at home and took it round for us to have it all together at Julia and Geoff's. Although Julia joined us for half an hour, she was obviously not well and didn't really join in the conversation. All of us were subdued and although we kept chatting to make the atmosphere light, it felt heavy with sadness and concern. At 11 pm that evening, the phone rang. A quiet, panicky voice was on the other end of the line, saying she was frightened. Geoff had gone to bed and fallen asleep early (9.00 pm!), and Julia was feeling very anxious as she had no one to talk to. After I had spoken quietly and reassuringly to her on the phone, she began to feel more in control. "Please pray for me, Mum," was her request, so I prayed with her over the phone asking God to fill her with His peace. Putting the phone down, I cried out my tears of frustration to God. *"God, what are you doing? You say you answer prayer, I may as well be talking to a brick wall!"* But it wasn't long before I was saying, *"Thank you that you alone see this situation from a heavenly perspective - thank you that you are the Creator and Sustainer of the universe, the Sovereign Lord over all."*

The next day at work Ken, our mental health facilitator spoke to me about Julia. He and Alison had been discussing different options to try and get relevant help for her. They had discussed a number of possibilities: referral to a psychologist for cognitive behaviour therapy; or an assessment with a psychiatrist. On hearing the word psychiatrist I just broke down - having heard stories of how some psychiatrist's treat people with M.E., there was no way I wanted Julia to go through this. I suggested the logical thing would be to phone Julia's consultant in Essex who worked with a multidisciplinary team. As Ken went off to report my thoughts to Alison, I was left feeling isolated and helpless. I would have liked to have been involved in their discussion - after all they were talking about my daughter. But I wasn't invited. Although still her mother, I had to accept the fact that I was no longer responsible for her - Geoff was her next of kin - although he wasn't in on the discussion either! Once I had thought all this through, I found the situation easier to accept. Fortunately the outcome worked out well as Alison arranged for a multidisciplinary team to see Julia at home.

Calling round to give Julia frequent baths, I became increasingly upset to see her so ill. Although I would appear bright when I was with her, invariably I came away with tears of sadness. One day, I was crying out to God to give me a Bible verse that would sustain me with hope. *The Lord will sustain him on his sick-bed and restore him from his bed of illness* (1) was the reply. Reflecting and meditating on this verse has given me a new way of praying for

Julia. Over the first years of the illness I asked God to heal her; then when she became very ill I found myself not having the faith to pray like that, so asked God to sustain her with His grace; now, having heard God speak this verse to me, every day I declare this truth. *"Thank you Lord, that you have sustained Julia on her sick-bed, and promise to restore her from her bed of illness."* Standing in faith, waiting for this promise to be fulfilled is not easy. I believe that this will come about in God's time - and that might mean, not until eternity.

Within a month Julia had significantly improved and was soon able to make the short walk out into their garden. Feeling strong enough for a short journey, she and Geoff managed to get away in August for a pre-booked holiday in a nearby cottage. John, Fiona and I visited them there for a meal one evening, and it was encouraging to see Julia with more energy. On our way home, Fiona remarked, "How good it is to see Julia so much better and more like herself." Indeed, it was heartening to see her over the summer months, climbing back up the hill. That summer was the first time in seven years that John and I didn't have Julia either at home, or have the responsibility for caring for her at the flat. Knowing that she was in a recovery phase enabled us to enjoy our new freedom as we began to have time for each other again.

Feeling better, Julia began thinking about having a cat for company, to break up the loneliness and monotony of the day. Medical establishments throughout Britain recognise the value of companion animals. An animal psychologist points out: "You need someone to say, 'You're wonderful, you still matter'. Pets do it so generously and continuously and without complaint," (2) and this was true for Julia.

Without Julia having to use up any energy, God met her desire by bringing a stray cat into her garden - it was a wonderful hidden treasure. Julia's befriending of this very timid, but affectionate cat, meant Tabitha soon became an accepted and loved member of her household. Sitting and relaxing with Tabitha on her lap, stroking her thick, silky hair, was of immense benefit for Julia - although to begin with on more than one occasion she was able to chuckle inwardly as she wore herself out coping with Tabitha's erratic attempts at toilet training!

We felt as if I had been walking through a dark tunnel during the years when Julia had been so ill, and out in the light I began to identify treasures that I had found in the darkness. Down through history it can be seen that out of adversity many a gem can be found. In the darkness of a prison, John Bunyan wrote a priceless treasure, *Pilgrim's Progress*. Joni Eareckson Tada, paralysed by a diving accident, found treasures in her darkness and shared them with the world through her paintings, writings and radiant life. I don't fully understand why God chose to lead me into the darkness, but a possible answer is revealed in words that Isaiah spoke, *I will give you the treasures of darkness, riches stored in secret places, so that you may know that I am the Lord.* (3) Finding my dreams for Julia shattered, I believe that I have discovered treasures in the darkness of suffering that I would never have found in the light.

I have come to accept that adversity doesn't always make sense, nor does there have to be any obvious purpose in it. When C S Lewis was at the end of his emotional tether in mourning the death of his beloved wife, his colleagues didn't know what to say. They were all academic dons and highly intellectual, and couldn't connect with Lewis' grief on an emotional level. One day, a friend asked him, "Is there anything we can do"? "Just don't say it's all for the best, that's all," came the reply. I wouldn't have chosen to suffer the pain of the last eleven years, nor would I want to repeat the experience! There were times when I fought my inner pain, and times when I allowed it to be built into the fabric of my being, believing that God was bringing me into a greater place of wholeness. When the going got tough I found that there was more to life than my circumstances and my feelings indicated at that moment. What seemed at the time cruel, cold, bleak, and never ending eventually became a means of drawing me closer to God. As I was stripped of my self sufficiency and independence I found myself standing naked before Him, feeling vulnerable and humiliated. It was at this place that I found a priceless treasure - I experienced God's love and acceptance at a much deeper level than ever before, and became more fully dependent on His grace - a gift which I didn't deserve.

Suffering is often spoken of in terms of the refining of faith, just as metals are refined by fire. Only precious metals like gold are worth refining and this process is carried out by subjecting the metals to intense heat. By passing gold through a bed of white hot coals all the impurities are removed, in the form of dross. It is only when the metal has been subjected to a certain heat for a certain length of time that it is refined sufficiently to be complete, reflecting the refiner's face. This image is found in scripture, *I will thoroughly purge away your dross and remove all your impurities.* (4) Adversity gets rid of the dross of the supports on which we foolishly base our faith. The apostle Peter wrote, *Pure gold put in the fire comes out of it proved pure; genuine faith put through this suffering comes out proved genuine. When Jesus wraps this all up, it's your faith, not your gold, that God will have on display as evidence of his victory.* (5) With many of my props stripped away my faith has grown stronger as I have learnt to trust in a faithful God and lean on Him in a new way. After all the refining, my prayer is that people will see in me something of the reflected face of Jesus.

Another treasure I have discovered is that pain and suffering has given me a new platform from which to view the world. We are so caught up as mothers wanting our children to achieve their potential, that we can lose sight of their uniqueness and preciousness. Of course, the pain is still with me - and it will be there unless and until Julia is completely well again, but it's no longer so important to me that Julia can't do what others her age can do. Yes, she misses out on things like a social and family life, and I would dearly love to see her able to do these things, but that's not everything. I enjoy the person that she is, and seeing her do the simple things in life that many take for granted. My eyes have been opened to appreciate so much more in life. In today's modern world, we can be so focussed on achieving and doing, that it is easy to miss the priceless treasures that are to be found hidden in our children. Even if they have gone off the rails, and turned to drugs, or drink and have ended up in prison, there will always be something good to find in them. I counselled one lady who couldn't find one good thing to say about her daughter who was a drug addict. However, as we began to explore various issues, the mother began to see some positive attributes in her daughter which she had never seen before. Consequently mother and daughter began to enjoy something of a relationship again.

Motherhood is not for the fainthearted. It is a privilege which brings responsibilities. We are called to mother, whatever the circumstances. Just as Christ loves and accepts us, we have a responsibility to love our children - that means to accept them where they are, and how they are, irrespective of what they achieve. If our children do not feel accepted by us as mothers, it is almost impossible for them to feel loved. I have counselled many women who have said that they don't feel loved by their parents, because they have never felt accepted for who they are, or lived up to their parents' expectations. Have we ever stopped and thought whether we make unrealistic demands upon our children? Perhaps secretly we long for them to turn out how we wish *we* could be; or we want to see them achieve in ways we never did; or that they turn out better than our neighbour's child. Setting ourselves up with too high a goal for our children can leave us battling with a sense of failure when they don't reach it, leaving us feeling guilty that we are to blame for poor mothering. Guilt is an occupational hazard of motherhood - putting rigid demands upon ourselves as mothers will invariably cause us some degree of emotional disturbance. Our children need our encouragement and acceptance in reaching their potential, but we cannot live their lives for them. My experience of mothering

Julia was all about facing the pain of dashed hopes and shattered dreams, but being committed to mother her anyway. At times I found it hard to accept the place she was in, and had to continually work at this. But I always accepted her as a precious daughter.

With Julia away for another respite break in Burrswood, I found myself preparing to lead a quiet day at the Acorn Healing Trust, near Alton. Basing the talks on Jeremiah, I took as my theme, "Finding God . . . . . . in my outer world, in my inner world and in my future." It wasn't difficult for me to empathise with Jeremiah, as I found him so open and honest about his struggles, *Why is my pain unending, and my wound . . . . incurable?* (6) However the verse that really stood out for me was, *This is what the Lord Almighty, the God of Israel, says to all those I carried into exile from Jeremiah to Babylon: "Build houses and settle down; plant gardens and eat what they produce".* (7) These words were part of a letter sent from Jeremiah to the Israelites, who were exiled in Babylon. Being in exile was a terrifying and traumatic experience. They were uprooted from the land that had been promised to them and forced to journey across 700 miles of desert, leaving behind their comfortable and familiar life. Moreover in the new land of Babylon, the customs were strange, the language incomprehensible and the landscape different.

The exile experienced by the Hebrews is a picture of how many of us feel at times. The essential meaning of exile is that we are separated from our home, from the place that is known and feels comfortable - it is a place where we would not choose to be. It was in this situation that Jeremiah encouraged the Israelites to do something positive - build houses, rather than sit around and complain; and become a productive part of their community by planting gardens. It's as if Jeremiah was rebuking and challenging them; don't sit around having a pity party - instead make the most of your opportunities by living at your best in this place. Then Jeremiah offered a promise, *"I know the plans I have for you," declares the Lord, "plans to prosper*

Hidden Treasure

you and not to harm you, plans to give you hope and a future". (8) The Israelites found out what it meant to be God's people in a place they would not have chosen to live in, and this resulted in a very creative period in Hebrew history. Finding oneself in exile can be the worst that reveals the best in us. When the non-essential is stripped away we find the prime source of life - and that prime source is God. He is the one who carries us through.

At the end of that Quiet Day, it was very encouraging to hear that many of the people attending had picked up the concept of being in exile and it was wonderful to hear how God had spoken to them. One lady came to me in tears, saying that she now knew why life was so difficult for her - she was in exile. She was a widow and had moved to live closer to her daughter in the South, and although she loved her daughter dearly, she felt exiled from the North. Just being able to identify that, gave her a new understanding and a new sense of peace in her place of exile. Another mother spoke of how she had always felt she was in exile through having a son with special needs, and how she was struggling to have faith for God's plans for their future. In the quietness of the chapel, God spoke words of comfort into her life, reassuring her that He was with her in that difficult place.

On Julia's return from Burrswood we spent time catching up with each other. To our amazement we discovered that the Chaplain there had suggested to Julia that she read the very same verses in Jeremiah. We had a very open and honest time together sharing our experiences of being in exile, and what God had shown us in that place. Finally we reminded each other of the Lord's promise, *"(I) will bring you back to the place from which I carried you into exile"*. (9)

With an Autumnal feel in the air, on most days Julia was able to walk either down the garden or up the road for two minutes and appreciate the changing colours of the season. Life was picking up.

She was well enough to enjoy a wedding, without any damaging cost to her energy levels as four days later she was out in her garden planting bulbs. I smiled inwardly at a comment she made the following week when her husband was off school sick. "Oh, it's boring with Geoff ill." She was obviously feeling better!

This improvement continued. The length of time Julia could walk was slowly increased, so that soon she could take a four minute walk to a nearby park - her horizons were broadening. In fact she was so thrilled with her improvement that she said, "It's exciting what I am beginning to plan to do." We were all encouraged and decided to celebrate together by going out for a meal as a family, all six of us - something we had never done because Julia hadn't ever been well enough since our two sons-in law had come on the scene. Once again our plans were thwarted as Julia had a minor set back, suffering with a virus. We quickly shrugged off our disappointment and just accepted that one day we would all make it out together.

Christmas 1998 loomed up fast and furious and we all enjoyed being together as a family under one roof. Julia's physical improvement was maintained and her concentration and quick mind were returning. This was demonstrated in her beating us all at Boggle! Towards the end of January, 1999, John and I, with Julia and Geoff, went away on a CiCP weekend at Ashburnam. For Julia to be well enough to go away with us to a Christian conference was a dream come true. Fortunately the meetings were held in the library where soft easy chairs and sofas were to be found, so at least when Julia managed to get to one of the sessions, she was able to relax in a comfy chair. We shared a ground floor flat together and back in our room after the Saturday evening meeting the four of us had an hilarious time, acting the fool and singing. It was one of those treasured moments when somehow we all sparked each other off - we not only feasted on spiritual food that weekend, but also enjoyed a lot of fun together. We were making up for lost time!

Hidden Treasure

With Spring just around the corner, Julia was breaking new ground with a number of memorable achievements:- the joy of being able to walk independently 100 yards down the road to a small corner shop and buy something; the spontaneity of just dropping in on John and me, as she and Geoff returned from a trip into the countryside; even flying over to Northern Ireland for the Easter wedding of one of her nursing friends. They planned this trip very carefully and went out a week before the wedding so as to give time for Julia to recover from the journey. When John and I collected them from Heathrow, I was a little nervous as to whether Julia would be absolutely exhausted and be in a heap. But as Geoff pushed the wheelchair through the doors, my anxieties were allayed as they were both beaming. Once Julia had spotted us in the crowd she smiled and waved - to see my daughter well enough to do that was another tear jerking experience! Strapping herself into our car for the last leg of their homeward journey, Julia said, "I've made it. I've had my tough moments, and haven't felt well at times, but I've done it . . . . . where next?"

Inevitably Julia paid for this trip. Not only did she have a stomach upset within a few days, but she took months to regain her previous energy levels and sadly has never been able to walk the distances she was walking before she went to Northern Ireland in 1999. That summer Julia struggled on with anaemia, palpitations and a loss of confidence and life continued with her being more or less housebound, apart from managing an outing once a week. Because my life was busy and fulfilled I chose to ignore Julia's bad days, focussing on the good days which were full of smiles and laughter. Two incidents bought me face to face with the fact that without being aware of it I had put on blinkers so that I didn't see what I didn't want to face. The first was when Julia's Disability Living Allowance application had been turned down and in order to put together an Appeal, we had gone to an agency for help. As we faced the searching questions, I realised that I didn't want to hear Julia spell out exactly how ill and debilitated she was. I wanted to hear her say that she could cook a meal - but she couldn't. I wanted to hear her say that she could walk down the road to the shop - but she couldn't. With my blinkers on it had been easy for me to pretend that things were better than they were, but the true picture was being thrust under my nose, whether I liked it or not. I had to dig deep and find the courage to face the fact that Julia could only do very little. It was as if the old deep wounds of pain and sadness were reopened.

The second incident occurred a week or so later. After nine years as Lay Ministers, John and I were leaving our church for a sabbatical, taking time out from church responsibilities as John was returning to full time work for a year, and I was planning to write this book. Saying goodbye to friends was very emotional as we had given so much of ourselves to God's work in that place. But I found the added factor that made it even more poignant was that throughout our entire nine years there, Julia had been ill, and we were now leaving with her still unwell. We were closing the curtains on our time at the church, but it was even more painful that we could not draw the curtains on M.E. As I said my goodbyes and thanks to the church, I expressed how much John and I had appreciated all their love and support for us in our caring for Julia. I thought I had all my emotions buttoned down, but much to my surprise, and slight embarrassment, I started to lose control as I found my voice cracking and tears welling up. My pain button had been pushed. Once home, I took myself off to a quiet corner to sort myself out with God! I knew that I had to take my blinkers off, face reality and release the pain. We can only expect God to deal with us when we open ourselves up and allow Him to peel away the layers of self-deception and fear that stunt our growth. Only then can we stand in His strength and not our own.

That Autumn I had to go into hospital for an operation which left me in excruciating pain whilst I was recovering. I was really touched that Julia came home for a few days to care for me in as much as she was able. She could do little things like get me drinks, cold packs for my wound, and rub my back - but more than that she was such good company. I was in so much pain that I could have cried, but together we ended up laughing, particularly over a bag of frozen peas that I used as an ice pack. When John came home at the end of one day, she teasingly said, "Dad, do you want to go on a long walk or a short walk"? He replied, "I'll go for a short walk with you." "Aah . . . . I'm on the long walk today, just up to the top of the road. Mum is on the short walk, just to the front door," she said with her voice ringing with delight. It was all relative! But it was her sensitive, caring nature that really shone through. She would have made a good nurse.

Over the last eleven years there had been a softening and a smoothing out of the rough edges with a growing sensitivity to God working in her life. The earmarks of her immaturity were being dissolved within her by a divine touch. One person said to me, "How beautiful Julia is. Although not physically well, her inner beauty shines through." A W Tozer commented that God cannot use a person until he or she has been hurt deeply. Through all the pain and heartache Julia has visibly grown in grace. God has formed something deep and beautiful within her, like a pearl is formed in the darkness and place of irritation. To John and me, our daughter is a priceless treasure - a precious jewel, a jewel shaped in the adversity of suffering.

As the Autumn months passed, Julia continued to have good days, interspersed with difficult ones, but was just well enough to travel down to see Fiona in hospital in Bournemouth, where she had just given birth to Joshua, our first grandchild. Although Julia was thrilled for Fiona and Paul, this inevitably gave her some heartache as she and Geoff long to have children. Hopefully one day when she is strong enough their hopes and dreams for a child will be fulfilled.

With the passing of another Christmas, the year 2000 was nearly upon us. With the whole country celebrating the Millennium, John and I arrived home from a party in the early hours of the morning to continue watching the festivities on TV. To our surprise the front door bell went around 1 am. Bursting with shouts of "Happy New Year," Geoff and Julia came in giggling and laughing, en route home after a party. John and I relished the joy of seeing Julia full of fun and able to join in something as significant as celebrating the beginning of the year 2000 - it didn't seem to matter that she was ill for the following week! Her year had started with a bang.

As the year progressed Julia's recovery was not consistent. Better months were followed by months when she couldn't do much again, and she was discouraged. After several attempts to increase her mobility over a period of six months, she would get so far, then slip back again and lose it. However looking at the situation positively she has had no major dips since that time and overall there has been some improvement. Her rate of moving forward is at a snail's pace, which not only tries her patience, but tests me at times as well. One day we reminded each other of the story of the tortoise and hare. So for a bit of fun I bought her a tortoise, (a soft toy), which now sits in her lounge to remind her that even though she can only move forward slowly, she will cover new ground.

One way in which Julia achieved this new ground was by making a conscious decision to invest her energy into non-physical activity. It was a real triumph for her to be able to attend a Christmas craft fair and sell the cards she had made so creatively over the previous months. As I looked back over the year 2000 I put aside the memories of seeing Julia curled up on the sofa looking really ill, and chose to remember the good times:- Julia and I jumping up and down on an old wind surfer at the bottom of her garden, only to find Geoff had returned home early and caught the pair of us shouting around like two kids; having a fun time holidaying all together as a family, with Julia well enough to enjoy baby Joshua; Julia's enthusiasm and sparkle for life when well. These are the memories I treasured. Recalling them helped me through the bad days when Julia wasn't well. These are the days when I put a brave face on and hid behind the smile that says, "I'm OK," although I was crying on the inside. But life goes on. I wonder how many of us as mothers have become very clever at hiding what really is going on.

All too often we pretend to other people that we are in control and that we have it all together! This can be partly to convince ourselves that we are not inadequate failures, and partly to protect ourselves from vulnerability. But let's face it, we are all messed up people one way or another. When a friend read the first draft of this book, she made a comment that in one chapter I came across as too perfect! Consequently I had to retrace my steps, asking God to stop me at the places where I was too proud or too frightened to commit to paper my inner weaknesses. Having stopped at these places I hope I have redressed the perfect mother image - for I am far from it! Openly sharing my weaknesses was something I wanted to do in the writing of this book, as I hoped it would help other mothers in their place of adversity. May these words spoken by Paul constantly ring in our ears, *Be strong in the grace that is in Christ Jesus.* (10)

Over these difficult years I have found reading stories of other people's honest struggles with life, themselves and God - an inspiration which has helped me to press on. We all struggle in different ways. It is not unspiritual to wrestle with life; in fact someone once defined a mature person as someone who struggles well. We are all on a journey and we struggle on the way; only the immature think they have already arrived, and have no problems, difficulties or hang-ups. It is better to struggle in our pain and confusion, (asking God the questions that bug us, even if we don't get easy answers, or the ones we want to hear,) than to pretend to ourselves everything is OK and there is nothing to struggle about. As I have written about my struggles as a mother I have tried to be honest and admit where I have felt confused and hurt, even although I know God is in control. I hope and pray that you will find this book a source of comfort and strength as you face your own process of coming to terms with what life has thrown at you.

It would be wonderful to write at the end of this book, that Julia was well . . . . but she isn't. This isn't a happy ever after story, but one of how God in His grace, has met us in different ways, in different stages, in different circumstances and with different people. His love has sustained us and is carrying us through.

As I look back over the years I see a little girl with a jigsaw puzzle, feeling frustrated and disappointed that the pieces do not fit together to make up the familiar picture on the box. Her Dad quietly walks into the scene with another box lid. Removing the old familiar one, he replaces it with a box lid that has a new picture. Feeling very confused the little girl looks up at her daddy and asks, "What are you doing?". Bending down and giving the little girl an encouraging pat on the head, he softly says, "If you work at rearranging your jigsaw pieces, you will make this new picture."

Although my dreams have been shattered into pieces, God has come alongside and helped me to create a new picture. My life now tells a new story, Julia's story too, continues to unfold.

Throughout 2001, Julia's mobility has remained limited, as she can walk only about 20-50 yards once a day. However she has been well enough to become more involved in life: discipling a young person, leading a bible study, going out more to visit people, completing a 50 hour basic counselling course - although the recovery time after this was two weeks!

She was also able to share in the joy of the birth of Fiona's second son, Ethan, and continues to have a wonderfully special relationship with Joshua, aged two, who adores his Aunty Julia. All this has helped her build confidence, and now Julia sees herself, not as someone who is ill, but as someone recovering and rehabilitating. Her latest step is the acquisition of a power bicycle. What a joy it was to see Julia taking off across the park for her first ride and vanishing into the distance. How we all cheered when she returned, breathless and tired , but exhilarated. She can only manage the bike for a few minutes at a time at present but it is another vital milestone in her path towards independence.

As for me, I continue to learn that whatever the hopes and dreams we have for our children, something priceless can be found in the midst of our disappointments. For as we see our dreams lying in broken pieces, and recognise that we can do nothing to restore them, we are stripped bare of all our independence. In our vulnerability and weakness God is able to melt away our shame and fear with His love - a love which reaches down and gathers us in his arms, holding us close to His heart. As we relax, and nestle into him, we sense the pulsating of his heart, and hear the comforting words of a loving Father. Out of all the pain and dark times, we find a priceless treasure - a greater intimacy with God.

> "Then shall I know . . . .
> Not till the loom is silent
> And the shuttles cease to fly
> Shall God unroll the canvas
> And explain the reasons why
> The dark threads are as needful
> In the weaver's skilful hand
> As the threads of gold and silver
> In the patterns He has planned."
> *Author unknown*

Bibliography/References

Chapter 1
(1) Psalm 57:10

Chapter 3
(1) *All hail the lamb*, Bilbrough David   1987 Dave Bilbrough songs/Thankyou music
(2) Dawes Belinda and Downing Damien, *Why M.E.?* Grafton Books 1990
(3) Kushner Harold S, *When bad things happen to good people*, Pan Books Ltd 1982
(4) Helmut Thielicke, *A Thielicke Trilogy*, Grand Rapids: Baker Book House 1980
(5) Pearson Althea, *Growing Through Loss and Grief*, Harper Collins Publishers 1994
(6) Johnson Barbara, *Splashes of Joy in the Cesspool of Life*, Word Publishing 1992
(7) John 11:35

Chapter 4
(1) Psalm 22:1
(2) Johnson Barbara, *Splashes of Joy in the Cesspool of Life*, Word Publishing 1992
(3) Kushner Harold S, *When bad things happen to good people*, Pan Books Ltd 1982
(4) Frankl Victor E, *Man's Search for Meaning*, (New York; Washington Square Press Inc. 1963)
(5) John 7:37
(6) Psalm 42:5

Chapter 5
(1) Proverbs 12:18
(2) Johnson Barbara, *Fresh Elastic for Stretched out Mums*, Marshall

Pickering 1996
(3) Proverbs 3:5,6
(4) Isaiah 40:13
(5) Luke 7:23 (The Amplified Bible)
(6) Ephesians 4:26
(7) Psalm 51:1,7 (The Message)
(8) Philippians 4:12
(9) Hebrews 12:27-29 (The Message)

Chapter 6
(1) Isaiah 43:2b
(2) Matthew 26:39
(3) Hughes Selwyn, *Every Day with Jesus*, July/August 2000
(4) John 21:22
(5) John 21:21
(6) 2 Corinthians 12:9
(7) Swindoll Charles R, *Maybe it's time to . . . Laugh Again,* Word Books, Milton Keynes 1992
(8) Wheeler Wilcox Ella, "The Wind of Fate", in The Best Loved Poems of the American People", comp Hazel Fellman, Garden City, N.Y., Garden City Books 1936

Chapter 7
(1) Isaiah 40:13
(2) Love that wilt not let me go, George Matheson (1842-1906)
(3) Daniel 3:17-18
(4) Romans 8:28
(5) Seerveld Calvin, *"Take Hold of God and Pull",* Paternoster Press

Chapter 8
(1) Psalm 77:7-9
(2) Psalm 77:11,12
(3) Psalm 69:20,29,30

Chapter 9

(1) Psalm 6:3
(2) Psalm 13:1
(3) Psalm 80:4
(4) Psalm 89:46
(5) Psalm 90:13
(6) Job 1 and 2:13
(7) John 9:1-3
(8) John 3:16
(9) 1 John 4:9-10
(10) Guinness Os, *God in the Dark*, Hodder & Stoughton 1996
(11) Malte Paul, *"Why Does God Allow Suffering"?*, St Louis: Lutheran Laymen's League 1965
(12) Psalm 51:12
(13) *"Faithful One, so unchanging,"* Brian Doerksen   1989 Mercy Publishing/Thankyou Music

Chapter 10

(1) Psalm 57:10
(2) Isaiah 26:3 (Translation from German Bible)
(3) Isaiah 41:10
(4) St Matthew 16:24, 25
(5) Griffiths Trevor Dr, *"Lost and Then Found"*, Paternoster Press 1999
(6) Psalm 115:3
(7) Job 42:2
(8) Hughes Selwyn, "Every Day with Jesus", May/June 2000
(9) Castle Fiona with Jan Greenough, *"No Flowers . . . . . just lots of joy"*, Kingsway 1996
(10) *"For the joys and for the sorrows"*, Graham Kendrick   1994 Make Way Music
(11) Castle Fiona with Jan Greenough, *"No Flowers . . . . . just lots of joy,"* Kingsway 1996

Chapter 11
(1) Lamentations 3:22,23
(2) *"The steadfast love"*, Graham Kendrick   1989 Make Way Music/Thankyou Music
(3) Ward Heather, *"Streams in Dry Land"*, Eagle 1993
(4) Psalm 27:14
(5) Luke 1:6
(6) Job 23:10

Chapter 12
(1) Song of Songs 8:5
(2) Romans 5:3-5
(3) Isaiah 53:7
(4) *"The Joy of the Saints"*, Darton, Longman and Todd
(5) Song of Songs 2:10-13
(6) Hosea 2:14,15 (New American Standard Version)
(7) Genesis 41:52 (New American Standard Version)
(8) Proverbs 13:12
(9) 1 Corinthians 10:13 (The Message)

Chapter 13
(1) *"For this purpose"*, Graham Kendrick   1985 Make Way Music/Thankyou Music
(2) McGrath Alister, *"A Journey Through Suffering"*, Hodder and Stoughton 1992
(3) Psalm 55:22
(4) Isaiah 46:4

Chapter 14
(1) Psalm 41:3
(2) Peter Browne, "*The Healing Power of Pets*", Reader's Digest July 1996
(3) Isaiah 45:3
(4) Isaiah 1:25
(5) 1 Peter 1:7 (The Message)
(6) Jeremiah 15:18
(7) Jeremiah 29:4,5
(8) Jeremiah 29:11
(9) Jeremiah 29:14
(10) 2 Timothy 2:1

WORD FOR LIFE TRUST Publications

Living Word Series, *titles include:-*

Alternative therapies by Michael Harper and Elizabeth Brazell
Forgiveness by Elizabeth Brazell
Freemasonry by Ron Graham and Elizabeth Brazell
Gender by Elizabeth Brazell
Gifts in Ministry by Elizabeth Brazell
Listening by Elizabeth Brazell and Fran Hawkins
Prayer and Bible Study by Elizabeth Brazell
Prophecy by Elizabeth Brazell
Suffering by Elizabeth Brazell
The Cross and The Resurrection by Elizabeth Brazell
The Holy Spirit by Elizabeth Brazell
The New Age by Beverley Risdon

Heart to Heart by Hilary Brinckman

A book of poems and pictures telling a story of personal faith and healing.

For a full list of publications and prices please write to:
The Publications Department
Word for Life Trust (WFLT)
3 Danestream Close
Milford-on-Sea, SO41 0UR, U.K.
or e-mail us at wflt@wflt.org